THE ⱼ

and

SCALPEL

****

Scientific Proof of
Extraterrestrial Implants in Humans
Second edition revised 2004
Updated 2005

Dr. Roger K. Leir D.P.M.

The documented true story of one surgeon's research into
the retrieval and analysis of what seem to be alien implants
in humans

The Book Tree
San Diego, CA

DEDICATION
To the individuals who became my surgical patients.
Their lives touched mine in a most unusual way.

ISBN: 1-58509-106-5

Visit Dr. Leir's website:

www.alienscalpel.com

****

Published by
The Book Tree
P O Box 16476
San Diego, CA 92176

We provide fascinating and educational products to help awaken the public to new ideas and
information that would not be available otherwise.
Call 1 (800) 700-8733 for our FREE BOOK TREE CATALOG.

Author's Statement

I am taking this opportunity to thank readers around the world who took their time to read the first edition of *The Aliens and the Scalpel*. Please understand that my work is ongoing and continuing at the time of this writing. As you will notice, I have made certain modifications to the original material but some of my relationships are now different than when the book was first written. I hope you will enjoy the new context as much as in the original version. I'm sure you will find this second edition as interesting, with new chapters and much expanded data.

Between the publication of this version and the time of this note, the 11th surgery has been performed. This surgery consisted of the removal of a small metallic rod from the patient's cheek area. The patient is female with an abduction history. The object is currently undergoing examination by several scientific specialists. The metallic rod measures about 6mm in length and is as thick as a pencil lead. It is highly magnetic, covered with a slightly different biological coating. This data will be available later and I will keep my readers informed.

Please be on the lookout for another new book authored by me. The title is *UFO Crash in Brazil*, the story of my in-depth investigation of the Varginha, Brazil UFO crash and sighting of non-terrestrial beings. Further information can be found in the very back of this book. Available soon will be the taped version of the original *Aliens and the Scalpel*, narrated by me. Look for it at your favorite bookstore or on Amazon.com. Remember, the proceeds from the sale of all books and products are used to fund future research through our non-profit organization, A&S Research.

Dr Roger K. Leir, podiatric physician and surgeon, attained his Bachelor of Science degree in 1961 and his Doctor of Podiatric Medicine in 1964. He has been in private practice since that time. Dr. Leir has participated in research that included the study of regenerating tendons and the use of artificial substances used in foot reconstruction procedures. Dr. Leir's interest in Ufology began at age twelve with the clear  recollection of his father reading the newspaper headline about the Roswell incident to his mother. In the late 1980's he became a member of MUFON, the Mutual UFO Network, and eventually functioned as an investigative reporter for the Ventura-Santa Barbara chapter's monthly periodical, *The Vortex*. Dr. Leir then began his pioneering work with the medical and surgical aspects of alien implant research. He has presented his research all over the world and was one of the seven American researchers to be keynote speakers for the opening of the UFO-Aerospace Museum in Japan. Some of Dr. Leir's numerous media appearances include The Art Bell Show, Jeff Rense's Sightings on the Radio, The X-Zone Radio Show, Heironymous & Company Radio Show, Hard Copy, The Dini Show, Strange Universe, Beyond Bizarre, Fox News, KTLA News, UPN News, and Confirmation, a February, 1999 two-hour NBC special.

Acknowledgments

Writing this book has been an occasion for me to reflect gratefully on some people who have profoundly influenced my life and consequently, this book.

The first and foremost was my dear father, Joseph Leir. When I was a child, he impressed me with his general knowledge and understanding of the world. I wondered if he derived it from his experience as a 32nd degree Mason and Shriner or whether he had an uncanny ability to read between the lines and see the truth.

My cousin, Dr. Kenneth Ring, also influenced me through our conversations and through his book *The Omega Project*, which is concerned with near-death experience and UFOs. I extend my heartfelt appreciation to Ken for his advice and friendship.

My wife Sharon, though not directly involved in the work reported here, has been of enormous moral support to me, and I am deeply thankful to have her beside me in life.

I am fortunate to be surrounded by the wonderful people of the Ventura-Santa Barbara (California) MUFON organization. They assisted me in organizing and preparing for the surgical procedures described here. One of the most creative and thoughtful of them is our state Section Director, Mrs. Alice Leavy. This fine lady encouraged me to perform in areas far beyond what I had originally considered to be my field of expertise. Her encouragement has been pivotal to the course I am now pursuing.

My thanks also go to:

Whitely Strieber, probably the most famous abductee in the world, and his wife Anne, who inspired in me the courage to pursue the scientific study of objects which are not only foreign to the human organism, but also to our planet itself.

Raymond Fowler, one of the most outstanding researchers in the field of ufology, who took an interest in my work and gave me the honor of contributing to his latest book *The Andreasson Legacy*.

Robert 0. Dean has given me great encouragement to continue my abduction research. he has pointed me in the right direction and made me aware of the importance of the line of research I was pursuing.

My dear friend, Dr. Tal, who stayed at my side and helped me with his medical and surgical skills, guiding me through troubled times of financial despair. Because of Dr. Tal's myriad abilities, I was able to proceed with the research reported here.

Table of Contents

PREFACE

"I have been frequently faulted by ci itics...for not dealing... more fully with the physical evidence that does exist for UFOs and abductions. But it is important to keep in mind that every aspect of the physical evidence... is. .. subtle, elusive, and difficult to prove."
—John E Mack,M.D.,

Abduction: Human Encounters with Aliens

My intention in writing this book is to provide a clear, concise account of how I applied my skills in medicine and science to a phenomenon which has not been looked at seriously by the scientific and medical establishments. This resulted in the most astonishing findings of any like research to date.

Yes, there have been many investigations of UFOs and hundreds of books and articles written about the phenomenon. And, yes, there have been a few notable scientists who have performed some of those investigations, such as astronomer Dr. J. Allen Hynek, atmospheric physicist Dr. James D. MacDonald, computer scientist Dr. Jacques Vallee, psychiatrist John Mack, M.D., and nuclear physicist Stanton Friedman. But fifty years after the modern UFO era began, the phenomenon remains mysterious because, for the most part, mainstream science and medicine regard the UFO phenomenon and study of it as foolish, fringe pseudoscience. If the field were to be studied seriously by those establishments, there would be multi-million dollar funding of a well planned and coordinated global research effort. Instead, ufology gets along as best it can with minimal funding raised largely by public membership in various UFO research organizations and by small grants to individuals from daring philanthropic individuals and funds.

The story of my own research efforts is one of coincidence, driving curiosity and struggle against numerous obstacles, including the search for funding. I don't mean to glorify myself or make grandiose claims, yet I feel in all honesty and humility that I have made a significant breakthrough in solving the question, "Are we alone in the universe?"

Harvard psychiatrist John Mack, whom I noted above, writes in his book *Abduction*:

When we explore phenomena that exist at the margins of accepted reality, old words become imprecise or must be given new meanings. Terms like "abduction," "alien," "happening," and even "reality" itself, need redefinition lest subtle distinctions be lost. In this context, thinking of memory too literally as "true" or "false" may restrict what we can learn about human consciousness from the abduction experiences I recount in the pages that follow.

In using the medical-surgical approach to the phenomenon known as alien abductions, I too have stepped into that realm where conventional terms become imprecise and must be carefully redefined in order to describe experiences which seem so far from everyday reality. This narrative takes you, the reader, along with me on a journey into the unknown. I present my thoughts as various experiences occurred and decisions were made by me to go forward into a mystery. I also recount the actual statements of the abductees on whom I performed the surgeries.

Chapter 1

A LOOK AT MY CREDENTIALS

I am a native Californian, born in San Francisco and have resided in Southern California since 1948. I pursued my undergraduate education at the University of Southern California and San Fernando Valley College. I received a Bachelor of Science degree in 1961. Upon graduation from the California College of Podiatric Medicine in 1964, I was awarded the degree of Doctor of Podiatric Medicine. After graduation I continued training with a year preceptorship in surgery. In addition I continued to hone my skills, working with senior foot surgeons in a multitude of southern California hospitals. Following this I became Podiatric Director of Residency Training at Simi Valley Doctors Hospital. I continued this for three years. In the following years I served as Chief of the Diabetic Foot Clinic at Cedars of Lebanon Hospital in Hollywood. During this period I opened a private practice and continued in this capacity until present.

My interest in the subject of Ufology dates back to July, 1947. This date was impressed indelibly into my memory with vivid conscious recall of my father walking into our kitchen and announcing to my mother that the United States Army Air Force had just captured a flying saucer. I recall how he showed her the newspaper headline and proceeded to explain his views on the subject of UFO's. He discussed in depth his belief in extraterrestrial visitors. He also expressed his opinion about how "the powers that be" were keeping it a secret.

It wasn't until some years later that I found myself involved with this subject again. A friend asked me if I would be interested in attending the local MUFON lectures. I told him that I would, and accompanied him. The presentation was so interesting that I decided to attend future meetings. Following this I became a member of both the local and national MUFON organization.

Coincidentally, at this time my very close first cousin, Dr. Kenneth Ring just finished his book entitled *The Omega Project*. After reading his book I was amazed to learn that the subject pertained to UFO's and NDE's.

I telephoned Ken immediately and asked him about his book. I told him how surprised I was that he had written about the subject of UFO's. He explained that it was a one-time shot and he had no further plans to continue on in this subject. He went on to state that because of time constraints and a heavy work load, he was no longer able to pursue the subject of Ufology. He asked if I would like to continue this research in his stead. After careful consideration I finally agreed. From that time on I began to receive large amounts of pertinent literature, videos, recorded lectures and other related materials from Kenneth. It didn't take long before I found that no matter how much time I was able to donate to this subject, it would be impossible for me to digest all the information and keep current at the same time. It was also evident that most current researchers had participated for many years in their quest for knowledge in this subject. This left me with a feeling of acute inadequacy.

It was during this period that the local Ventura-Santa Barbara Mufon group changed their monthly written publication to an all new format. The editor asked me if I would be willing to become a contributory author. This interested me. I accepted the position and continued in that capacity.

Because of my new chosen pursuit I felt an obligation to attend as many live lectures as possible. I reported on these events, carefully presenting the facts as I saw them. Each event was scrutinized and committed to print.

Later I became an advisor to the board, and a medical consultant. With my interest growing, I decided to study for status as a Field Investigator. Within a few months I passed the examination and was officially designated by the national organization.

Through the years, my involvement with MUFON became more complex. I consider myself responsible for starting a trend within our group to seek out knowledge and "go where no man has gone before," as Star Trek puts it.

There is a high probability of a relationship between my implant research and the growing interest by the membership of the group. There are times when our guest speakers are forced to relinquish time from their topic to an audience clamoring for new data on the implant project.

In addition, my thirst for the newest knowledge in this field has thrust me upon the lecture circuit. I accepted an offer to present my material to the National MUFON Symposium in Greensboro, North Carolina. Following came another presentation at the Awareness Conference in Tampa, Florida; and also at the UFO Awareness Week Conference in Chicago, Illinois.

In addition to the lecture events, great interest has been aroused in the radio and television media. The response from print media has been overwhelming.

One of the most common questions I have been asked pertains to persecution by my peers or governmental agencies. It is with great pleasure that I am able to say so far, the answer is none. My friends and colleagues have stood by me, demonstrating sincere interest in my scientific endeavors. I have succeeded in networking with an increasing number of medical practitioners who specified a sincere interest in this field. There has been an increasing number of calls from numerous scientists with divergent fields of expertise who offered their help and expert advise.

I regret I can't find hours in the day to answer the deluge of phone calls and email responses. There has been a tremendous outpouring of interest from the public at large, regarding the abduction phenomena in general.

I am thoroughly convinced that the much talked about Roper Poll only presented a conservative estimate as to the number of individuals involved in the alien abduction phenomenon.

I am overjoyed by the offers of other well known, qualified researchers in the field of Ufology who have offered to assist me in my quest for knowledge. With the help of colleagues such as Robert O. Dean, Colin Andrews, Phillip Mantle, Jaime Maussan, Budd Hopkins, and numerous others, we have been able to make gigantic leaps forward. I sincerely thank these exceptionally kind and dedicated individuals for their support.

I have personally grown both psychologically and spiritually, expanding my depth of knowledge one hundred-fold. This subject of Ufology, with all its twists and turns of mystery, has become one of the most influential factors in my life.

Chapter 2

MY PERSONAL NDE'S

Soon after my initial telephone conversation with my cousin Ken, I became interested in ufology and this started a new phase of my life. Ken, in friendly fashion, became rapidly interested in my new pursuits and offered as much help as he could within his time constraints of full-time university teaching, researching, and writing his books on near-death experience.

Not long after the second set of phone calls, a plan began to take shape. What I suggested was a cousin reunion. Ken and I have two other first cousins. Don is a professional jazz musician and Cliff is a cardiologist. Don lives in New York City, Cliff lives in northern California. Again, a strange set of circumstances was about to bring us all together. Don was scheduled to give a concert in Oakland, California, at the same time Ken was coming to the area to visit his mother. All I had to do was arrange my schedule so I could meet them in Oakland and we would have our reunion.

The gathering of the cousins took place without a hitch. I also met separately with Ken and we discussed his work. As I listened to his views on the subject of ufology, I soon learned that we had a divergence of opinion. Although he had performed a great deal of research in preparation for *The Omega Project*, he had also become strongly convinced that the UFO experience had to be relegated to the spiritual, or to at least the realm of the mind—what he called the "imaginal realm," meaning real but non-physical. Because of my own experiences, it seemed to me that the only way I was going to convince him of the material reality of the subject was to drag a flying saucer onto his front porch and have him touch it.

Our conversations about the near-death experience were more pleasing to Ken because we had a common view of the subject. I was amazed that our lives had taken so many divergent twists and turns. He was totally unaware and amazed that I had undergone two NDE's. He listened intently as we sat quietly drinking coffee while I related my experiences. He said, "You truly had the classic experiences, didn't you?" It was the first time I had told anyone about them. He was able to guide me through some of my hidden feelings and I began to release emotions which had been repressed for many years. I am very thankful for our reunion and for how Ken was able to help me during our talk.

I have had two NDE experiences, which he considered to be of the classic type. The first occurred in 1965 at a time when I found myself in both acute stress and dire poverty.

I had just completed medical school and started an office practice in a small town in the San Fernando Valley. Before I entered school, I was fortunate to have made the acquaintance of a general practitioner who, through the years had become a close friend. He welcomed me into his office with open arms. I shared the facility with a dentist and an optometrist. It came as quite a shock when my life-long friend suddenly passed away shortly after I arrived on the scene. He was 39 years old and died a horrible death. He was a kind and generous person but had a major character flaw: he always had to be right and never could be wrong. This type of thinking, coupled with foolishness and some amazingly bad luck, drove him to an early grave. The poor man suffered constant abdominal pain and had diagnosed himself as having abdominal cancer. It was only after a twelve-hour operation in a gallant attempt to save his life that he found out that he was wrong. The surgeon found that he had a severely ulcerated stomach which had involved other abdominal organs. His true diagnosis turned out to be only a severe peptic ulcer, which he had neglected. He became worse and hemorrhaged profusely. In other words, he simply bled to death.

I was severely affected by the loss of my friend and the only immediate emotional Band-Aid was to work long hours in an attempt to forget. During this time I realized that financial reward for my previous educational endeavors was much slower in coming than I had anticipated.

In my dire straits, I sometimes provided entertainment for my colleagues by becoming the recipient of some cruel jokes. One notable example, was a time when I had continuous and severe bouts of bronchial asthma. It became my habit to bring home a generating tank of pure oxygen and administer this gas to myself. I would isolate myself in a semi-darkened bedroom, apply the face mask and breathe this soothing gas deeply into my lungs. Soon I would drift off into the quiet oblivion of sleep.

One depressing evening I went home early with a severe coughing spell and decided that I would take a treatment in the comfort of my bedroom. I set up the apparatus, adjusted the flow of gas, made myself comfortable and drifted off into deep sleep. Suddenly, I was out of my body and floating someplace above it in a position to watch my poor pathetic self laying on the bed with the mask in place and peacefully absorbing the flow of gas.

Soon I found myself bathed in a bright light and being drawn into a tunnel of light. This was the most peaceful light I had ever encountered. It was as if the light energy itself was alive. In addition, the intensity of this beautiful luminosity was beyond description. I was at peace in the most profound sense of the word. This was a feeling of non-temporal existence which cannot be described in words. I was pulled through this light tunnel without any apparent force and I became aware of some sort of an opening distantly ahead.

Suddenly I heard an all-encompassing voice which was commanding in character. It was a voice without apparent gender and it spoke to me in no uncertain terms. It commanded me, "Go back." I didn't want to! I was well satisfied where I was and wanted with all my heart and soul to continue on this magnificent journey of peace. But efforts to mentally argue against this command were futile and I felt myself being propelled back, the way I had come—through and out of the tunnel. Immediately I felt as though I was literally slammed into my body. My body consciousness returned and soon I began to gather my wits. I looked over at the tank of gas and noticed that the gauge read empty. There was no gas flowing. I could not imagine what had happened.

The next day I performed a careful examination of the apparatus and found that someone had adulterated the oxygen with nitrous oxide gas. This is the so-called laughing gas. I didn't think it was funny at all and let the guilty individuals know that in no uncertain terms.

Nevertheless, it had been an unforgettable experience which I mulled over and over in my mind a thousand times. I was puzzled and couldn't understand what had happened. Being scientifically oriented, I began to question my mental processes. Perhaps I was a victim of the pathophysiology of nitrous oxide, my experience merely being its effect on my brain. If this were the case, then how could I explain the profound feeling of reality and how could I float above myself and consciously recall this visual event? The most logical conclusion that I could finally draw was that during the course of the experience, I had become toxic with the nitrous and had entered the realm of death. In other words, I was just plain dead. But apparently it was not my time to enter that state of existence permanently. Was it a coincidence that the bottle of gas ran dry? Was it fate or part of some divine plan of greater design? These questions will always be with me.

My second NDE occurred on August 16, 1973. My recollection is vivid because this incident was so traumatic it literally changed my life.

On a warm summer evening my close friend Jack, my wife and I arrived at Van Nuys airport about 5:30 p.m. We were going to fly to Bakersfield for dinner. I am a licensed pilot and I had made arrangements with the Fixed Base Operator to have an aircraft ready and waiting. We parked, locked the car, walked to where the FBO promised to leave the key and the log book for the aircraft. We made our way to the parked airplane and proceeded with the pre-flight inspection. To my dismay I found the fuel tanks almost empty. Never before had I rented aircraft with so little fuel on board. I went to the nearest pay telephone, called the FBO at the other end of the field , and arranged for the gas truck to meet us. We climbed into the plane. I started the engine, called Ground Control for clearance and taxied toward the north end of the airport. It was only a few moments until we arrived there, met the waiting truck and issued instructions for the type and amount of fuel needed. At that point I made my way to the pilots' lounge and checked the weather for our visual flight rules from Van Nuys to Bakersfield. The weather was reported as clear, light winds, and unlimited visibility.

The flight would take about an hour. I considered this a short hop, one I had taken many times before. My passengers and I climbed back into the waiting aircraft, secured our seatbelts and settled in for a pleasant, routine dinner-hour flight. Jack sat to my right, in the co-pilot's seat; my wife sat in the right rear seat. The pre-flight check had been carried out. I started the engine and tuned in the Van Nuys ATIS (Air Terminal Aviation Service) radio station. When I had the necessary information, I changed frequencies and called Van Nuys Ground Control for clearance to taxi to the active runway. We proceeded with our taxi roll to the run-up area just short of the active.

All that was left to do was to finish the pre-flight checklist and the final engine run-up. One by one I went carefully over the list. All lights were on, all instruments checked and set. We were ready for take-off.

Night was rapidly enshrouding us. I called the tower for take-off clearance. Permission for take-off was given so I taxied into position on the runway and slowly advanced the throttle until the engine was running at full take-off speed. I carefully pulled back the stick and instantly we became airborne. After we started to climb, I commented to my passengers that it appeared we were going to be late for dinner.

The departure was uneventful and routine. The atmosphere aboard was relaxed. I made the standard departure and headed the nose of our aircraft directly toward the predetermined compass heading. I set the navigational side of the radio for a (V-O-R) frequency heading toward the Gorman V-O-R. This was the radio halfway point to our destination. The needle slowly began to center and at a cruising altitude of 10,000 feet I leveled the nose of our little bird for a calm and smooth flight.

Everything was functioning normally. It was the beginning of a beautiful flight. We were starting to see lights below as the dusk melted into the blackness of night. The panorama appeared crystal clear, just as the weatherman predicted. I asked Jack and my wife if they were enjoying the flight. They seemed relaxed and in awe of the beautiful scene below.

Time passed quickly and we started to approach the Gorman VOR. The needle on the Omnigator started its slow swing from the indicted "To" to a "From" configuration I reset the radio to a Bakersfield frequency, but nothing happened. This didn't disturb me because there had been previous times when this had happened. I simply tuned Van Nuys back in and started to fly a "From" radial, continuing on my original heading toward Bakersfield. But then, much to my surprise and dismay, no "From" heading registered on the gauge. We were experiencing complete radio failure. The only noise from it was the constant sound, pop!pop!pop! over the speaker system.

It was now evident that we had lost all communication. I looked ahead and still could not see the loom of light emanating from the Bakersfield area. This was strange because at our altitude it should have been visible. Perhaps there is ground fog in the Bakersfield area, I thought. If that was the case, I did not want to attempt a landing without radio communication with the ground.

To my right was the pitch blackness of the desert. There was no moon to guide us. I noticed that two beacons were visible and in an instantaneous decision I changed course and headed toward those lights. I gave a short explanation to my companions and tried to reassure them. I simply told them that we were having a navigational problem and we would be changing destinations.

Soon we were crossing the rugged Tehachapi Mountain Range in the cold dispiriting night with absolutely no visual reference below and knowing there was desolate desert terrain ahead.

Suddenly the aircraft was gripped in violent turbulence. Everything in the cabin began to float or stick to the ceiling, including my charts and other navigational aids. I desperately fought the controls to stabilize the aircraft. I concentrated deeply with my eyes glued on the instruments. All at once the gyrocompass started a slow roll and all attempts to "cage" it and stop the malfunction proved fruitless.

My God, I thought, what more can happen? I wondered if the engine might be next. I decided to fly toward the beacon to my left, thinking it would be China Lake Naval Air Station. The light to my right would then have to be the small city of Inyokern.

To my left I could see one row of runway lights in the pitch blackness of the land below. I couldn't tell which side of the runway was represented by that ridiculous lighting pattern. There were no taxi lights, no ILS, no background lights and no threshold lighting system. There was a rotating beacon which appeared to be coming from the tower.

I took up a new heading directly toward the tower. Next, I executed the emergency signal, which consisted of turning my landing lights on and off in rapid succession and waving my wings. I peered out of my little left hand window looking for some response from the tower. It was only moments before I got my first surprise. It came in the from of a steady red light. This meant, Do Not Land!

I was shocked and wondered what would happen next. Fortunately I kept my eyes glued on the tower and was surprised to see a steady green light shining at me.

At that point I chose to inform my passengers of our true situation. I told them that we were attempting a landing at an alternate airport due to radio failure and other instrument problems. They seemed to have confidence in me as the pilot in command and responded to my directions without argument. I told them to make sure their seat belts were firmly fastened and to be prepared for an abrupt landing. They became quiet and asked no questions.

I was now cleared to land. I started my downwind approach, using the one row of lights below as a guide. Without a radio I was unable to set my altimeter, so I had to guess at an approach of one thousand feet above the ground. What I could not know or see was that the desert floor below was slowly rising.

The desert night air was hot and I could feel the radiant heat from the ground below. Next I slowed the aircraft to 120 miles per hour and put down 20 degrees of flaps. I lowered the landing gear and waited for the indicator light to show that the gear was down and locked. My prop was set at full pitch and I maintained what I thought was an altitude of 1,000 feet above the ground. I proceeded with a shallow base turn. Instantly my landing lights illuminated the desert floor: sand, cactus and sage. Panicky thoughts flew through my mind; an extreme emergency situation had just begun. I knew that if I hit the ground with a nose down position we would all perish. There was only time to utter a few choice curse words. My actions which followed were purely automatic behavior.

My right hand shot toward the throttle control and with one swift motion I pushed the throttle to its maximum full open, "fire-walled" position. I pulled back on the yoke and assumed straight and level flight. This was an effort to prevent a "stall" configuration. I knew that we were going to hit the sand, so I wanted the nose of the aircraft as high as possible. I kept the stick pulled back into my lap and watched in horror as I saw the left wing impact with the ground. We were instantly propelled forward, sliding in the hot desert sand, listening to the sound of the ripping and tearing of metal around us. The nose of the aircraft came down with a tremendous jolt and I watched as the mighty three-bladed propeller took a bite out of the earth, which ripped the entire engine from the fuselage. It was the moment the entire aircraft hit the ground and slid toward the threshold of the runway. We came to rest only 500 feet from the distant edge of this isolated military runway.

The facts pertinent to this discussion involve my feelings at the time of impact and shortly thereafter. I had made every effort to cushion the impending collision. I felt the jolt of the crash and then everything went black. Suddenly I felt myself rushing toward and finally into a tunnel of light. A feeling of absolute calm was upon me. I was surrounded with an aura of blissful peace. There was the distinct feeling that I had been in this place before. It was not long on this journey when I heard a stern, commanding, peaceful voice ordering me, "Go Back"! There was an implication that I should have known better than to proceed and that I did not belong in this place at all.

Shortly after this directive, I was jolted into consciousness and found myself rubbing my eyes and thinking that I was blind. I rubbed away some of the blood which had saturated my eyeballs and realized that I could indeed see. Then I knew I was staring out a blood smeared window. Yes! Yes! I was still alive - and so were my wife and friend.

Recently I discussed this NDE with a learned colleague. He pointed out that this could be classified as an "angel experience." This was an unfamiliar term to me. I asked him to explain what it meant. He merely asked how long I thought it took for all the events of the crash itself to have taken. I pondered the question for a moment and answered, "Probably only a fraction of a second." He then posed the question of how I was able to recall the events that happened at the moment of impact so well. It was as if I was seeing everything in slow motion. It didn't take me long to realize that this was a physical impossibility. He then reiterated, "I think that you might have had an "angel experience." As I reflected on it, I could not disagree.

Chapter 3

FAMILY INFLUENCE

My parents, Joseph and Shirley Leir moved from New York to the San Francisco Bay area in the 1930s and I was born there in 1935. My mother had two sisters and two brothers, who also lived in the Bay Area. Although they experienced dire poverty when they were children my mother's family managed to keep their spirits high.

My father's background was much different from my mother's. He, his sister and two brothers were raised in an even stricter family environment, dominated by their mother. Their father was a skilled tailor who emigrated from Russia and was able to make a living almost immediately because of his craft. My father's life seemed to center around a sense of independence that was drummed into his character starting at a very early age.

During the Great Depression, he met my mother, married and ventured to the West Coast. They were soon followed by my mother's two sisters and their husbands, then in short order, her parents and, finally, her brothers. Most of the family settled in San Francisco proper, although both sisters settled in nearby Oakland. His siblings drifted between California and the East Coast. Eventually, my uncle Fred permanently took up residence in California.

So my parents had a very extended family in the immediate area, and it was soon enlarged by children born to my aunts and uncles. With many cousins, I grew up with a powerful sense of family. Although I was an only child, I felt that my cousins were much like brothers.

When I was about five years old, we moved to a small town on the San Francisco peninsula called San Bruno. Almost every weekend, we would trek across the Oakland Bay Bridge to the East Bay area. Since both of my aunts lived there, it provided a central meeting place for all the sisters and cousins to gather on a regular basis. Sometimes all four cousins, Don, Cliff, Kenneth and I would be together during our East Bay visits.

As the years went by, the interests of we cousins turned in different directions. Don began to take piano lessons and his parents became convinced he possessed an innate talent for music. Cliff and Kenneth had a greater inclination toward the academic world and pursued interests in that direction. I was constantly reminded of the very good grades they achieved in school, compared to mine, which were just average.

As a young boy, I often went outside at night, just to gaze up at the sky. I was fascinated with the stars. When I was old enough to use the library, I centered my attention on astronomy books. Since I was too young to comprehend the writing well, I concentrated on the pictures. Soon I was able to pick out major constellations and, with the help of my older friends, apply the correct names.

One day I announced to my parents that I wanted to be an astronomer. They laughed and said that my math grades were not good enough for that field of study. Disappointed by their lack of encouragement, I gave up the idea. Privately, my interest never waned.

I don't know whether it was my environment or my genetics which endowed me with a vivid and wild imagination. Somehow, I became convinced that I could actually fly. In many of my nighttime dreams, flying was second nature to me. My friends were also convinced that I could fly. Perhaps, as a group, we all became caught up in my spirited imagination.

One of my earliest heroes was Superman. My grandfather, a tailor, presented me with one of the best birthday presents I ever received—a hand-sewn Superman cape. I was so proud of this garment, and so convinced that somehow it enabled me to fly, that I would not allow any of my friends to wear it.

****

As the years passed, my cousins and I followed paths which separated us geographically. Don moved to New York to pursue his musical career. As the years went by, he became a noted jazz pianist, playing with some of the greats, such as Dave Brubeck. Cliff became an M.D., specializing in cardiology at a variety of institutions, including Stanford University. Ken earned a Ph.D. in clinical psychology and began teaching at the University of Connecticut. He gained a lot of public attention by collaborating with Dr. Raymond Moody to study near-death experiences. Soon after, he began writing books based on the research he was performing at the university.

Thus, over the years, our close relationship as cousins waned as we went our separate ways. Reading Ken's book, *The Omega Project*, in 1989 revived many old memories, and I felt compelled to call him. We had remained in contact by telephone and mail, but had not seen each other for years.

During the phone conversation with Ken, I asked if he was in touch with our two other cousins, with whom I'd also lost contact. He said he was and had stayed with Cliff when he, Ken, made one of his quick trips to the San Francisco area. His mother, my aunt Ro, was living in a retirement home in Berkeley. He also told me he had recently had dinner with Don in New York City. I was overjoyed to hear this news and suggested it would be wonderful if all the cousins could get together for a reunion. He enthusiastically responded, "That's really a great idea. Let's give it some thought."

We agreed to check our schedules and get back in touch soon. After hanging up, I sat deeply in thought. The years of my childhood flashed by as if I were watching a motion picture. I couldn't wait to tell my mother.

My father had died a few years before and my mother's health, both physically and psychologically, was gradually deteriorating. Her hearing and vision were poor, and she had suffered a stroke. Although there was no acute paralysis, she was left weak and unable to take care of herself. I was fortunate to find a woman to take her into her home and care for her full-time. Today at 95, my mother is alert and often asks questions about my cousins and her one remaining sibling, Ro. Those family ties are still strong.

When I told her about the proposed reunion of the cousins, she was deeply moved. Tears ran down her cheeks when I related the conversation I had with Ken.

Due to our busy schedules, several months passed before Ken and I were able to touch base again. He had talked with Don in New York and found out that Don would perform a jazz concert in Berkeley in May. Ken said he might also be making a trip to the Bay Area about the same time. He asked if I could fly up.

I replied, "I'll call Don to find out exactly what date he will be arriving so I can make plans."

The conversation ended on that note. I was about to begin another great adventure and suddenly felt emotional and nervous. The next day I called Don. He seemed pleased to hear from me. It had been a while since we had talked. He told me the date for his trip to California was May 12 and that he would have about five days to spend before he had to return to New York. I told him I would let Ken know and that the date sounded like it would work just fine for me.

As I hung up the phone, I was filled with joy. I shouted to my wife, "Sharon, guess what? The cousin reunion is really going to happen."

Surprised, she looked at me and asked, "Are the wives coming?"

"I forgot to ask," I replied sheepishly. "I'll find out in a few days, though."

During the next two weeks, our plans solidified. It seemed that the wives were not going to attend, which did not displease Sharon, since she had made tentative plans to visit her relatives during that same time period.

I began to plan for the event, making arrangements to take time off from my practice. The surgical schedule was not heavy at that point and my secretary only had to move a couple of cases. The next few weeks seemed to drag, until finally, the day arrived. My flight from Santa Barbara was uneventful. I arrived at Oakland on schedule, gathered my baggage and headed toward the car rental counter. Outside, the temperature was cool and crisp, but the sun felt warm on my face.

It wasn't long before I found myself heading north on the Nimitz Freeway toward Berkeley. It had been quite a few years since I had traveled that highway but my memory served me well. After only half an hour, I reached my turnoff. Then, the streets became unfamiliar and I turned to the directions I had gotten from the innkeeper over the phone. Soon I found the small hotel recommended by Cliff.

On reaching my room, I discovered a note from Ken taped to the door. He had arrived a day early and made plans to meet me that afternoon with his mother. I was to wait in my room until contacted by him or Cliff.

Minutes later, I heard a knock on the door. I jumped to my feet and pulled the door open. There stood Ken and, behind him to one side, his mother, my very dear Aunt Ro. Ken stood framed in the doorway, silhouetted by the dim hall light. He appeared taller than I remembered; I had forgotten that he was over six feet tall. His curly blond hair hung loose and he wore casual pants and an untucked shirt.

"Hi, hi, hi, please come in," I stammered emotionally as I waved them into the room. We greeted each other with hugs and kisses. The tears welled in my eyes. I reached for a tissue and dabbed them dry, doing my utmost to control my emotions. It had been many years since I had seen Ken; however, I had seen my aunt recently.

Within a few minutes, the mood became lighter as the formalities were dispensed with. I had brought my video camera and Ken suggested we take advantage of the opportunity and videotape his mother answering questions in reference to incidents which only she would know about. Ken did the interview and I filmed it. Both of us were amazed at the new stories she told. It was a very enlightening experience for us as family members.

Little did we realize then that the video interview would go on to become the cornerstone of our cousin reunion. It set the format for events yet to happen. Ken and I agreed I would take the tape home and make copies for all the cousins.

With this activity complete, I asked Ken what the plans were for the rest of the day. He said he had to take his mother back to her residence and asked if I would follow him in my car. Then we would go to Cliff's house, where Don was to meet us. This idea sounded fine, so off we went.

Cliff's home was nestled in the hills of Pinole, a small community in the hills of the east Oakland Bay area. Ken and I had been there for only a few minutes before the doorbell chimed and in walked my cousin Don. Again, there was a warm round of hugs. After dinner we sat around the kitchen table for hours bringing each other up to date. Our lives had taken distinctly different turns, but the feeling of a blood bond was still there. I felt overwhelmed by the emotion of the moment. It produced a profound sensation that I had contacted my inner self.

In the days that followed, our reunion was filled with emotional events that reconnected me to my youthful fascination with the stars. It would be difficult to determine exactly which event had the greatest influence. Perhaps it was a combination of witnessing Don's performance at the concert which stirred and fired my emotions, together with the many intimate talks I had with Ken regarding my near-death experiences and other psychic experiences. I confessed some of my deepest secrets to him, while he listened intently, using his professional psychological skills to guide me in reaching new conclusions. I also took the opportunity to question him deeply about his NDE research.

One particular night, alone in my hotel room, I looked at myself in the mirror. This was not the face of a young boy who played with his close cousins, but a middle-aged man who was growing older. As I stared at my face, my thoughts and emotions began to churn. Within me was a growing awareness that, while I had succeeded financially in my career, and had a loving wife and beautiful daughter, there was a vague feeling of emptiness inside...a sense that I was not fulfilling my greater purpose.

Perhaps I was experiencing a proverbial mid-life crisis, I thought. I quickly realized that I had little control over the aging process, and that the most important thing I could do was to discover the purpose for my existence. The mere action of self-questioning was part of the process of maturation. I wondered what the real reason was for my visit to northern California. Why was I striving to recall memories with my cousins? Why at this particular time was I assessing my life's values? Was this all part of some great synchronous plan?

I was not raised in a religious environment. My father often criticized organized religion, because of its vast wealth when many of its followers were poor, yet he still believed in the existence of God and the power of prayer. He always said that instead of praying in a multimillion-dollar building, he could do a better job by kneeling under one of the Lord's own trees in open sunlight.

I was quite close with my grandfather on my mother's side, an orthodox rabbi who shared private thoughts with me which seemed diametrically opposed to his chosen profession. Once he confided that, while studying to become a rabbi, he had secretly read material from both the Talmud and the Kabbalah — esoteric Judaic scripture forbidden to any but the holiest of men. He never told anyone what he had read, but he emphasized that the nature of this life was not the way it appeared, including religious belief. He told me that the essence of what we were taught about life and spirit was incorrect. This left me insecure in my own belief system. I realized that I was a spiritual being, but what that meant exactly was not yet made clear to me.

My grandfather also stressed his belief in something I never forgot: we are not alone in the universe. Decades later, alone in a hotel room, I marveled that this statement felt as true to me as my belief that I could fly had been when I was a child. Was this the key to my purpose? Did my destiny somehow involve the subject of unidentified flying objects? It all started to make sense. Suddenly I became aware that I was a part of some bigger picture. I was being guided to do what I had to do. My consciousness was expanding and, as a result, I was starting to ask questions of a spiritual nature.

I knew beyond the shadow of a doubt that I was set on a new course to follow, searching for knowledge I would eventually share with the entire world, fulfilling my destiny.

Chapter 4

THE MEETING

June of 1995 was filled with a myriad of projects for me. It seemed as though I was spending more time on ufology than my chosen profession. My phone was ringing off the hook. Most of the calls were from MUFON members asking me if I could do one thing or another. I tried to accommodate everyone who called, but it didn't take me long to learn I couldn't please everyone, nor do everything asked of me.

My practice was feeling the effect of Managed Care, with a consequent decline in the number of private patients and a significant income loss. I thought about what I might do to supplement my earnings, and one of the activities I chose was to write articles for newspapers, and a few select magazines, pertinent to my field of practice. But I had no idea of what that would lead to.

The local MUFON chapter to which I belonged was having severe financial problems. I felt an obligation to offer some help. The officers had changed many times, some leaving the organization permanently, others switching posts within the group. The position of Section Director was occupied by Alice Leavy, a dedicated person who had a multitude of personal experiences in the UFO field. The Assistant Section Director, Kathy Epperson, was also a person of high integrity and ambition, with the additional talent of baking the greatest-tasting chocolate chip cookies I have ever eaten. Kathy and Alice had been part of the original group which established the local MUFON branch. The other members of the board of directors were also people with dedication and high standards. I couldn't understand why, with all this excellent people-power, there should have been financial problems.

Meetings were held in a low-rent building located centrally for the area. It wasn't fancy, but served the chapter's needs in a sufficient manner. One of my suggestions was to change the meeting location so more people could attend, increasing the amount of money taken in per meeting. I was pleasantly surprised to find my suggestion implemented. Future meetings were scheduled to be held at a local Days Inn hotel.

Another suggestion was to try a fund-raiser. Alice and the board liked the idea, but were unsure of what type of event would make money. I suggested we put on a classic car show. For many years I had been an avid classic car collector and knew a lot about that field. Since neither Alice nor the board members had any experience at that sort of thing, it became my responsibility to convince them it could be a money-making project. I drew a chart showing all the pros and cons of the proposed event, as well as the amount of money that could be raised. The idea was unanimously accepted and the car show took place without any problems.

Although the cash flow improved from these events, there nevertheless seemed to be a constant shortfall. This prompted me to supply more suggestions. I came up with a plan to redesign our monthly MUFON newsletter and re-title it The Ventura-Santa Barbara Vortex. The committee asked for volunteer writers. Naturally, all heads turned in my direction. What could I do? Suddenly I had the post of an investigative reporter for the new publication.

As I sat at my computer pounding the keyboard for long hours, I learned what the term "deadline" meant. Sometimes the pressure was tremendous. Although my position was purely voluntary, I was driven to get the job done.

I felt it was my duty to cover as many events as I could. It was fun to attend lectures, listen intently, make notes, and then write it up in a way that would allow me to express my own opinion, while providing an objective account of the event. At one of these gatherings I met a man who would change my life forever.

In June, that same month of 1995, I received word that the UFO Expo-West, a major public event, was going to be held in Los Angeles. The literature was quite intriguing so I made arrangements to attend. I would be wearing two hats: enthusiastic ufologist and investigative reporter. I could look, listen, enjoy, and be critical all at the same time. I would write accurate reports, but I was free to say exactly what my opinion was.

Alice accompanied me on the trip. We arrived at our hotel late in the afternoon, but before the lectures began. This allowed us to get settled and look at the exhibits. There were many types of vendors present, about ninety percent of them related to the field of ufology. Included were merchants specializing in video tapes, T-shirts, jewelry, dolls, publications, and a few other items only slightly pertinent.

As we walked through the display areas, we were greeted by many familiar faces.

Some were surprised that I was there; others accepted it without batting an eye. The surprise seemed to stem from a prevalent opinion that people in the medical profession didn't—perhaps shouldn't—spend their time at UFO conventions. "Well," I thought, "if I'm going to be stared at, then so be it!"

The next day I arose early to attend as many of the lectures as I could. During my simple breakfast alone in the coffee shop, I planned out my day, using the conference program as a guide. I wondered where Alice was, but knew she would catch up with me later.

The organization of the conference required each presenter to give a 45-minute lecture, which was included in the cost of admission to the expo. During their presentation, the speakers would give the audience reasons to attend the companion workshop, for which there was an additional charge. I was a bit shocked to learn the presenter did not get paid for his or her lecture by the promoter, but only derived a share of the proceeds taken in from the workshop—sometimes less than forty percent. At that time I really didn't understand what motivated the speakers to settle for a deal like that. Only later, when I became aware of the entire operation of the speaking circuit, did I understand. My education in public presentation was just beginning.

I took voluminous notes during the first lecture to give me a good start on the article I would write. Afterward, I ran into Alice. We exchanged greetings and I told her my plans for the day. The next lecture was by an abduction researcher. Alice asked if I knew who he was.

"Yes, I've heard about him, but have never had the opportunity to hear him speak," I answered. "I believe he speaks on the subject of alien abductions. Would you like to attend his lecture?" She nodded, so we headed toward the lecture hall.

The room was quite large with its seats laid out theater style, filling the entire center section of the room. Along the walls were tables with various displays of pictures, books and other pertinent materials.

We wandered around the right side of the room, and then crossed to the opposite side. I noticed a long table displaying several photographs and what appeared to be medical and scientific data. "Hey, Alice! Come over here and take a look at this," I said.

We approached the table together. The first item we saw was a display of foot x-rays depicting some sort of foreign object in the big toe area. Standing by the table was a tall, good-looking man engaged in conversation with several other people.

He turned and looked at Alice. "Hi there," he said stepping forward to shake hands with her.

She replied, "Hi, it's very nice to meet you. I'm Alice Leavy, the Section Director for the Ventura-Santa Barbara chapter of MUFON. I'd like you to meet Dr. Roger Leir. He's our medical consultant."

He stuck out his hand and gave me a hardy handshake. "I'm very happy to meet you," he said graciously. There was something about him which immediately caught my attention. Perhaps it was his eyes; it seemed as if he was capable of looking right through me.

I gestured toward the x-rays. "Do you mind if I pick these up and have a look at them?" I asked.

He reached over and handed me the x-ray films in one swift motion. "Take as long a look as you want, Doc."

As they resumed their conversation, I held the films up to the light and scrutinized the foreign objects. My initial impression was that they looked very similar to stainless steel sutures commonly used in foot surgery. I thought to myself, "This is a total waste of time. I'm not giving any more attention to some guy who displays x-ray films of some previous foot surgery, and makes a big deal out of the whole thing." I gently laid the films back down on the table and started to walk away, leaving Alice to fend for herself.

Then I heard Alice's voice calling me to return, so I moved back to the table. She grabbed my arm and said, "I think you should listen to what he has to say. It's really very interesting."

I gave her a nudge and she moved toward me to hear what I was about to whisper in her ear. "Alice, come on, let's not waste anymore time with this guy. It's a bunch of nonsense! It's just someone who's had foot surgery and is claiming some absurd story about alien implantation."

She looked at me as if I had just come down with the plague. "Roger, you aren't being fair. You should give him a chance to tell you what this is all about."

"Okay, I'll listen to what he has to say. But remember, I'm only doing this because you asked me to," I said grudgingly.

The researcher was now surrounded by a large crowd of people who were listening intently to him. We edged our way closer and at the appropriate opportunity Alice jumped into the conversation. "Please tell Dr. Leir what you were explaining to me about this case with the foot x-ray."

"Oh, yes, I would be most happy to," he replied.

I listened closely as he began to relate the story of an individual's abduction history and the events that lead to an x-ray being taken. I asked him about any previous foot surgery. He said none had been performed. I then asked if he could present proof of his statements, and to my surprise he led me to a gigantic pile of folders. Leafing through several stacks, he came up with a thick medical file with the name of the patient covered over. He looked directly into my eyes with his powerful gaze. "These are her medical records. Would you like to go through them?"

"Sure, I'd love to take a look," I answered.

I reached and he gave me the file. "Would you have any objection if I took this data to my room, where I can go over it in peace and quiet?"

He responded by handing me another stack of documents, saying there was additional information and reports from the University of Houston. I thanked him for his trust, put the package of documents under my arm, and with Alice following, walked briskly away. We pushed our way through a small crowd of people gathered at the doorway and proceeded to gather in the hall. "Well, that was quite an experience," I commented. Alice agreed and suggested we take a break for lunch.

The hotel food was in the "not too bad" category. Soon our repast was completed and we sat looking once again at the lecture and workshop schedule.

"I see that our researcher friend is going to be giving a lecture at 3:00 this afternoon. I'd like to attend. Wouldn't you?" Alice asked.

"I guess we could do that," I responded. "First I want to unload all this stuff that we got from him in my room. I'll meet you back down here in about twenty minutes."

When I arrived at my room, I had to return some phone calls waiting for me. My office made sure I didn't forget that my primary obligation was still to my patients.

When I returned, Alice was waiting, almost in the exact same spot where I had left her. She was surrounded by a crowd of people. I recognized some of them as members of our own MUFON group. Some of the others whom I did not recognize turned out to be members of the Los Angeles or other local chapters of MUFON. Alice introduced me to the members I didn't know.

The lecture room was crowded with people. Apparently, the latter part of the day attracted more attendees. We managed to find two seats near the front of the room. Soon the moderator came to the lectern and introduced the speaker to the audience. Gradually a hush came over the room.

He entered from stage left and took his place at the lectern. He opened with a pleasing joke and continued in a very light vein. I realized almost immediately that this man knew how to work the audience. During his speech, the crowd reacted like a finely tuned orchestra responding to a skilled conductor. They oscillated from rapt silence to outright laughter.

First, he described his background and mission in life. I pulled a pen from my pocket and began to take notes. After all, this was the primary reason for me being present at this conference. I would critique his lecture as I would any of the others.

The speaker told us that he serves as the Chief of Abduction Investigations and Director of Physical Investigations for the Houston UFO Network in Texas. He himself is an abductee who has spent nearly 30 years gathering hard physical evidence on the abduction phenomenon, including a variety of alleged implants and an alleged artifact from the UFO which crashed near Roswell, New Mexico, in 1947. I was impressed by his extensive training in clinical hypnotherapy, hypno-anesthesia therapy, master level Neurolinguistic Programming (NLP) and graphology, all of which he includes in his investigative technique. For years, he has provided investigations and hypnotherapy at no charge to persons involved in alleged abductions and human/alien contact events. He is also a former senior military police officer and former CIA agent (covert operations).

He said that his mission is to bring credible, scientific findings about UFOs and abductions to the medical and scientific communities. He has spoken before a group of 250 physicians at a major U.S. hospital regarding medical implications of the phenomenon and has been invited to appear on a medical panel with Dr. John Mack and best-selling author-ufologist Budd Hopkins. Papers about his work have been written for a forum at the world-renowned Massachusetts Institute of Technology (MIT).

He went on to talk about the abduction cases he has investigated over nearly three decades. He was careful not to divulge the information everyone most wanted to hear, those tantalizing tidbits being saved for presentation at his workshop. The lecture ended with an impressive round of applause.

Alice and I parted company. She had made plans to staff one of the tables for an attendee who was displaying literature and other materials related to the abduction phenomena. This left me free to do as I pleased for the balance of the afternoon. I made a beeline for the next presentation I had marked in my program.

At dinner, Alice and I were joined by a host of other presenters. One of the individuals that she was working with was Yvonne Smith, who had a fast-growing reputation as an authority in the abduction field. She had accumulated a great number of abduction cases and was the force behind an abductee support group called Close Encounter Research Organization (CERO). About a year earlier, Yvonne had asked me to become the medical consultant for that group, and I was happy to accept the position. She had undergone training with Budd Hopkins and by doing so had established herself as the West Coast standard. During dinner, many people dropped by the table to say hello to both Alice and Yvonne. They were all introduced to me and I felt honored.

By 10:00 p.m., I was eager to return to the peace and quiet of my room. I said good night to Alice and her friends. At last I was alone. I took advantage of the time by perusing the voluminous amount of medical material I had obtained. The more I read, the more intrigued I became. There was not only a lack of medical evidence to suggest this individual had a foot surgery, but the records also contained a report from the physician who took the x-rays. He stated that the patient had been queried regarding the objects in her foot. She had denied having any medical or surgical intervention whatsoever.

In addition to the medical records contained in the file, there were other documents relevant to this and other cases. One document was a report from the University of Houston by a professor in the Physics Department. Its contents pertained to an analysis performed on an object, obtained from one of his abductee clients, who reported to him that it came from her eye. It was an in-depth report that was quite impressive. Attached was a photomicrograph of the object. The analysis showed a number of unusual properties. There was speculation that it might be the housing for a biological camera installed in the client's eye during an abduction episode.

Finally, I turned out the light, propped up my pillow and prepared to drift off into a peaceful sleep. However, I was too restless; my mind was filled with thoughts of the day's events...abductions, implantations and alien entities.

The next morning, as I sipped a cup of hot coffee in the coffee shop, I heard a familiar voice say, "Hello." Alice joined me and we mapped out the strategy for the rest of the day, deciding to attend some of the lectures together..

The day passed quickly. Both my mind and the yellow note pad were clogged with information. I rushed down the hall toward the room where a workshop was scheduled. I could tell by the crowd gathering at the door that this was going to be a packed room. A young man was standing at the doorway taking tickets for the event. He asked me for my ticket, and I told him that I didn't have one. I asked him to summon the speaker, explaining he had invited me and a colleague to his lecture.

"It's okay, they're my guests," the speaker said, escorting us to seats at the front of the room. I told him I'd gone over the medical records and found them quite interesting. I asked why he didn't just have the objects removed and analyzed. He explained that the client had no medical insurance and couldn't afford to have the surgery performed.

I thought deeply for a moment. "Would the lady be willing to come to California to have the surgery performed?"

He looked at me and said, "I don't see any reason why she wouldn't."

"Well, I'll tell you what," I responded. "If she would be willing to come here, I'll perform the surgery without charge."

He stepped back about three paces with his eyebrows raised, and asked incredulously, "Do you really mean that?"

"I certainly do." I quickly replied.

He shook my hand vigorously. He turned to walk away, then quickly looked back, saying in a loud voice.

"Have a seat and enjoy the lecture."

During the course of his presentation he mentioned the case that he had discussed with me, explaining that I had just offered to perform the surgery without charge. He said that was a major step for research, but the woman couldn't afford the airfare from Houston to California. Next, with what I would learn was typical aplomb for him, he asked if anyone in the audience would volunteer to pay it. Then he finished his presentation. The audience responded with thunderous applause.

As the crowd was leaving, I heard a voice over the loudspeaker system: "Dr. Leir, please come to the podium. Dr. Leir, please come to the podium."

Holding Alice by the arm, I forced my way through the crowd. Our friend was talking to a man. Unsure of why I had been paged, I went up to him. He looked at me, beamed a huge smile, and said, "Dr. Leir, I'd like to introduce you to a gentleman who had just agreed to foot the bill for the airfare."

****

In the weeks that followed, we spoke often times by phone, and during one of these conversations, he asked me if it would be possible to do two separate cases.

He had another individual with a foreign object in his hand. I told him I thought it was a good possibility, explaining I would have to set up an entire team, not only to perform, but also document the procedures. He seemed satisfied with what I had told him, and asked me to let him know when the event could take place.

There were many times I pondered the situation, considering what I might be getting myself into. One of the requests I had made was that he send me the x-rays, so I could take them to a qualified radiologist prior to performing any surgeries. I also explained to him that both surgical candidates would need to have laboratory examinations done prior to coming to California. I would supply both candidates with the orders for the type of lab work needed. In addition, they would be required to start on antibiotics two days prior to the surgery. He agreed to these conditions. I was ready to embark on my first trip towards the unknown.

Chapter 5

THE PLAN

Only a few days after the Expo West, the phone rang shockingly loud at 7:45 a.m. I am a "night person" and my office hours are tailored to my lifestyle, so I was jolted awake. I picked up the receiver. "Hello," I said hoarsely.

"Hi, Doc! This is your friend in Texas. How are you doing this fine morning?" My mind not yet fully conscious, I thought to myself, "Who in the hell is this person?" At that point my memory began to function. Apparently, the two-hour time difference between Texas and California might become a problem with my newfound colleague in Houston.

Deliberately, I responded, "I am just fine. How is every little thing in the great state of Texas?" He seemed to pick up on my facetious mood.

"I hope that I didn't get you up."

"Oh, no," I lied politely. "I was just heading for the shower."

As my senses sharpened, it sunk in that I had volunteered my services as a surgeon to this man. I told him that I could speak more intelligently about the case when I had the information in front of me, and asked him to supply me with some particular data about the proposed patient.

"Would it be convenient for you to call me back this afternoon at my office?"

"I can certainly do that," he answered. With that, our first conversation ended.

I decided to take advantage of the extra time by going to the office early. I quickly showered and dressed. My wife was already up and bustling about the kitchen.

"Sharon, I'm getting an early start today."

"That's great; I know how often you get an early start," she teased, laughing.

I grabbed a cup of tea and a banana on my way to the door, and heard Sharon say, "Have a good day and don't forget to call before you leave for home."

It was a typical day at the office. The caseload was light and I managed to get through the morning without spending time on the telephone. For some reason, people have a tendency to call when I am in the middle of a surgical procedure or just as I am about to examine a new patient.

Upon returning from lunch at 2:00 p.m., I picked up a stack of personal phone messages from my office manager, Janet. I quickly perused the pile and came across a message from the Texas researcher. Over the intercom, I asked Janet when the best time would be for me to make a lengthy phone call. She got back to me a minute later, after checking my schedule.

"You have a break at 3:15, if you stay on schedule," she said.

"Don't worry about that, you know I'm always on time," I laughed, poking fun at myself. I have a well-earned reputation for running late.

At 3:05 p.m., I was actually ten minutes ahead of schedule. Soon I had him on the phone.

First, we chatted about the conference. I offered to send him a copy of my article for the Vortex when it was printed (I had reviewed his lecture quite favorably), and told him we would add his name to our mailing list.

Then he got down to business. "Doc, have you given any more thought to the surgery? I will advise my client as to any details you would care to present to her."

"To be quite honest, I have not really had the time to give it much thought, but I will call you back in a few days." He seemed satisfied and we ended the conversation.

Over the next few minutes, it dawned on me that I had pledged my services without considering some important factors. I wondered whom I would be able to confide in on a professional level. What about the criticism I might receive from my colleagues and peers? With a wife and a little girl to raise, I couldn't afford to give up my practice at this stage in life. Maybe I should have thought of those things before I opened my big mouth. I came close to calling him and canceling the entire plan.

At the end of the day, I called Alice. "I'm concerned that I might have bitten off more than I can chew in regard to the promise I made," I confided. "You know, I might get into serious trouble professionally by proceeding with this."

Alice asked many questions about my profession and how I could get into trouble. I explained that performing the surgery was one thing, but the required documentation, if published, could damage my credibility in medical circles. She felt that I was overreacting and cited other professionals in MUFON who had no problems due to their UFO-related activities. To her, I was just making a mountain out of a molehill, creating unnecessary anxiety.

I postponed making any decisions at that point. As promised, I called my wife to let her know I was leaving. On the way home, I picked up a bouquet of flowers to surprise her.

The evening passed quickly. Fatigue fell upon me like a ton of bricks, and I headed to bed early. In my warm pajamas, I slid under the covers. It felt just wonderful; there was always a comforting sense of security in my bed. Sharon climbed in next to me, reached over and pushed the button on the television remote control. "I'm just going to watch long enough to get sleepy," she said.

With that I shut my eyes and drifted off into dreamland. Perhaps it was the day's events that forced my mind into one of my most adventurous dreams ever.

******

It was a beautiful, bright sunny day. The air was cool and crisp. I looked up at the sky and it seemed as if someone had just freshly painted it a deep blue. I thought this was the most vivid blue sky I had ever seen. As I looked about me I could see I was in some sort of jungle. The foliage was thick and the atmosphere dense. I could smell the moisture dripping from the vines and leaves. What am doing here? I thought. I don't remember getting here. How did I get here? Wow, this is crazy!

Without warning I was jolted by a blood-curdling scream that sounded like a cross between a bull elephant and a tortured human. As the ground began to shake, my first thought was that it was an earthquake. Gripped with fear and panic, I ran as fast as my legs would carry me and jumped up on a low hanging branch of a tree. With my hands securely around the thick branch, I hoisted myself into the upper portion of the tree. I looked ahead into a small clearing. There stood the source of both the terrifying noise and the ground tremors.

It was a gigantic beast with a long neck and a very small head. The face seemed to be looking directly at me and for whatever the reason my fear suddenly vanished. I knew instantly this creature was a species of dinosaur called Brontosaurus. I felt as if I had been with this creature many times before. As I looked out from my perch, I began to notice other prehistoric creatures. I knew them all by habit and name. It was as if they were all my friends.

I reached up to tear a large branch from the tree. I opened my mouth to speak and a strange sound escaped from my larynx. I was shocked. How could I have ever made that sound? There wasn't much time to consider the possibilities. The next thing I knew, that giant beast was heading directly toward my tree. I stared at the approaching creature in awe but without the slightest fear. Soon he stood below me. I reached out, holding the leafy branch in my hand. The beast reached up with his mouth and took the entire offering. There was a look in his eye as if he was saying "Thank you." I watched as he devoured the leafy branch. I felt like saying, "Nice boy, you can go home now."

My lips, however, were held tightly shut. I was making every effort to prevent a sound like the one I had made previously. After the beast finished, he turned and slowly walked away. Each step he took jarred the earth and made the safety of my tree seem less secure. When he was a safe distance away, I slid down the trunk and walked a few feet into the clearing. A huge, strange black flying creature sailed over my head. I knew what this creature was and after spending more time in this strange place I realized that I knew every creature I saw, including their names, as well as habits. Shortly after this final realization, the scene began to fade.

******

All at once I was back in my bed. The sweat poured from my face; I felt nauseous, my head hurt and my ears were ringing, as if I had the flu. My attempt to get out of bed was painful. Somehow, I managed to make my way to the bathroom. I washed my face, downed a couple of aspirin and stumbled back to bed. That was the last thing I remembered until my alarm woke me at 7:30 a.m. the next morning.

It has always been my habit to spend what my wife considers an inordinate amount of time in the shower. This was one day I needed as much as I could get. The soothing pressure of hot water streaming over my body was "just what the doctor ordered." It was certainly more than cleanliness that made me scrub my entire body. It just felt good.

All of a sudden I noticed something unusual on the palm of my right hand. Rinsing off the soap, I saw what appeared to be a line connected by three symmetrical dots extending upward across my palm to the third finger. One dot was at each end of the line and one was placed centrally in the crease of the finger. I thought that I must have marked myself with a ball point pen. Scrubbing forcefully with a wash rag and soap, I tried to remove the mark to no avail. It would not come off. I figured that whatever made the mark was insoluble in plain water and soap, so I planned to remove it with alcohol when I arrived at my office.

The time had gotten away from me and I found myself making a mad dash for the door in my typical Dagwood Bumstead fashion. I said a quick good-bye to my wife and hugged my daughter all at the same instant. The drive to the office only took about fifteen minutes.

Janet immediately confronted me with my tardiness and advised me how many patients we were already behind. My response was to ask for a cup of hot coffee. I quickly donned my white smock and raced into the bathroom. I took a bottle of alcohol from the medicine cabinet and scrubbed my strange mark with a saturated cloth. To my amazement, the mark remained.

My mind raced. How was I going to touch patients with this ugly mark on my hand? I reached for a bottle of nail polish remover. We sometimes used this to remove polish from a toenail which was going to be operated on. I scrubbed again. Nothing happened! I was flabbergasted.

"Janet," I yelled, and she appeared in the doorway.

"Yes, what do you need, Doctor?"

I showed her my marked hand and said, "Please get me a large Band-Aid, so I can cover up this ugly mark."

Janet returned shortly with a one-inch wide bandage. I peeled the paper free and placed the patch over the mark.

"Where in the world did you get that weird mark?"

"To tell you the truth, I don't know. I just woke up that way this morning," I grumbled.

The day proceeded without further aggravation or unusual happenings. The thought of my dilemma gnawed away at the back of my mind. I had to let him know something soon. I was about to leave when Alice called to ask if I was going to be on time for the meeting. I had completely forgotten about that night's MUFON meeting. I told her I would get there as soon as possible and to start the meeting without me if I was late.

When I arrived, the room was filled with people and Alice was at the podium giving her welcoming speech. It was usually my role to introduce the evening's speaker. I waited for my cue from Alice and hastened to the podium. After I addressed the audience, the speaker came up and I retired to the back of the room.

Alice told me one of our board members had brought some strange material she had taken from her front lawn. She showed me the plastic bag and asked if I could take it out to my car and test it for fluorescence with the black ultraviolet light I had there. I took the bag and headed for my car, with Alice and a few others on my heels. Curiosity was running high. Mary Helen, the person who brought in the sample, told Alice this substance appeared on her lawn overnight in the form of a ring.

I opened the trunk of my car and took out the black light. One of our group held the bag open as I shined the light so all the material could be exposed. There was no obvious fluorescence. Abruptly, Alice shouted, "What is that all over your hand?"

I shined the light on my palm. The bandage I had applied earlier was falling off. The area of the mark was fluorescing a brilliant green color. I stood there in shock. The Texas researcher had described a brilliant green fluorescence appearing on the bodies of approximately 5% of alleged abductees. Suddenly I remembered my strange dream. I thought to myself, This is nonsense! This can't be happening to me. I turned to Alice and the group and announced that I must have smeared my hand with something but assured them it would wash off. If only I could believe what I just said, I thought.

After a restless night, I arose in the morning with a nagging question on my mind. Had I become a victim of the very phenomenon I had recently become involved with? I immediately knew what I had to do.

The phone rang three times before a male voice answered, "Hello, may I help you?"

"Hi, this is Roger. I've been considering the surgery and want to start making preparations as soon as possible. I will fax you the information I require on the patient." I gave him the details of what had to be done and some general instructions pertaining to the requirements.

Saturday morning found me sitting quietly in my office preparing to make the necessary arrangements for the impending surgery. Almost as if he were reading my mind, he called on my private line at that instant.

"Hi, Doc. I hope you don't mind me calling on your inside line but I got the number from your wife and she said it would be okay."

I told him that he could call me anytime on that number. He asked me some questions in regard to the lab tests I wanted. I supplied him with the information and then he sheepishly asked, "Doc, do you think that you could arrange to do another surgery in addition to the foot case?" He explained that a man who was an alleged abductee had some sort of a metallic object in the back of his left hand. I asked him if he had seen the x-rays and he replied that he had. In addition, he had known this person for quite some time and was convinced of the sincerity of his encounters.

He also advised me that both surgical candidates had never undergone hypnotic regression. Little did I realize, at that point, how important this would become. I told him I would attempt to arrange for another surgeon to do the hand case, ending the conversation on an uplifting note.

Accomplishing the surgical procedures within the time constraints allowed required a considerable amount of preparation. The first task was to make a list of highly qualified and open-minded individuals. The second consideration was the time and place of the event. I would also need a detailed list of necessary supplies and materials.

My initial decision involved an appropriate co-surgeon. Since the second case involved hand surgery, and podiatrists are limited to foot surgery, I had to consider several possibilities: an orthopedic surgeon, a plastic surgeon, a specialist in family practice, a dermatologist or a general surgeon. After careful thought, I decided to go with a general surgeon. My primary reason for choosing this specialty was the need to have someone who would be prepared to handle anything unusual.

I finally chose a friend I had known for many years. I shall refer to him as Dr. A. Not only was he was a close friend, but his qualifications were impeccable. He was in professional retirement and would perform the procedures without charge.

Next, I considered the need for a well-qualified Ph.D. psychologist. I turned to the roster of members for our local MUFON group and came up with a perfect individual. Christie was doing her doctoral thesis on the subject of hybrid children in relation to the alien abduction experience. She was extremely gentle with her patients and always willing to learn, as well as being a hard worker and ambitious. I knew she would be thrilled with the opportunity to participate in the project and would not ask for monetary compensation.

It was vitally important to have an attorney on our team. Because the entire procedure would be documented for research, all the paperwork, such as consents and releases, needed to be handled impeccably. I had known many attorneys over time, but most of them would not perform pro bono services or stick their necks out to endanger their careers.

One likely individual did come to mind, however. Jerry was more than an attorney; I had known his family for many years and had worked with him on several legal matters. His specialty was patents and copyrights, and he served as legal advisor to his family's pump manufacturing business. I knew I could approach him about the project. I also knew he might laugh at the whole idea but if he thought it could possibly be fun, he would throw himself into the project wholeheartedly.

The next member of the professional component was pivotal. Without him, the entire procedure could not take place. This was our researcher friend. It would be necessary for him to coordinate the entire event from his home in Houston, Texas. In addition, he would have to arrange the air and ground transportation to convey the two surgical patients from the airport to the surgery site. He would also have to act as a conduit between the patients and myself. I would be sending him prescriptions for the patients' lab work and preoperative antibiotics. He would be required to see to it that the patients reacted in a positive manner and have all the lab results sent to me well in advance of the proposed surgical date. This would be no easy task because the surgical candidates lived far from each other and from Derrel.

The Texas researcher would also perform in a professional capacity as hypnoanesthesiologist. I had decided to perform one case with the use of hypnosis and one without. This would add another medical research factor to the picture. We would then be able to do a comparison study in reference to healing, reaction to medication and the requirement for postoperative analgesics. This would be independent from the alien abduction research component.

After the principals were selected, I turned my attention to the remaining portion of the team.

I realized that my surgical nurse should be someone who was not only familiar with my surgical techniques but also a person I could trust completely. After careful consideration, there was only one person who would fill the bill: my daughter-in-law, Denise. I knew she would be fascinated with the procedure and felt secure in the knowledge that she was fully trained by me. Before giving birth to my granddaughter, Denise was a trusted employee in my office and only gave up that position to become a full-time mother. Denise was also trained and certified as a phlebotomist. She would be the one to draw blood which would later come to serve as the transport media for our specimens.

My next area of consideration was recording the entire event. This aspect was most important because it was, above all, a research project. I decided to record the proceedings in comprehensive fashion, using both still photography and video. In addition, written documentation would be necessary.

I needed a very special person to operate the video camera. I did not want an individual who would watch the procedure, become shocked or revolted by the sight of blood and cause a disaster by fainting directly into the surgical area.

I pored over a list of candidates from among the MUFON members. All at once, the name Mike Evans popped into my consciousness. By gosh, I thought, he would be perfect for the job. Mike was a registered nurse employed by the Veteran's Administration. A native Californian, he held a Bachelor's degree in psychology and an Associate in Arts in anthropology, in addition to his nursing degree. Mike had been with the Ventura-Santa Barbara MUFON group since 1987 and was previously the State Section Director. He was also responsible for video recording all of our local MUFON meetings. I was thoroughly satisfied with this choice.

The next position on the team would be the one to coordinate the entire event. I decided this would become a shared position. The individuals chosen were my office manager, Janet, and our current MUFON State Section Director, Alice Leavy. Janet had been part of my office staff for almost five years and was responsible for all the fine details pertaining to my medical practice. Alice had been active in MUFON since 1989. She considers herself a native Californian. Born in Michigan, she migrated to California with her family when she was a toddler. Alice had multiple UFO experiences dating back to the 1970s when she resided in the San Fernando Valley. Both Alice and Janet would be ultimately responsible for the total flow of events which would occur at the time of surgery.

Manual recording of this event required the involvement of professional writers. I looked first at my circle of friends, as well as the MUFON list. My choice narrowed to Jack and Ruth Carlson, who possessed professional writing skills. Ruth was past president of the local writer's club. Jack had previously been in charge of the Assistant Directors training program for the Association of Motion Picture and Television Producers in Hollywood. He had also written numerous articles for the Ventura MUFON Vortex.

Last but not least, I selected members of the team who could perform other tasks necessary to the project. One such person was Bert Clemens. Bert has been a MUFON member for many years and has first-hand knowledge of the abduction phenomenon. As a general contractor with skill in electronics, Bert's talents would be vital to the project. He would make sure all the equipment functioned properly. I decided to transmit the event to an adjoining room where our guests could witness the surgery independently from those who were present in the operating room itself. In order to accomplish this task, cables had to be connected from the camera in the operating theater to the adjoining room with the television receiver. I knew this would be an easy task for Bert. Other electronic equipment which might be necessary to the surgery would be in Bert's domain. This would be decided at a later date.

I was quite satisfied with my preliminary personnel decisions.

Next my thoughts were drawn to the selection of a suitable surgical site. The apparent choices were a hospital, an outpatient surgical center or one of my offices. I had to consider that a hospital would provide a better facility with more equipment, but the amount of people involved in the project was a major drawback. Also, the television equipment would be cumbersome and take some very special politicking. Using an outpatient surgical center presented similar problems. The only logical alternative was one of my three offices. I decided my Camarillo office fit most of the criteria.

This facility was shared with two dentists. If I performed the surgeries on a day when they were not in the office, it would provide us with the ideal location. A single phone call would settle the matter, and since there's no time like the present, I dialed the number and reached Dr. King's answering service. The woman who answered agreed to track him down for me. As I waited for the dentist to come on the line, I wondered what to tell him. I didn't know just how far I could go with him because we did not know each other on a social basis. I thought it best to simply ask about the surgery and leave it at that.

"Hello, this is Dr. King. Can I help you?"

"Hi, Larry, this is Roger. I'm sorry to disturb you. I hope I didn't take you away from anything important."

"No problem, Rog. I just got in and was about to kick off my shoes and watch the news on TV," he responded.

"Larry, I was wondering if there would be any problem with me performing a surgery in the office one Saturday? I know that you and Dick usually don't come in on weekends to see patients."

There was a brief moment of silence as he pondered my request. "I really don't see any problem with that. When do you think this would be?"

I realized I was going to have to nail down a date, right then and there.

"Hang on a second and I'll take a quick look at the calendar," I replied. With that I grabbed my desk calendar and flipped through the pages.

I thought to myself, We're rapidly sailing through the month of July. It's already the 8th of the month. I flipped the page to the next month. August 19 fell on a Saturday. My mind raced. Could I possibly get everything ready by that time? Would this be a satisfactory date for the patients? On the other hand, if I pick the date now and it turns out to be inconvenient for anyone, I can always change it.

We agreed on August 19th and hung up. At that point I realized that I was committed to the event.

I immediately called our researcher friend to report my progress and the decisions which I had made during the last few hours. He seemed pleased and said that he would get in touch with the surgical candidates and advise them of the surgery date.

The next day just flew by. I could hardly wait to take the next step. I planned to be on the telephone for quite some time that night, calling all those whom I had hand-picked for their various roles in the upcoming event.

After three hours of phone calls, I was still sitting in the very same spot without a sign of fatigue. Usually by the middle of the evening, I started to drag a little. That night, I was all fired up and ready to push onward. I had completed all calls but one and the results had been very heartwarming. Absolutely no one had turned me down and everything was all set to push full steam ahead.

The only person I had left to call was Dr. A. I left him for last because I knew his schedule was a little erratic. There was only one phone number where I could contact him. The phone rang about ten times and a female voice answered. I knew from her voice that it was his sister. "Hello, Sadie. Is your brother there?" I asked.

"No, he isn't, but I expect him shortly. Do you want me to have him call you?' she replied.

"Yes, that would be really great. I'm at the Thousand Oaks office. Please have him call on the back line and I'll pick it up," I said.

I went back to the lounge and poured myself a cup of coffee. There was an extension phone there and I could watch for the back line to ring at that location. As I sat there, I began to think about my friend, Dr. A. He was a most unusual soul. His life directed him through a wide variety of experiences.

At one time, he had been part owner of a prominent southern California bank. I recalled the experience I had with him as one of his partners in a land deal at Lake Arrowhead. He managed to acquire the only piece of vacant property on the lake and divided it up into lots. There were plans to build some very high quality homes. As it turned out, about six were actually constructed. He took one for himself, but never occupied it. I used to visit the house and the property with him, and asked many times what he was going to do with the house, but I never received a satisfactory answer. He eventually sold the entire property and all the partners ended up with a tidy profit.

Dr. A. had also been a part owner of a local hospital. The facility did very well financially, but some of his partners could not get along with each other. This resulted in a series of monthly meetings which soon turned weekly and sometimes twice a week. He became extremely tense and irritated with the entire project. Many times I accompanied him to these meetings and was shocked to witness the irrational behavior of the participants. Finally, it was agreed to sell the hospital. Some of the partners who were over-anxious to get out of the deal gave their full shares away for prices in the neighborhood of $75,000 to $100,000. Not Dr. A. He held his ground and found an insurance company as a potential buyer. I recalled that negotiations proceeded for months. I was always privy to the inner happenings because Dr. A. considered me a close friend and sometimes took me along to witness the events.

I will never forget one of those marathon meetings which lasted all night. The members of the board were negotiating the sale with the buyers. The room abounded with sounds of shouting and the crash of objects being thrown at the walls. It was impossible for me to believe that professionals could behave in that manner.

About 6:00 in the morning, Dr. A. walked into the doctor's lounge. He had a full day's growth of beard and his suit was wilted. He showered and donned a clean suit, complete with shirt and tie. Now, he appeared fresh as a daisy. He turned to me and said, "I'm going back in to close the deal. I'll be back shortly."

I sat on the couch, unable to keep my eyes open any longer. I dozed for a while. Suddenly I felt a hand on my shoulder. Dr. A. had a smile on his face. "Let's get out of here and get something to eat. I'll tell you all about it on the way."

We got into his car and headed for one of the few restaurants we could find open. "Well, come on! Tell me what in the hell happened," I asked with bated breath.

Smiling, he quietly told me how he had gone back into the cigarette smoke-filled room and taken his place at the conference table. All the other board members were half asleep, exhausted, spent and disgusted. Dr. A. slowly reached into his pocket, pulled out a neatly tied package of documents, laid them out on the table for everyone to see and proceeded to pick up the negotiations with a very tired buyer. It took him less than fifteen minutes to convince the buyer that if the sale of the hospital did not culminate then, there and now, another pending sale would happen with another company. With that, a deal was struck which resulted in each full partner being paid over one-and-a-half million dollars.

The sound of the telephone ringing jolted me back to the business at hand. A quick glance at the telephone button panel told me it was the inside line. I picked up the phone, relieved to hear a familiar voice on the other end.

"What are you up to this time of the night?" asked Dr. A. "I figured you'd be home with your wife and kid."

"When you hear what I have to say, I think you'll understand why I'm at the office," I responded.

"Okay, let's hear what's got you so excited this time."

"I'm going to tell you something and I want you to promise you won't laugh."

Dr. A. assured me that whatever I had to say, he would take it seriously. I explained to him that I had gotten interested in the field of ufology. At that time, I had not mentioned this to even some of my closest friends. I explained to him what had taken place with my coverage of the UFO Expo, how I became acquainted with Derrel and how this lead up to the impending surgeries.

The tone of Dr. A.'s voice became quite serious as he asked, "How do you know you can trust this guy and how much faith do you have that these patients will even show up?"

"Actually, I don't really know him at all, but I am trusting my gut. Also, my friend Alice, who is the head of MUFON out here, seems to have great confidence and respect for the man," I answered in one breath.

"Well, if you think this is actually going to happen, I'll help you as much as I can. Remember I am going to Europe. What date is this event scheduled for?" he asked in a very matter-of-fact manner.

"I have it marked on my calendar for the 19th of August. Will that date work for you?"

Dr. A. said that he would set that day aside and wanted to get together with me several times before the event to discuss the matter in greater detail. He asked to review the medical data as well as preview the x-rays. I told him that would be just fine and promised to call in a few days to set up our first meeting.

I took a quick glance at my watch and was flabbergasted to see that it was already 11:30 p.m. I telephoned Sharon and explained I was delayed at the office. She knew that I came home late on occasion so this was nothing new. She asked if I would be eating dinner at home and I said yes.

.The next few days flew by. I had time to consider some of the unknowns regarding my upcoming surgical event. I certainly didn't have to consult the books regarding the procedures for removing foreign bodies. I had performed this type of surgery hundreds of times before and always had great success. During my years of practice I had removed numerous objects from the human foot such as shards of glass, wooden splinters, pieces of metal, needles, plastic and even hair. My concern was that I knew nothing of so-called alien implants. I decided that my collection of UFO literature must contain some information regarding this subject.

I took advantage of the weekend to pore through the literature. There really wasn't much information on this subject. What little I came up with seemed to point to the fact that there had never been a successful implant extraction surgery performed.

In one agonizing instance, Budd Hopkins recounted in Intruders, a physician had removed a small BB-like object from the nasal passage of a woman and then simply thrown it away. I learned of another woman named Cheryl Fernandez, who supposedly had an alleged alien implant surgically removed from her leg. In addition, there was a Canadian physician who reportedly removed an object from an individual with an alien abduction history. I could find no published analysis of this object.

One of the most notable cases involved an alleged abductee from New York state named Richard Price, who had an implant in his penis. Over time, the object emerged on its own and Price was able to remove it himself. He then offered it to Dr. David Pritchard of the Physics Department at the Massachusetts Institute of Technology. Dr. Pritchard initially examined the object by electron scanning microscope, but did not find any unusual compounds or persuasive evidence that it was of extraterrestrial origin. It is my understanding that these tests were financially supported by Robert Bigelow of Las Vegas, Nevada, who was apparently dissatisfied with the results and persuaded Dr. Pritchard to perform some further testing. The final conclusion was that the object was interesting and remained an unknown.

Faced with tales of frustration and failure by others to obtain hard evidence of the reality of alien implants, I was certain I had to take every precaution in order to prevent similar occurrences from happening to me.

The scant literature indicated that a few objects which had been successfully removed had strange things happen to them, resulting in a complete lack of analysis. There were tales of surgically removed objects turning to powder, becoming liquid, vaporizing and other strange phenomena which were equally as peculiar as the subject itself.

One of the most important objectives was to not only extract these objects, but also to preserve them in a way that they would not rapidly degrade. I gave this matter long, hard thought and came up with a plan. The safest medium to place these specimens in would have to be a biological fluid belonging to the patient from whom the object was extracted. The simple answer dawned on me.

All I had to do was to withdraw blood from each one of the patients, spin it down in the centrifuge and separate the serum. The serum would be mixed with a preservative and, without the presence of cells, would not coagulate. This, then, would become the ideal transport medium.

With the basic plan in place, I decided I would just relax and let things happen of their own accord.

The next few weeks were filled with numerous meetings and phone calls from all the parties involved. Alice was more than helpful. I learned that she had an abundance of skills, especially her ability to organize and get the job done.

As the day of the surgery approached, plans became solidified and all the pieces started to fall in place. I was confident that I was ready for my journey into UFOland.

Chapter 6

THE FIRST SURGERIES

A thousand thoughts raced through my mind while sitting there devouring my snack. The events of the day flashed by. It had been a long day, yet we were far from finished. My thought processes focused on the selection of the surgery site. This had been totally left to my better judgment. I had carefully considered whether to use a hospital setting, an outpatient surgical center, or one of my offices. I took into account the number of personnel required, the need for privacy, the filming equipment and a myriad of other factors, such as the date and time of day preferred. It was my decision to perform these procedures in my office. I decided that my Camarillo facility would fill the bill.

August 19, 1995, happened to fall on a Saturday and that would leave the Camarillo office completely available and free of the other doctors and their staff who shared the facility.

The time had passed rapidly and soon the day of the surgery was upon us. One by one the members of the team began to arrive. It was only a short time before the office was bustling with activity.

I was very pleased that everyone apparently knew their job and went about it without much direction. Dr. A. was one of the first to arrive. The surgery room was carefully prepared for both surgery and videography with the installation of all the video equipment. Television cables extended from the room like a nest of snakes all heading in different directions and for a multitude of purposes. One destination was the room adjacent to the operating room. This area was equipped with a color television monitor and numerous chairs. It was designated as a viewing room for those individuals who were there to witness the event but were not permitted in the operating room.

Most of the preparations were completed by noon. All that was needed were the patients. Our abduction researcher had made arrangements with a man who had been introduced to him previously at a local conference. The man had offered to convey our two surgical candidates from the airport upon their arrival and bring them to the office. Our patients were due to arrive at about 10:00 a.m.. The driving time from the airport to my office was about one and a half hours. If they ran into heavy traffic, they nevertheless would have arrived by noon.

Time passed slowly. Soon it was 1:00 p.m.. Still there was no word from the driver or the patients. We began to wonder about the correctness of the flight information and suggested that we call the airline and ask if the flight had arrived on time. Janet called and we were informed that all of the flights that morning had arrived on schedule. We also considered the possibility that there may have been an accident on the freeway tying up traffic. Alice suggested that we check with the Highway Patrol. A phone call was placed and the information obtained indicated that traffic in that area of Los Angeles was flowing normally.

It was now 2:30 p.m.. There was no word on the whereabouts of our missing guests. The surgery crew was becoming irritated and our patience was wearing a little thin. I asked, "Is there anyone here who might know where this pick-up person lives?" No one did.

People began to take turns nervously peering out the reception room window to look for newly approaching vehicles in the parking lot.

3:30 p.m. arrived and still there were no patients. At this point we began to discuss whether to cancel the surgery and try to reschedule it. Our still photographer had another shoot to perform elsewhere and had to leave. "Could you please wait just a little while longer?" we cajoled. Our efforts were most persuasive and she agreed to give us a little more time.

Suddenly I heard a ruckus coming from the waiting room. "What's up?" I yelled. A voice from the front of the office replied, "I think they're here." The excitement in her voice stirred everyone. We immediately ran to the window and peered out.

Our Texas researcher shot outside and could be seen greeting three people climbing out of a rather shabby car. One was a lady who seemed to be in her early fifties. The second was a man of large stature. He was wearing a pair of blue denim coveralls and sported an immense gray beard. "My God," I thought, "this man looks exactly like Grizzly Adams from TV." The third person was of average height and build and was not very impressive. He would have been difficult to pick out of a crowd.

The entourage was soon through the front door and introductions were made. A small group gathered about the driver to ask about the delay. His statement almost caused a riot. "What delay are you talking about? I gave these folks a nice tour of the beach area and my house."

The driver was asked, "Didn't you realize that we were waiting for these folks to arrive and that their surgery was scheduled for this morning?"

"I knew they were supposed to have surgery today, but you didn't tell me when," he retorted.

"My God man! Its almost five o'clock! When did you think they were going to be operated on? Midnight?" We asked.

"May I suggest that we not waste anymore time and get on with the surgery," I interjected.

The surgical patients were escorted to the appropriate areas of the office and each began a processing procedure in the predetermined manner. A complete medical history was taken. Next, each underwent a thorough psychological examination which involved their abduction history and psychological states. This information was recorded for later transcription. All paperwork, including the consents and release forms were signed and placed in the patient's file. A chart was then prepared as a permanent record for each patient. All laboratory tests and pertinent data was reviewed by Dr. A. and me. Next, each patient was brought to the x-ray room and new radiographs were taken and processed. They were also thoroughly reviewed. Each patient was then placed in a treatment room and my surgical nurse, Denise, withdrew the prescribed amount of whole blood.

As I explained earlier, since the literature contained many stories about surgically removed suspected implants disappearing, evaporating, turning to powder, etc., I decided the best transport medium would be the patient's own body fluid. After the blood was withdrawn, it was placed in a serum separator tube and then centrifuged so that the serum portion could be isolated and poured off. This separation technique caused the serum to contain both an anticoagulant and preservative. The liquid was poured into separate vials and became our transport medium.

With the initial preparation completed, our first candidate, Patricia, was brought into the operating room and positioned on the operating table. With video rolling, our nurse/camera operator Mike Evans, focused on the hypnotic induction.

I savored the moments of relaxation in the doctor's lounge, but realized that the job was only half done. Our second patient awaited.

Dr. A. poked his head in the door and said, "Shall we do it?"

"OK, let's get it on," I responded, then jumped to my feet and headed swiftly out the doorway to the scrub sink. I donned a clean cap and mask, turned on the water, took one of the sterile scrub brushes from its holder and began the scrub process.

A quick glance at the clock told me that I had a full five minutes remaining to complete the required surgical scrub time. Next to me at the adjoining sink stood Dr. A.. He was about a foot taller than me and seemed to stoop a bit while scrubbing.

"Are you ready to go fishing?" I asked.

"You know me, Rog, I've been doing this type of surgery for thirty years and I've never failed in finding an imbedded foreign body. I hope that this will not be the first." We both let out a loud chuckle.

Denise popped into the room in time to open a package of sterile towels. I reached out and took the first towel. Dr. A. followed suit and took the next one. Soon our hands were dry and we removed the new, fresh sterile green gown from their wrappers. Denise stood behind us and tied the last of the knots on the rear portion of the gown.

The small surgery room was filled with eerie silence as our first patient, a woman, got on the operating table. I took my position sitting at the foot of the table. To my right was Dr. A. The camera operator was positioned so that he had a clear and wide view of the surgery site. Our surgical nurse, Denise, would provide service from my left. The Texas researcher was acting as the hypnoanesthesiologist, which placed him at the end of the table near the woman's head.

The surgical prep had already been performed and the injection of my local anesthetic mixture carefully administered. I applied an elastic tourniquet to the big toe. I looked at Denise and said, "Number 10 scalpel blade." She responded with the usual surgical pass and handed me the surgical knife. Although I was prepared to find pieces of metal or shards of plastic, suddenly I realized that perhaps history was about to be made. I took one final, calculating look at the x-rays on the view screen. With the surgical knife confidently in by right hand and without hesitation, I pierced the skin making the initial shallow incision.

Thus I began the surgery on Patricia, the first of our two patients. A trickle of dark red blood began to ooze from the wound. Dr. A. responded by dabbing the area with a dry gauze sponge. The gauze square began to swell with its new burden of the thick red liquid.

"Number 15," I said. Denise placed the second surgical knife in my right hand. I began to deepen the wound by a sharp dissection technique. This started the process of our virtual fishing expedition in search of the mysterious metallic foreign body.

At this point Dr. A. placed the retractors carefully into the wound area. A forceful stream of bright red blood shot out of the wound and splashed against my crisp sterile green gown.

"Clamp!" I almost shouted. Denise responded with a mosquito clamp. Dr. A. pulled on the retractors as I isolated the small bleeding artery and applied the clamp. The bleeding stopped instantly. We were now free to carry on with the procedure.

"How is our patient doing," I asked our hypnotist. He responded with a hand signal indicating that everything was A-OK. The room filled with the constant drone of the hypnotherapist's monotone voice as he continued to reinforce the hypnotic anesthesia. "More blue, that's it, put some more blue into your toe. You are doing just fine." I was impressed with the effectiveness of the hypnotic anesthesia and firmly convinced that the patient would feel no discomfort, I administered a good healthy dose of my own concoction as well which consisted of a long-acting anesthetic mixed with a quick-acting one.

Time passed quickly. We continued in our search by using the instruments at hand to dissect the soft and fatty tissue of the toe, trying to visualize the sought after object. Everybody's eyes were keenly fixed on the open wound. Suddenly Dr. A. said, "What's that? I see something." Everyone held their breath. Was this finally the object? I interrupted the procedure, sponged the wound with a clean sponge and carefully inserted forceps to get a better look. There was some tissue discoloration noted but, alas, no solid object.

Almost one hour had passed since the initial incision was made and I could feel the tension mounting. Occasionally our photographer would enter the room and peer over my shoulder to try to get a firsthand glimpse of the proceedings. She was stationed in the room next door, which was the viewing room for our guests who were not allowed in the operating theater. This area was equipped with a television monitor which was being fed a signal from the camera in the operating room.

Denise was asked to reposition the x-rays on the view screen so that we could take a fresh look. The wound was retracted widely as I continued my probing efforts.

All of a sudden the patient shrieked in pain and pulled her foot from our grasp. We were utterly shocked! An anesthetized patient isn't supposed to do that! I reached up, grabbed her gyrating limb and forcibly brought it back down to the table. Our hypnotist immediately began to reinforce the trance state. I called for more local anesthetic and swiftly infected another large dose of the magic mixture. It was only moments before things returned to the previous calm.

"What happened?" He inquired. I explained to him that the only time I had seen anything like this was when the surgical procedure technique involved direct pulling on a nerve which was outside the field of anesthesia. The Texas researcher looked at the clock and with a slightly sarcastic tone of voice said, "Doctors, where are my doggone implants?"

"Be patient," I replied. Dr. A. also chimed in with a few comments. We silently continued with our quest.

All at once, the sound of a crisp metallic click was heard. It broke the dead silence and reverberated in the small room. Everybody chimed in. "What was that?!" I had touched something with my probe and it had made a noise. Again our patient instantly objected with a violent movement. "Don't move," I gasped. "I think we've found something. Denise, pass me a Kelley clamp quickly now!"

My outstretched hand felt the pressure of the new instrument. Everyone in the room remained still and silent. I carefully inserted the clamp into the wound, spread the jaws to their maximum, reached in and grasped a solid object.

"Okay, nobody move now," I said. "Number 15 blade, please. Thank you. Let's do it!"

With that, I began the careful dissection to free the foreign body from its fatty and fibrous tissue attachments. In just a few moments I announced, "Here it comes!" and with one final tug, the object came free from the inner confines of the toe. The patient winced in pain and had to be made peaceful with more anesthesia.

A shout of "Hooray" was heard from the viewing room next door. There was a sudden hustle and bustle in the operating room as we transferred the small object to a white sterile gauze sponge. All eyes were fixed on the peculiar object. Dr. A. peered intently at it and then glanced at me with a quizzical look. "What in the hell is that?" he quietly exclaimed.

I found myself staring at what appeared to be T-shaped or a triangular-shaped mass that was dark gray in color and slightly shiny. It looked fleshy, not metallic, and was about one-half centimeter long by one-half centimeter wide.

The still photographer moved into position and started to photograph the gauze sponge and its strange contents. The flashing of the camera bulbs added to the excitement of the moment. Soon it was our videographer's turn to record the object on video.

Dr. A. took the initiative and suggested that we find out what was inside this exotic gray cocoon. Without waiting for an answer or comment, he handed me a fresh surgical knife. I clamped the specimen with a heavy duty surgical clamp and began to gently incise the biological covering.

"What in heaven's name?" I exclaimed. "I can't cut through the damn thing!"

I asked for a fresh blade and made a second attempt to cut into the object, "No,, it just doesn't want to give. Here, you try."

I passed both the object and knife to Dr. A. and assisted him in securing the specimen. He carefully began to stroke the tough gray membrane with the scalpel blade.

"Rog, I don't think that I am getting anywhere with this. I'm just not doing any better than you did. Let's put it aside for now and try again later." With that, he handed me the sponge containing the specimen and I, in turn, passed it to Denise. She asked if she should place the object into the solution for transport and I said, "Yes."

I was deeply concerned about the transport solution before the surgery was performed and I had spent quite some time researching the attempted recovery of alleged implants. I found that nobody so far had really come up with anything concrete. There were tales about the recovered objects vaporizing, turning to powder, and just plain disappearing. I did not want to take any chances. It seemed to me that a good transport medium would be comprised of the patient's own body fluid. With that in mind, I had ordered Denise, a trained and licensed phlebotomist, to withdraw whole blood from each of the surgical patients, spin it in the centrifuge and pour off the serum. The serum separator tube comes with both the necessary anticoagulant and preservative. This would then become the biological transport fluid.

Once the extracted specimen was put carefully to bed, it was time to begin the second procedure. I released the tourniquet from Patricia's toe with a resounding snap that was heard by all. The release of pressure allowed blood to course through the toe and enrich the tissue with fresh oxygen and nutriments prior to beginning another lengthy procedure.

I asked the Texan if Patricia was prepared for the next surgery and he responded with an affirmative nod. For the moment a quiet calm settled on the little surgical room as I replaced the constrictive band around the big toe. Dr. A and I again peered at the x-rays on the view box. Then, with a fresh surgical knife I carefully made a superficial incision on the opposite side of the toe. Slowly the tissues began to separate. As I deepened the wound, small bits of fatty tissue were removed and placed in a regular specimen container. We knew that this object was going to be more difficult to find than the first one because of its position and smaller size. Time raced on and I could tell that the surgical team was becoming tired and anxious. Our best efforts at finding this one were of no avail so far. We removed the retractors from the wound and took a second look at the x-rays. We decided that perhaps we were not quite in the right area due to the angle the x-ray was taken.

I had been surgically removing foreign bodies for almost thirty-two years and was aware of most of the little helpful tricks surgeons have developed. Some of those involved triangulation by needles or the application of superimposed radio-opaque grids. I have found that by and large these techniques are no substitute for just plain skill and luck. The only devices which are truly of assistance are those sophisticated x-ray instruments such as a lixiscope or fluoroscan. Unfortunately, these were not available to us on our limited budget.

After viewing the x-rays a second time, we repositioned the limb and extended the incision toward the main body of the foot. With this new approach we were able to see a new area which, previously, we could not see. Only a few minutes passed before I spotted a small segment of abnormally appearing grayish tissue.

"What's that?" Dr. A. shouted. The team clustered around me, trying to get a peek into the wound. I gently inserted the probe and touched something solid. The patient winced in pain. "More local anesthetic," I told Denise. She passed me the syringe and I injected another two cc's of the numbing anesthesia.

Tension mounted in the room as I inserted a clamp and attempted to latch onto the object. A bead of sweat rolled from my brow onto my surgical mask. I was too close to my goal to stop to have someone sponge my forehead. I removed the empty clamp and asked Dr. A. to hold the retractors so that the wound was stretched to its maximum. This produced a welling of deep red venous blood in the wound area.

"Sponge please, Denise," I directed. She leaned over our hands and pressed the gauze sponge into the wound area. I immediately took the clamp and re-inserted it into the open wound.

Suddenly I felt the jaws close on something solid. "Denise, 15 blade, please" I said. With my left hand firmly holding the clamp, I inserted the surgical knife. With my right hand I meticulously loosened the soft tissue attachments holding the object.

With gentle upward pressure I was able to bring the object almost out of the wound. There seemed to be one final strand of tissue which needed coaxing. Dr. A, sensing the problem, reached for the dissection scissors and carefully cut the remaining attachment. A loud cheer went up from both the team and the adjoining viewing room. I tried to ignore the excitement as I placed the specimen on a clean sponge and began to take measurement.

The cameras once again came to life and the flashing lights were reflected by all the bright metallic objects in the room. Because the pitch of excitement was at such an extreme level, one of our team members got in the way of the video camera which resulted in a beautiful view of somebody's back, just at the time the object was pulled from the wound. We, of course did not realize this until the tape was reviewed after the surgery was long over.

Once the commotion was past, we were able to get back to the business at hand. This object appeared like a small cantaloupe seed with a few tiny tendrils dragging from its ends. We were amazed to see that this newly acquired specimen was also covered with a smooth, glistening, dark gray covering.

This time it was Dr. A.'s turn to attempt to open it. I passed him the surgical scalpel and the gauze sponge containing the specimen. Since this one was much smaller than the first, it was impossible for me to assist by holding onto it while he attempted to open it. We all stood and watched, our breathing almost stopped as he took the blade and gently tried to pierce the coating. We looked at each other in amazement. This was just like the first object. It resisted our attempts to open it.

"Let's get on with the business of closing the wound," I snapped. I felt it was more important to sew the wound closed and get the patient out of the operating room. Denise passed me the needle carrier with the suture material clamped in its jaws. I decided that it would not be necessary to use deep sutures.

I began to suture the wound closed. I placed each stitch so that it would pull the wound edges together with just the right amount of pucker. Each one was then tied in the usual surgical knot. Once tied, each tail was cut to length by Dr. A.. With all of his years experience as a general surgeon, he functioned like a well lubricated automated machine.

Soon the wounds were fully closed. The tourniquet was then removed and I watched as new blood flowed into the part and the color changed from a rather pale white to a bright pink. Circulation was restored and the wounds were ready to be dressed. Dr. A. said, "Excuse me folks," removed his gloves and stepped out of the room.

Denise handed me the dressing materials and I applied them to the foot. I asked how our patient was doing. Patricia herself piped in, "I'm doing just great. How are you doing?"

I told her that the surgery was over and everything was just fine. Denise began the procedure of checking and recording the patient's vital signs. The patient was on her way to the recovery area as I slipped out of the door, took off my gloves and headed for the doctor's lounge.

It felt good to have accomplished the task I set out to perform. I slipped out of the soiled surgical gown, removed my mask and took a deep breath, bent over, stretched, twisted and rolled by neck to limber up. Alice, our surgical coordinator, stuck her head in the doorway and said, "Gosh, you guys must be exhausted. Can I get you something to munch on before the next case starts?" This sounded really good to me and I replied "yes." I stepped to the sink and washed my hands. Within moments, Alice was back with a sandwich and a drink. I slowly sank into a chair and began to relax.

Our second surgical patient, Pat had replaced Patricia on the operating table. The table itself had to be rearranged due to the fact that the surgical area involved was Pat's left hand. I recalled that he reminded me of the TV character, Grizzly Adams. He was a large, bearded fellow, who took up most of the space on the table.

As we entered the room I noticed that he shifted his eyes to meet mine.

"Hi Pat, how are you doing so far?" I asked.

"OK," he muttered under his breath just barely audible.

Dr. A. moved quickly to his position at the patient's left hand which had been placed on an arm board. This was an extension I added to the table for the purpose of supporting the patient's arm.

Dr. A. looked over the top of his surgical mask and fixed his gaze directly at the patient's eyes.

Pat's outstretched hand, palm down, looked bright orange due to the spray applied during the surgical prep. This color extended from the fingertips up to the elbow. The skin had a rather awesome appearance because of the lack of hair. Denise had performed the prep well. She had shaved the skin of both the hand and arm. Dr. A. took a surgical magnifying loop and began to peer closely at the skin of both the hand and the arm areas.

"Rog, come over here and take a look." I did so and gazed through the loop, investigating every crack, pore and orifice that I could view with the device. There was no evident portal of entry, no scar or any sign of any type of skin interruption that would have allowed the foreign body, visible on the x-ray to have entered the body.

"Excuse me! Let's stop right here," I said in a rather loud voice. "Bert, could you please bring in the gauss meter?"

Bert entered the room and passed me the instrument. I took a sterile towel and carefully wrapped the device so that the gauge could still be read. I placed it slightly above the back of Pat's hand and pressed the on-off button to activate the meter. Suddenly the room was filled with a strange, pulsating, buzzing sound which emanated from the gauss meter.

"My God". What in the hell is that?" Dr. A. shrieked.

"I'll tell you what it is. This damn thing is putting out one giant electromagnetic field," I replied, meaning the object in Pat's hand.

At this point, Mike Evans, a trusted member of our Mufon circle, and Bert both chimed in to suggest that perhaps the device was being activated by all the electronic equipment in the room. Mike then suggested that we take the patient out into the parking lot which is far away from any electronic influence, and test it again. I looked at Dr. A. and he nodded in agreement. This meant we had to get the patient off the table, take him outside, do the test and bring him back into surgery. That, in turn, meant the prep and positioning of the camera and cables would all have to be done over.

I looked about the room and said, "There is no choice. This is too important. Let's get on with it. Have somebody get Alice or Janet and tell them what's going on so they can relate this to our guests in the other room. Let's be very careful and try to maintain those areas that are still sterile.

With that, our group made its way from the surgical room, down the hallway through the waiting area and out the front door of the building. The parking lot was dark and only some isolated cars were seen scattered about the area, but a few small lights were visible from the distant advertising signs.

"Let's try it here. Bring over the instrument and let's see what she does," Dr. A. commanded. I was still holding the gauss meter in the sterile towel as I ran over to Pat's waiting hand. "OK Pat, just relax now. Let's have a look at the back of your hand again.

Pat responded by holding his arm out straight. I moved the detection device into position and once again pushed the button. The still night was suddenly alive with a second chorus of that strange pulsating and buzzing. "Wow! Look at that will you! It's pegging the damn meter!" I exclaimed.

Dr. A. responded. "Let's get our patient back into surgery and get this thing out." With that we hastened back into the building and our ultimate destination, the operating room.

Dr. A., standing near Pat's left hand, had his eyes fixed on Pat. He said in a very calm voice, "Can you tell me where you think this object in your hand might be located?" Pat moved his right hand and with one large bulbous finger pointed to spot on the back of his left hand. "I think it's right about here," he muttered in a quiet voice.

With that Dr. A. flashed a fully loaded hypodermic syringe. The needle was just inches above the skin of Pat's left hand. Our rough and tumble patient suddenly lifted his head from the surgical table and exclaimed, "Damn, Doc, you don't have to poke me with that. Just go ahead and cut that thing out!" I edged forward, looked our surgery patient squarely in the eye and said, "Pat, just lay back and let the doctor do his thing." There wasn't another word said and soon the exposed part was numb with anesthesia.

Dr. A. started the surgery with a superficial incision using a number 10 surgical blade. The wound welled with bright red blood. Performing as a second surgical nurse, I reached over and applied pressure with a sterile gauze sponge. Dr. A. was quick to continue the procedure deepening the wound with a number 15 blade. Instinctively, and without hesitation, my hand shot forth with another sponge. The wound was now bleeding profusely and soon several small rivers of red liquid were flowing down Pat's arm and into the receptacle below.

"Could you hold the rakes for me, Rog?" Dr. A. inquired. He had placed the two small retractors into the wound and with a modicum of gentle pressure I pulled the sound edges apart. With that, the process of fishing for the mysterious foreign body began again.

The process was slow and tedious. We probed the wound, sponged the blood, looked at both x-ray views and peered deeply into the wound. One hour had gone by and the elusive object was nowhere to be found.

Dr. A. asked Mike to remove the radiographs from the view screen and bring them closer so that he might get a little different perspective. We gazed at the x-ray films for several minutes and discussed the possibilities of malposition of the hand during the time the x-ray was taken. We finally came to the conclusion that the object was much deeper than was originally thought.

Dr. A. placed a self-retaining Wheatlander retractor into the wound. This is a small device with teeth and a trigger. When the trigger is squeezed, a mechanism causes the jaws of the instrument to diverge from each other. This results in the wound edges being pulled apart both deeply and superficially. he extended the incision slightly and increased the depth of the wound. The tendon structures glistened in the strong light of the operating lamp. Dr. A. delicately retracted the tendons and exposed the deep tissues below.

All at once an audible click was heard. "I think I just touched something," Dr. A. said excitedly. I held my breath.

Pat suddenly piped up and said, "Hey, guys, that hurt!" The tension sprang across the room like a tight wire stretched to its maximum and ready to snap.

"Clamp" Dr. A. commanded, without taking his eyes off the gaping wound. I reached over and sponged the area of bright red blood as it welled up and pooled in the center of the open cavity. The surgeon inserted a clamp and gently squeezed the handle. The jaws closed. He glanced at Denise and in a very calm and confident voice said, "New 15 blade, please." She picked up the waiting Bard Parker handle with its fresh 15 blade attached and deftly passed it into Dr. A's outstretched hand. He once again entered the wound with the new blade and in a fraction of a second pulled out the clamp which had a small, dark colored object sandwiched in its jaws.

With that, a sudden vocal clutter swept the operating room. "Is that it?" "Did you get it?" "What is that thing?" Everyone was questioning and seeking the knowledge of the moment. There was a sudden flurry of voices emanating from the viewing area. The room was lit by the flashing of camera bulbs. Mike turned the video camera toward the new specimen and adjusted the focus.

"Hold on, everybody." I tried to press for calm. "Let's take a look and see what we have here." The little gray object was then placed on the waiting stark white sponge. I was shocked. It looked exactly like the little object that I had removed from Patricia's toe just a few hours earlier. It was shaped like a small cantaloupe seed and appeared to be covered with a dark gray membrane. Dr. A. picked up a knife with a sharp 15 blade and started to cut the object open.

"What the hell! I can't seem to cut into the damn thing. Its just like the other one!" He handed the sponge containing the specimen to me and I passed it off to Denise, who in turn placed it into the waiting transport container. It only took Dr. A. a few minutes to suture the wound closed and apply the dressing.

The second and last case was not completed. Our visitors and witnesses began to pour out into the hall. The mood and comments were upbeat. The gathering showered us with compliments and affection.

Dr. A. followed as I led the group down the hall to the lounge. The activity for the day was far from over. There was much more to be done. Not only did the patients require our immediate post-op attention, but also it was necessary to re-evaluate them psychologically.

The day ended late in the evening when the last person left the facility and the dead bolt finally latched the outside door. But it ended with everyone feeling a tremendous sense of satisfaction and eagerness to get on with final identification of the three mysterious objects we had removed.

Chapter 7

THE VEGAS CONNECTION

I took the luxury of resting over the weekend to mull over the recent events and discuss them with my wife. Although Sharon was interested, her attitude was rather nonchalant. She wisely reminded me that each day brought new thoughts and ideas, and advised me to move one step at a time before jumping to any conclusions.

Monday found me back at my usual routine, seeing patients. After completing the day early, I began preparing the surgical specimens to be sent out for pathological testing. Our Texas friend had taken the objects and their containers with him back to Texas, leaving me with the soft tissue specimens. Since all the studies were to be double-blind, I had to decide what information I could include with the request form. I invented a fake research project dealing with soft tissue reactions in foreign body surgery. By using this as an excuse, I could query the pathologists without them raising an eyebrow.

Since I was probably going to need all the help I could get, I made the decision to send one specimen at a time to the same laboratory. This could lead to the development of a relationship with the head pathologist.

I removed the specimens from the refrigerator in my office lab. The pathology lab forms were rather simple to fill out. The diagnosis was "soft tissue adjacent to foreign body." The location was "big toe." Removing the specimen from its container, I placed it on a gauze sponge, sectioned off a small piece and sealed it in the laboratory container. I placed the specimen and the forms into a locked box, strapped it onto the front door of the office and called the lab for a pick-up.

I did not submit a rush order for the results of the analysis. I wanted the lab technicians to take their time and do a thorough job. Also, since there was no suspicion of malignancy, a rush order would not be justified.

Meanwhile, the plan was to remove the gray membrane somehow and send the metallic portions to a laboratory at the University of Houston, where he had a Ph.D. friend who would perform the analysis. When we spoke, I explained to him how I was going to handle the biological portions of the specimens and told him that I thought we were going to get back results that were quite typical of soft tissue foreign body reactions. He vehemently disagreed with me, theorizing that the tissue would be devoid of any type of inflammatory reaction whatsoever and most probably would contain nerve tissue.

It was all I could do to refrain from bursting out laughing. Over a period of thirty years, I had removed foreign bodies and looked at hundreds of pathology reports. I knew that the absence of any inflammatory reaction was impossible. I had studied the process of inflammation since the early days of my medical education and as far as I knew, the body reacted to all foreign bodies with the standard inflammatory process. I considered the times I had implanted metal screws, plates, pins and the like into the human foot. Some of these had to be re-operated down the line and the metallic material removed for a variety of reasons. In each and every case I witnessed the metal changing color with mild oxidation and the formation of fibrous tissue around or adjacent to the screw heads. Also, when the specimen tissues came back from the path lab, they all showed signs of chronic inflammation.

The next few days flew by and were filled with routine daily duties, including composing my article for the MUFON Vortex. In numerous conversations I had with Alice about the surgeries, she insisted on telling me what I had done was vitally important to the progress of proving the reality of the abduction scenario. At this point I thought she was exaggerating tremendously but was entitled to her opinion, so I politely agreed with her. She also inquired about the progress of the analysis and I readily informed her of the situation.

About two weeks after the surgery, Janet said there was a new batch of pathology reports on my desk to be reviewed before they could be filed into the patient's charts. This was one of those paperwork chores I had performed many times. As usual, I left that tedious endeavor to the end of the day.

I wished that my attitude was as fresh as the cup of coffee Janet had set on my desk, next to the pile of paperwork. Most of the pathology reports were routine and pertained to bunionectomies, hammertoe corrections and ingrown nail specimens. Suddenly I found myself reading a report labeled "Soft tissue surrounding foreign body."

I sat up straight in the chair and my hand began to tremble as I slowly perused the page. I had not expected the results from the abduction cases so soon. As I read, I could not believe what I was seeing. There had to be some kind of mistake.

First thing in the morning I called Chris, the pathologist who did the analysis. After giving her the case number and patient name, I got right to the point.

"I sent you a specimen of tissue I had removed that was adjacent to a foreign body, and you send me back a report telling me that the tissues are totally devoid of any inflammatory tissue. Come on, you know that's impossible."

"Hey, I call them as I see them," Chris replied. "If I reported no inflammatory tissue, then by God, there wasn't any."

"Okay, okay. Maybe you could give me a clue as to why you are reporting this tissue loaded with nerve proprioceptors. The stuff was taken from the deep, dark depths of a toe, just adjacent to the bone. How can you find nerve proprioceptors in that area?" I asked impatiently.

Chris explained carefully, "Look, Doc, all I do is slice up the tissue, apply my stains, pop it under a microscope and report what I see. I really don't care if your specimen came from the moon. What I see is what you get. I'm sorry I just don't have the answers for you. Tell you what, I'll drag out the slides and take another look. Does that make you feel any better?"

It did improve my disposition. I offered to buy her lunch sometime, and asked that she call me when she was done reviewing the specimens.

I decided to prepare the next tissue sample, arranged for a pick-up by the lab and called Chris the next day to alert her so she could intercept the specimen and perform the analysis personally.

Her question took me by surprise. "Roger, what in heaven's name are you up to with these specimens?"

I had to think of something fast. If I told her the truth, it would ruin the double blind study. Yet I did not want to lie outright to her, either.

"It's no big deal. I'm just doing a little research project on foreign body reactions. By the way, I need to keep this kind of quiet. You understand, don't you?" I explained matter-of-factly. She seemed satisfied, and agreed to put a rush on the new sample when I told her I needed the results for a paper I was writing.

A few days later, I noticed another neat pile of lab slips on my desk. I sat down and quickly went through them. There it was! I hurriedly opened the envelope and began reading the document. I was dumbfounded. The report was almost identical to the first report. Nerve cells and no inflammation.

"This is too much," I blurted out loud to an empty office.

Although it was 6:30 p.m., I tried calling Chris at the lab. Fortunately, she was still there.

"Hi, Chris, this is Roger. I want to thank you for getting me the results back so soon. Also, could you verify the fact that you did this sample yourself?" I asked.

"Yes," she answered, "I was the one who did it, just as I promised you the last time we talked."

"Of course, you realize the results of this one are almost exactly the same as the previous specimen."

"Well, now that you mention it, I guess they are pretty similar. But what's the big deal? You said they were from a foreign body reaction and that's what you sent the first time, wasn't it?"

"That's true," I explained, "but this one was from a different foreign body and taken from a different place."

"Wow! That is a little strange but there is probably some logical explanation."

For the next 45 minutes, she presented one idea after another, which I would counter with a data point contradicting her theory. Finally, I asked if she would photocopy and send me information from the latest Robbins Textbook of Pathology—which is the Bible of pathologists—referring to inflammation and soft tissue foreign body reactions. She agreed.

I reasoned that the next specimen should be done by another individual in order to gain a fresh opinion and approach. I didn't call Chris about this one, and made a written request on the lab order form that Chris not perform the analysis of this specimen. I knew there were many other capable pathologists in the lab.

It was time for some serious research. I logged onto the Internet searching for information on foreign body reactions in the human body. My search took me to medical libraries at Harvard and Stanford Universities; the material was complete and I felt rewarded by my effort. Then I perused my own texts, some of which were outdated. My findings proved to me that the human body had not changed since the time I graduated from professional school. In essence, I found no reason for the lack of inflammatory response found in the microscopic analysis of my two specimens. Perhaps the third specimen would prove different.

It was almost a week before the results were in on the next specimen. By the time it arrived, I was primed and ready to be confronted by the same mystifying analysis. I was not disappointed. The new report was almost exactly the same as the previous two. The language was slightly different because the analysis was performed by a different pathologist. I decided to call our abduction researcher and update him on the analyses.

"Hang on to your hat," I prepared him. "Somehow, you were right. They essentially found the adjoining tissue filled with nerve proprioceptors and a total lack of inflammation."

"Well, well, well, what a surprise," he responded sarcastically.

"Okay, rub it in. I don't know how you could ever have guessed such a thing. Well, anyway, where do we go from here? Did you get the membrane off the objects and what about the metal inside?" I questioned.

"Before trying to remove the membrane, I subjected all the objects to black ultraviolet light and they all fluoresced a brilliant green color. This is the same color we've found on abductee victims following an experience. Do you think this is one hell of a coincidence or what?"

He went on to tell me he was able to remove the membrane from the metallic portion within by drying the specimens. He explained that the metal portions were dark gray in color and had an irregular surface. Also, they were highly magnetic and would stick to any ferrous metal object. He was waiting to hear from a friend at the University of Houston, who had a Ph.D. and had agreed to do the metallurgical analysis. I asked him to send me portions of the membrane so I could send them out for analysis.

Almost a week later, the membrane samples arrived by Federal Express. A note from him accompanied four small plastic containers of small dark particles. I gathered up the vials, headed for the office laboratory and placed them carefully in the refrigerator. I would send the specimens to the lab at the end of the day.

Days later, Chris called me from the pathology lab.

"What's this latest crazy concoction you sent me?" she asked, half-jokingly. "Are you playing one of your little games, trying to get even with me over the last go around?"

"No, this is not a game. What did you find?"

"There are only three components to this thing. They are protein coagulum, hemosiderin and keratin. I did an iron stain on the dark brown granules and they came back positive for hemosiderin."

"First of all, have you ever seen anything like this before?"

Chris had never seen anything similar, but attempted to hypothesize how the specimen could contain these substances. The only problem was that no suggestion made sense. She tried to explain the presence of keratin—which the body uses to produce hair and nails—by saying the substance must have been so superficial that when the surgery was performed, I probably dragged in a small piece of skin. I explained to her that the specimen came from an area deep within the toe and was not superficial. She tried to explain away the hemosiderin—a component of blood similar to hemoglobin—by rationalizing that the area probably hemorrhaged and the clotted blood left the hemosiderin deposit behind. I explained to her that there was no hemorrhage and, in one instance, the specimen had been contained in the body for over 40 years. For each of her postulates, I presented facts that made them impossible. I finally asked her if all the specimens were the same. She said they were, but was not surprised. She didn't know that one of the specimens came from a totally different human being.

Within two days, I received the written report. I made copies and filed the originals in the patient's charts.

****

Almost a full month went by before I talked with our Texan again. I wanted to know what progress he was making with the analysis of the metal portions. I was beginning to receive phone calls asking me what the metal portions were, and I had to put the callers off. When we spoke, he explained that there had been no progress on the metal analysis because the Ph.D. program at the university was on temporary hiatus. It would be at least another month until they were up and going again.

I suggested that we look elsewhere to have the tests performed. I knew we needed to get the funds to pay for the tests. The costs were expensive.

I spent the next few days making numerous phone calls to people whom I thought could help. I also asked Alice to look over the membership list to see if any of our members in MUFON could fill the bill. About two days later I received a call from Jim, a friend of mine, who gave me the name and number of a friend of his, John, who could probably help. We set up a meeting for the three of us in Ventura the following week, about a half-hour's drive from my office.

The lunch went well. John had a background in mechanics and engineering. He also confided in me there was a possibility that both he and his brother had an abduction experience many years ago. The more I talked with him, the more I realized he had some of the psychological traits of the typical abductee.

John said his brother used to work for a very large laboratory and he would ask him if he could get some of the tests done on our samples. There would be no charge because his brother still had a lot of favors coming from his friends at the lab. This was wonderful news and I was extremely excited. I told him We would get him the material samples.

After arriving back at my office, I immediately called the Texan and gave him the news. He would have to bring the samples to California as soon as possible. Within a few days, he arrived and we handed the samples over to John. The excitement was almost too much to bear. I began to believe we were on the threshold of a major finding. I had not felt this way prior to turning over the samples.

The Texas researcher went back to Houston and I continued with my life's routines. Several MUFON meetings came and went. At each meeting I was asked to explain what was new with the implant research. I felt an obligation to our group to keep them well informed of the latest progress. I was surprised when comments were made at one meeting about how long it was taking to get the results. I tried to explain the costs involved and how difficult it was to get favors done. Several individuals kindly offered their help.

Over the next couple of weeks I called everyone who was recommended. Some were quite congenial and others had either changed jobs or could not do the tests we needed done.

The following week we turned over the next set of samples to Brian, someone who was recommended by one of the MUFON members. He told us he would have the results back in two weeks. That sounded great and we were happy with our decision.

I got a call from John and set up another meeting. I was eagerly anticipating results from his brother's analysis. I drove to Ventura to meet again with John. We made small talk for a while, then John said he had some preliminary results from his brother. I took out my note pad and prepared to take notes. He told me that one of the compounds contained in the sample was called boron nitride. He did not know for certain whether boron nitride was a manufactured compound or one found in nature, but in his opinion, no such compound did occur naturally. He told me he would call his brother to find out. He also mentioned the presence of iron and magnesium.

I asked him if he knew what the ratios were or what type of tests had been done. He appeared insulted that I would have the audacity to ask him these questions.

I quickly changed the subject and told him we would be in touch by telephone. John promised the final analysis would be done as soon as possible.

Several more weeks went by and still there was no word from either of the sources we had chosen to perform the tests.

The following day, my secretary told me John was on the line and requested to talk with me right away. I was excited and thought he was going to tell me he had the final analysis.

"Roger, I heard from my brother and he told me that boron nitride was not found in nature and was some sort of a high-tech compound."

"Hey, that's really great. What else did he find?" I asked.

"What do you mean, what else?" John retorted. "I was excited he provided this much information. What else do you expect to find?"

I began losing my patience. I really didn't want to antagonize this person, since he was doing us a favor, but this was too important to let it go on any longer. Forcefully, I asked, "John, when do you think you can get us a written report?"

"Report! Report! Are you crazy? My brother is trying to do us a favor by having someone run these tests on laboratory equipment without them finding out about it so it won't generate a charge, and you expect them to write a report. Come on, man, it just doesn't work that way."

I was stunned. All this time we had been sitting and waiting and this was the result. Now, what was I going to tell those people who were coming down on us for not having the information?

I came to the conclusion that backdoor research was not going to work. We agreed we had to find legitimate funding and have these tests done by a reputable laboratory with results printed on valid stationery, signed by the scientist who did the test, and attested to by a witness. We also decided to pursue the contacts we were still involved with, such as the University of Houston and our volunteer from MUFON.

In addition, I called my cousin Ken to explain our situation and see if he had any suggestions. I explained what was happening on the UFO scene in general and what we were experiencing with the testing. I asked if he had any suggestions. He supplied a few names of people who might be able to help me.

One was Dr. John Alexander, a brilliant scientist with whom Ken had worked in the near-death experience field. He thought Alexander was now residing in Las Vegas and working with a research company. When I called, the company's name was given out as the National Institute for Discovery Science.

When Dr. Alexander came on the line, I introduced myself as a cousin of Dr. Kenneth Ring and told him of our research. He appeared to be very interested in the work we were doing. Surprisingly, he had knowledge of the surgeries I had performed. When I asked if there was any way he could help solve our problem, he requested that I fax him any data I could, and he'd get back to me quickly. I compiled the material and faxed it to him right away.

The next morning, my telephone at home rang at 7:00 a.m. I was sound asleep when Sharon shook me and handed me the portable phone. I couldn't imagine who would be calling so early.

"This is John Alexander. I received the information you faxed me last night and I have Bob Bigelow on conference with us."

The next voice I heard was that of Robert Bigelow. "Dr. Leir, do you mind if I call you Roger?" he asked. "Just go ahead and call me Bob."

"Roger will be just fine," I said, trying to collect my thoughts and wits.

Alexander explained about the National Institute for Discovery Science (NIDS) and what they were up to. The organization was set up by Bigelow to serve a dual research purpose. One line of research was into the nature of the mind; the other was the study of unusual aerial phenomena, namely, UFOs. Alexander was the director and Bigelow was the CEO. Alexander expressed deep interest in the project we were working on and said he was impressed by the biological data. He and Bigelow spent almost an hour asking me questions about the project and when they were done, we agreed to be in contact again shortly. They were going to present the material to several members of their board.

I was excited after the phone call and almost let out a scream. Later I had heard it was rumored that Alexander was a federal agent and still in the active employ of the government. As for Bigelow, the word was that he was a billionaire whose purpose in life was quite mysterious. He had offered a multi-million dollar research grant to three of the largest UFO organizations in this country, MUFON, the Center for UFO Studies (CUFOS) in Evanston, Illinois, and the Fund for UFO Research in Mt. Ranier, Maryland. Apparently, he pulled back the research funds without giving anyone the money.

Only two days later my secretary advised me that there was a Mr. Bigelow on the phone, who requested to speak to me immediately. I was shocked that he was calling me so soon. I excused myself from the patient I was involved with and made a mad dash for the phone.

In brief, Bigelow invited me to visit the NIDS offices in Las Vegas with the specimens. I told him I would get in touch with my research colleague immediately and arrange for a time. Once this was done, I would call him back and finalize our plans.

I ran back to the treatment room and finished with the patient. Then I called Janet and asked her to tell the remaining patients I was running a little late. My colleague consulted his calendar and told me what dates he was free. I chose a date I could get away and called Bigelow back. We agreed on the date and he supplied me with the address and directions to the office.

I made a hasty retreat from my office. I could feel Janet's eyes staring a hole in my back as I entered the treatment room. I was running at least half an hour late.

We were scheduled to leave the following Wednesday early in the morning, meet at the airport and share a cab to the NIDS offices. We would return the same evening. I would bring all the necessary data and other materials I needed to show our prospective benefactor.

****

In the Las Vegas airport, my friend and I greeted each other warmly and headed for the terminal entrance. We hailed a taxi, gave the driver the address and were quickly on our way.

The National Institute of Discovery Science was surrounded by a stone wall about six feet in height. As the driver pulled into the driveway, an armed guard appeared out of nowhere and approached the cab. Once he confirmed that we were in the right place, we got out and proceeded into a very strange-appearing building which looked like a cross between an apartment house and an office building. At what appeared to be a reception desk, we were asked to have a seat by the receptionist, who told us that Mr. Bigelow would be right down. We sat in two chairs which blended in with the decor of the room. This area of the building was paneled with the most beautiful wood I have ever seen. Every ounce of furniture appeared to have been specially made for the room. There was not a speck of dust to be found anywhere and every item was in its proper place. It seemed as if we were involved with someone of impeccable taste.

After sitting for about ten minutes, the secretary rose from her desk and started up a curved flight of stairs constructed of the same fine wood used throughout the office. In a few moments she returned with two men dressed in sport coats and ties. The gray-haired man introduced himself as John Alexander. We exchanged greetings and he introduced us to his companion, Robert Bigelow. I was a bit surprised at Bigelow's appearance. I had pictured him as a much older man. Although handsome and distinguished, he looked young, as if in his late thirties. I would soon learn, however, that he had grandchildren.

Alexander informed us that we were invited to accompany them to lunch and have our meeting upon returning. During the meal, we made small talk about how Las Vegas had grown over the years. I asked Bigelow how long he had lived in the area and he was quick to say that he was born there. I thought better of asking him what year that was.

The ride back to his office seemed to take only a short time. We soon found ourselves sitting in Bigelow's private office. It was a spectacular sight. The decor was magnificent and all the bric-a-brac melded with the ambiance of the room.

Then we got down to business. Alexander led the conversation. He reiterated that NIDS was formed for research in two distinct areas of interest: investigation of the mind and study of aerial phenomena. Both men explained the plans for future development of the organization. We each shared our mission and goals, and stated what we expected from NIDS.

Bigelow told us that he was impressed with our research and he would present our findings to the board, which was composed of 16 of the nation's top scientific minds. Alexander offered to drive us to the airport. We exchanged good-byes with Bigelow, gathered our belongings and followed Alexander to the car. The trip to the airport was very enlightening. Alexander explained how he became involved with Bigelow and what his role in the CIA was. He told us about experiments in remote viewing and psychokinesis, also his own participation in the development of this country's non-lethal weapons program. He was a most fascinating person. He also related his involvement with my cousin Ken and told us of his continuing interest in the study of life after death.

****

During the next week, there were few opportunities to think about the subject of UFOs, abduction research and NIDS. I had scheduled a number of surgeries; between attending to the surgical patients and the routine office work, I wound up with more than my usual dose of overwork and fatigue.

It was Monday morning of the following week when I was once again awakened out of a sound slumber by the jarring ring of the telephone. I picked it up groggily.

"Roger, this is John Alexander. I have Bob on the other line. We would like to take a few minutes of your time, if that is okay."

My gosh, I thought, both of them! What could they possibly want at this time of the morning? It didn't take long for them to get to the point. This time it was Bigelow who carried most of the conversation. He told me he had discussed some of our biological findings with several members of the board and they were interested in helping us. In fact, he had one of them standing by, waiting for a telephone call, and asked my permission to put him on the line. I agreed and soon we were having a four-party conversation.

The newest member to join in was proficient in two areas. He had a medical degree and, furthermore, was a board certified neurologist. He also held a Ph.D. in Physics. I was impressed, to say the least. Our conversation became more complex with a great deal of medical jargon and I am sure most of it was over the heads of our two telephone colleagues who stayed silently on the line. His questions were not antagonistic and gave me the impression he was sincerely interested in my answers.

The next portion of the conversation took place among the other three individuals as I sat there quietly listening. It seemed as though they thought it was a good idea to present this material to the entire board and asked me when we would be free to come back to Las Vegas. John reminded his colleagues that the board was scheduled to meet on a weekend in about two weeks. He asked if this was too short a notice. I told him we would rearrange our schedules accordingly.

Two events occurred in rapid succession. The first was the unexpected arrival of a package containing my itinerary and plane tickets to Las Vegas. The second was a phone call from my Texas friend telling me that he had received the same package. The flights were well coordinated so we would arrive in Las Vegas at approximately the same time and could come together to the meeting. I had also received a list of items I was to bring with me. One of the most important things on the list was the objects we had surgically removed.

Two weeks later, I found myself being escorted into the NIDS building by two armed guards. We entered what appeared to be a rather lavish dining area, replete with a multitude of tables covered with white linen table cloths. The silverware was displayed elegantly on cloth napkins. There were a few individuals milling around the room who seemed to be enjoying hors d'oeuvres. We were taken into a kitchen area and invited to help ourselves to any of the food that was displayed. One quick glance about the room aroused my appetite. There were platters containing every imaginable type of delicatessen cuisine. The bread-and-roll section looked like a miniature bakery. There were glass bowls containing all manner of salads. There was also an array of steam trays with heat and steam billowing up from around their lids. The aroma of fine food flooded my nostrils. We selected plates and began piling on fine delicacies. Then we found a table set for six and began to partake in the feast.

During the next ten minutes, the room filled with people. The background conversation hummed with the tone of scientific talk. We deduced that the board was taking their lunch break. Suddenly I heard a familiar voice across the room calling my name. It was Bigelow, surrounded by several individuals I didn't know. He gestured for us to come over. We made our way to the gathering. Bigelow excused himself from the crowd, stuck out his hand and gave us a greeting befitting two old chums. He then introduced us to members of the board and their guests. It seemed as if this meeting was to be more than just an ordinary board gathering. One of the distinguished individuals we were introduced to was Jacques Vallee. I had read much of this famous ufologist's works and felt it was an honor to make his acquaintance. Bigelow invited us to go back and enjoy the lunch. He informed us he would come over and talk about procedural issues of the meeting with us shortly.

We returned to our table. Just as we were about to have dessert, Bigelow approached the table and sat down. He told us there was a schedule and the format would be adhered to rather strictly. Our appointed time for the presentation was 2:00 p.m. He advised us to finish our lunch and take a stroll through the grounds. At the proper time he would send someone to get us who would escort us to the meeting room.

After dessert, we went outside onto the grounds of this magnificent business estate. The weather was just perfect with a 75-degree temperature and a slight breeze. As we started toward a chain-link gate, a voice behind us asked if we had ever been through this area before. We turned and shook hands with an elderly gentleman who said he was on a break and offered to show us around. We accepted his offer and were soon pleased that we did. He guided us down a path that took us through a beautiful garden filled with the aroma of roses and other flowers. The tour took us through canyons, mountains and bridges that crossed streams of flowing water—all artificial, of course. Soon we found ourselves deep within a darkened cave.

Our guide made his way to an area ahead of us. He reached up and with both hands began to turn a rock. All at once, a huge boulder began to slide out of the way, revealing a dimly lit secret chamber. He invited us in. There were several places to sit on what appeared to be seats carved out of the rocks. Our guide explained that Bigelow liked the outdoors and had all this constructed as a sort of getaway from the everyday world of business, finance and family problems. He also explained that next door was another fenced area he had constructed for his grandchildren. He offered to guide us through this area also, time permitting.

Soon we were out of the cave and again in the warm sunlight. We followed our guide as we wound through artificial forests and miniature mountain areas. Soon we were at another chain-link gate. Our guide opened the gate and we entered an area which could put Disneyland to shame. This area had the same artificially created beauty but everywhere we looked was some sort of a fun ride or game which children could play. We were told that Bob loved his grandchildren and built this area especially for them, so that when they came to visit, they could have fun together. When I heard this statement, my heart jumped for joy. I knew instantly that Bigelow was more than your everyday business tycoon. He was a man who gave every indication of being someone with a giant heart who loved his family and life itself. With this thought bursting through my consciousness, I heard a voice saying, "They are ready for you now."

Our guide took us back to the place where we had started. A guard appeared to escort us to the board room. He led the way up a spiral staircase and through an area I recognized from our previous visit. We were allowed to take a short detour to claim the items we needed for our presentation. Soon we were entering the inner sanctum of the Bigelow domain.

The boardroom was typical of what you might expect at a corporate giant such as General Motors. I did not expect to find anything resembling this in Las Vegas. The room was huge and constructed of the same fine wood seen in the decor throughout the structure. As I entered the room, my eye caught sight of a huge television screen. It was the type of monitor you see in a major-league stadium, composed of individual picture tubes combined to form one giant image. Hanging next to this was a pull-down motion picture screen sized appropriately for the room. The conference table was in the shape of a horseshoe with the open end pointing toward the multi-screens. There was additional space around the table area to accommodate not only the seats of the board members but also to provide additional seating for guests.

John Alexander made his way through the gathering and greeted us. He told us I was to do the entire presentation. My heart fell to the floor. My mind was in a whirl. I asked myself over and over again, What gives me the right to be here, on this day, with these people? I considered myself to be simply a little-known foot surgeon in a small southern California community. I felt I had no business consorting with some of the finest and foremost scientists in America.

I heard the door close with a dull thud and instantly the room became silent. Bigelow spoke in a soft authoritative voice. He directed the board's attention to me and made the introduction. He told them I would be presenting the material they had previously discussed, and also would show slides and video. After this was complete, they would be allowed to ask me questions.

Bigelow signaled me to begin my presentation. I felt petrified with fear. Yet there was nothing to do but go on, so I opened my presentation by telling everyone that I would pass out a prepared document. I reached into one of our briefcases and pulled out a bunch of them. After the shuffling of paper had stopped, I walked slowly to the middle of the presenter's area and resumed speaking to introduce our videotape of the surgeries. I knew what material they were interested in and felt prepared not only to present it but also to answer the questions it would draw.

Time passed quickly. The video presentation was over and the lights came back on. The beginning questions were all of a technical nature and I answered them to the best of my ability. As the questioning continued, I noticed that a portion of the board had suddenly taken my behalf and began to answer the questions for me. At this point, I knew I had made a favorable impression.

From then on it was smooth sailing. Whenever I was asked a question I could not satisfactorily answer, I would merely glance at one of my supporters and he would jump in to answer the question for me. The more I talked, the more confident I became.

My time came to an end. I do not know, even to this day how I knew it was all over. It was as if a mental clock just set off an alarm bell.

We gathered up our material and walked to an adjoining room replete with comfortable chairs and couches. There were also a number of ornate occasional tables. I was surprised when most of the members of the board began to gather around. They asked if they could see the specimens. We were quick to oblige and soon there was a standing crowd. We carefully explained the origin of each specimen along with the details of the particular abduction experience involved. I found this quite fascinating as the involved scientific types, I was warned, had no interest in hearing tales of alien abduction.

The board was about to convene again. One of the guards was sent to escort us back to the dining room where we had started the afternoon. We were invited to help ourselves to food, make ourselves comfortable and relax. We were told that someone would be coming down to meet with us periodically.

We took the time to review the situation, wondering what they would offer, if anything. It wasn't long before our questions started to be answered. Bigelow appeared in the doorway, walked over to us and pulled up a chair. He told us that in his opinion, we had made an excellent presentation and the board would be voting shortly on their decision. He told us that he would be popping down from time to time and keeping us apprised of the situation.

We sat looking at each other. A smile crept over my colleague's face and he said quietly, "Roger, I think we did it. Isn't it just great?" I agreed with him wholeheartedly.

I was just beginning to relax. I didn't know or ponder why I was feeling this way. The guard was joined by a colleague and they sat by themselves in a corner out of earshot.

Bigelow's trips up and down the stairs came at regular intervals. Each time he would bring us additional information. Finally, at about 5:30 p.m. he came down and asked if we were interested in taking a walk. We jumped at the chance to get some fresh air and exercise. Bob lead us into an area of his park-like garden. We strolled along and discussed the future involvement of NIDS as it pertained to our research. The conversation was upbeat and favorable. It was all said and done with a handshake. We agreed to turn over four of our surgical specimens for analysis.

There were certain stipulations to the agreement. The first was that we were forbidden to mention the involvement of their organization in our work. (Obviously, that stipulation has since been withdrawn.) The next was that a scientific paper would be written and published in a world class journal. (We were only too glad to comply!) Another pertained to the knowledge eventually winding up in the public domain. This was our stipulation and we said we were adamant about this point or the entire agreement would be voided. We also agreed to allow NIDS to select the laboratories of their choice. They were the experts and wanted to be in the driver's seat. Our working relationship had to be one of mutual trust.

We sat once more in the dining room. We gathered the specimens and began to code them. All tests were to be double-blind. Only I would keep the key which would tell where the objects originated.

Bigelow sat nervously waiting. I gave him the specimens and shook hands. I am sure that he was as excited as we were.

We said our good byes, gathered up our materials and were escorted to the vehicle which would take us to the airport for our return flight home.

Chapter 8

THE SECOND SET OF SURGERIES

I was assured by Robert Bigelow that N.I.D.S. funds would be forthcoming if I complied with the wishes of their board. Their first request was for me to send a detailed budget for the surgeries and related research. I had given this much thought and developed a general plan. My first task was to call the various individuals who would be involved on the professional level and obtain a cost estimate.

I went to my office one quiet afternoon when I was not seeing patients and made several phone calls. My first call was to Dr. Thomas Dodd, a friend who owned a large surgical facility in the San Fernando Valley. I told him that I was involved in a rather unusual research program and needed to rent his surgical facility for one day.

"I'm in need of some sophisticated equipment, such as a Fluoroscan and a C-Arm, which I know you have," I explained.

"How many hours would you be using it for and what is the date you had in mind?" Tom asked.

I gave this some thought. I did not want him to know my plan was just in the formative stage and that I was working on a budget for a third party who would ultimately be supplying the funds.

I answered, "I was considering a date in mid-May. This will depend on the patients' availability. I expect to do three or four cases and that requires some coordination. As far as the surgical time is concerned, I believe it shouldn't take more than one hour per case plus time for the anesthesia and prep."

Tom said that his office manager would get back to me about the costs involved, and added, "Remember, I also have to pay the entire staff for the time you keep the suite open."

I told him that I would wait for his assistant's call before I confirmed everything.

My second task was to find the chief surgeon for these cases, since Dr. A. would not be available. I reviewed my list of possibilities and decided to call another old friend, Dr. Cass. I had known him for many years and, although I hadn't seen him for some time, I felt sure he was still in practice.

My friend seemed enthusiastic about helping with the surgeries but unfortunately he was going to be out of the country when we needed him. He suggested a young surgeon he had worked with named Dr. Pratt, who had excellent skills, and would almost certainly do the cases.

I immediately dialed the number he had just given me and Dr. Pratt himself answered. I introduced myself and told him Dr. Cass had recommended him for the surgeries. He asked me a number of medical questions pertaining to the patients and seemed satisfied with my answers. He said he would be available on the surgeries' tentative date of May 18 and his charges would be $500.00 per case, or a total of $1,500.00 for the three cases. I told him the costs would be acceptable.

A few days later I began composing a scientific budget for the N.I.D.S. The surgical costs were running higher than I had anticipated. Dr. Dodd's office manager had informed me that the costs of the operating room alone would be $1,000.00 per hour. The additional cost to keep the remaining part of the facility open would amount to another $300.00 per hour. I tried to convince her to lower the price without success.

Next, I called Mike Portanova, who was the official MUFON photographer and also a member of the executive board, for an estimate of costs for the still photographs and processing. He responded with a figure in the $500.00 range.

So far so good; my budget was taking shape. The next consideration was the psychologist's fee. I called the woman we had previously used for the surgeries performed in August, 1995. Although she was eager to work with us again, she would no longer provide her services free of charge, which did not come as a shock Then she surprised me by saying that a portion of the testing should be performed by a clinical psychologist. She knew of someone who could do this for us and naturally there would be a separate charge for her services. The total of all these arrangements would add up to about $500.00 per case. I was taken aback but told her I would submit her figures in my budget proposal.

Over the next few days I asked several key people to critique the document. Once everyone seemed satisfied, I sent it to Derrel for final approval. He in turn called me and gave the go-ahead to send it to N.I.D.S.

The next week or so seemed to drag by. I did not want to make further arrangements until I had some word from Bigelow. Finally, late one afternoon, while I was busily engaged in my practice, I was told that I had a phone call from N.I.D.S. It was Anne, Bigelow's secretary.

"Mr. Bigelow asked me to call you in reference to the budget proposal. The board has been looking at it and has a few questions. They would like to know the name of the patients, their medical history, and their experiences as abductees. They also would like to know if they meet your original criteria and do they have demonstrable evidence which shows on an x-ray, CAT scan or MRI?"

I was stunned at the nature and thoroughness of these questions. Once I recovered my wits I told her I would happily provide all the answers and send them by fax shortly. I typed the answers that night and faxed them to N.I.D.S.

Several days went by before I received another communication from Bigelow's secretary. She told me the board had approved the budget and she was going to fax me a set of documents to read and sign, if I approved of them. On receiving the fax, I read it over and considered it a fairly straightforward agreement. I signed the documents and faxed them back immediately. It wasn't until later in the day that the realization of what had just transpired finally sunk in. My mood was elevated for the balance of the day.

This was the catalyst I needed to direct all my energies toward the project. The first step was to notify the patients that they would finally undergo the surgery. One by one I made the phone calls. It was a possibility that we would perform four surgeries instead of three. The fourth potential patient was none other than Whitley Streiber, world famous abductee and author of the bestseller Communion. We had been in constant contact over the previous months and he told me he thought he had an implant in his ear. He had been traveling around the world on the lecture circuit and was scheduled to be in the Los Angeles area at the time of the surgeries.

I advised him to have laboratory studies and an x-ray of the suspected implant region before any surgery could be performed, and said this information had to be received by me several days prior to the event. He agreed to all my suggestions. However he changed his mind at the last minute and decided not to have the surgery performed. He explained that he wanted to have the possible implant tested for function prior to having it surgically excised. He intended to have this done in Texas. I concurred with his decision because it would be a golden opportunity to have function studies to add to our pool of knowledge. But it was nevertheless disappointing.

I let my Texas colleague know we would only have the three original surgical patients, all of whom had passed the battery of lab tests and physical exams which cleared them for surgery. One of our surgical candidates had a severe allergy to all local anesthetics and the only way to perform the procedure was by using hypnoanesthesia. I suggested we invite a number of distinguished individuals to witness the surgery firsthand.

I thought this was a good idea and proceeded to arrange for an additional room at the surgical facility which housed a large projection TV, which would be used as a monitor to receive the broadcast from the surgery room. Realizing we could be deluged with people who wanted to see the surgeries performed, I decided to restrict admittance only to those who received a special invitation. Among those invited were Robert O. Dean, Cecelia Dean, Johsen Takano (Director of the Cosmo Isle UFO-Aerospace Museum in Japan), Michael and Debra Lindemann, Dr. John Mack, Budd Hopkins, Dale Musser (Chief Investigator for Saber Enterprises), Paul Davids (producer of the movie, Roswell), Larry Germain (producer), Toyo Secawa (H. Man International), Barbara Lamb, Walt Andrus, Yvonne Smith, Whitley and Anne Streiber, Melinda Leslie, Donna Higbee and numerous others...a virtual Who's Who in Ufology.

Meanwhile, Alice was assisting me with the numerous details which remained. She called the MUFON members who had participated in the previous set of surgeries and requested their help again.

Within a few days we started receiving responses to our invitations by mail and telephone. I was surprised by the number of individuals who asked if they could invite their friends and colleagues. If this situation were left unchecked, we would wind up with more witnesses than we could accommodate. After giving this problem much thought I decided I would personally extend invitations to anyone recommended by an individual who was on the original list. In that way, I could control the total process.

THE SURGICAL PATIENTS

We had received numerous applications from individuals claiming they had implants. From this list we chose only three whom we believed met our criteria—one male and two females. All three believed they had been involved in an alien abduction experience. The only slight difference was the male candidate who was not completely sure whether he had been involved with aliens or the U.S. military.

We knew from past experience that some of alleged abductees claimed military involvement, but this was difficult to prove because of what are termed as screen memories, which block full recall of the actual events. It would appear that abductors can easily play games with the minds of their victims. Sometimes they would play out a military scenario which was believable and in many cases would seem to be complete with the proper uniforms, weapons, underground bases, flying military aircraft and military ground vehicles. Of course, it's also possible that military abductions are quite real. It was because of these factors we chose our male candidate. The most convincing evidence was that this individual had a metallic foreign object in his left lower jaw. The object was easily demonstrable on radiographic examination. In addition he claimed to hear voices and related this to the object in his jaw. We told him that after the surgery was performed and the object removed he might continue to hear the voice communication. He understood this but nevertheless wanted the object removed.

The second surgical candidate was a female with an object in the front portion of her leg adjacent to the shin bone. X-rays taken showed only a small round radio-dense shadow in this area. In addition, there was a noticeable lesion on the skin which we classified as a typical scoop mark. This skin lesion has been found in a high number of alleged abductees. We considered this an opportunity not only to remove the foreign body embedded in the deep tissues but also to remove the superficial portion of the skin. This would allow for a separate study of the superficial tissues as well as the deep tissues and the object itself. This patient had conscious memories of an event which happened several years earlier and thought her abduction events were continuing. She also had a vivid memory of seeing a UFO over her home in the San Fernando Valley north of Los Angeles. We performed a battery of psychological and physiological laboratory examinations on her and found her to be a good surgical candidate.

The third subject, another female, appeared to be a classical textbook case of alien abduction. She had all the signs which appear in many books on the subject. In addition, she had a signed affidavit from her neighbor who lived across the street attesting to the fact that on the same night an abduction experience occurred she had witnessed a circular-shaped craft hovering over the victim's house. This sincere surgical candidate was able to clearly recall numerous details that occurred during her abduction experiences. She also had a demonstrable lesion on the skin of her leg which was red in color and raised. She described the history of this lesion and how it was treated by her doctor. She had a small surgery performed to drain the area and this resulted in delayed healing which took the better part of a year. She said that the doctor drained a copious amount of a purple fluid and was mystified about its origin. For some reason, no pathology examination was performed on the exudate. X-rays of the area demonstrated an object similar to that of the second surgical candidate. It appeared essentially as a small radio-opaque ball located in the soft tissues just below the area of involvement on the skin. A decision was made to use the same type of surgical procedure as on the second patient, which was to remove the skin lesion and all the tissue below, including the foreign object shown on the x-ray.

PREPARATIONS CONTINUE

The days passed quickly. Preparations continued and the closer we came to the actual surgical date the more nervous I became. One of many small items of concern was that I hadn't yet received any funds from Las Vegas, yet I became personally obligated for a large sum of money. I called Bigelow's secretary and explained my concern. She assured me that the funds would be forthcoming and that she would discuss the situation with Bigelow and get back to me shortly. As it turned out, I did not receive the funds until almost one month after the surgeries were completed. This delay in funding produced additional pressure. In thinking back, I now consider how lucky we were that only few demands were made upon us for payment during that period.

The RSVPs continued to pour in and with them came numerous phone calls from others who had heard about the surgery and wanted to come. This was another of my concerns. Although the facility was adequate in size, the viewing area only held just so many chairs. I didn't want a chaotic scene caused by an overflowing audience. I called Alice and sought her advice. She told me she would actively coordinate the event.

The non-professional portion of the team was going to be about the same as it had been with the first set of surgeries. Each individual had already performed once and the experience was certainly not easily forgotten. I thought to myself there would have to be just a few changes. Since all of the cases were to be done by the general surgeon, I felt it was imperative to have a highly trained surgical nurse. I selected Mike Evans, who acted as our videographer for the previous procedures. Mike was very accommodating and agreed to do the cases. There was no need to look for someone who would do the filming as I had made arrangements with a man who had been doing our MUFON photographic analysis, Jerry Barber. He agreed to film the entire set of surgeries using some high-tech equipment which included specialized cameras. Some of these cameras would be operating simultaneously and others were for extreme close-up shots of the specimens and wound areas. The MUFON camera would also be set up to record the event and broadcast the procedures to the viewing area.

Alice arranged for another MUFON board member, Peggy Portanova, to handle the food for the event, set up the kitchen and coordinate the feeding of all our guests. Her husband Mike would set up the still cameras and perform all the still photography. As in the previous surgeries, Jack and Ruth Carlson would record the event with a written document. Bert Clemens became our in-house equipment expert and would be responsible for the TV equipment and other electronic technicalities. Another board member, Leslie, was in the Navy and stationed part of the year in Antarctica. Fortunately, she was on furlough and would not return to duty for some time. She volunteered to bring two of her male counterparts who would serve as security for the event.

It was now May 12, only six days before the surgeries were to take place. I racked my brain to see if there were any details I hadn't considered and decided the only thing left to be done was to take the team to the surgical site and have a rehearsal. This would familiarize them with the facility and show me how smoothly things would run.

May 14 was chosen for the on-site rehearsal. I conducted a tour of the premises and helped everyone find their niche. There were many suggestions during the event which we evaluated and implemented as appropriate. After the dry run I was that confident all the bases had been covered.

On the morning of May 16, the phone rang and Sharon answered. She handed me the portable phone, saying it was a man whose voice she did not recognize.

"Hello, this is Roger. Can I help you?"

"Yes, this is Dr. Pratt. How are you? I hope this won't put you out but I am afraid I won't be able to do the surgeries I agreed to do with you on the 18th. My secretary scheduled another big case and I can't be in two places at the same time," he stated matter-of-factly.

I reached forward and steadied myself against the bathroom sink. For a moment I was speechless. His words echoed in my head. My mind began to race. I thought, This means I'll have to cancel the entire surgical affair. How will I explain this to the patients? What about N.I.D.S. and all the rest of the people involved?

Suddenly, my daytime nightmare was interrupted by Dr. Pratt's next statement.

"Oh, by the way, I have a colleague who has agreed to take my place. I took the liberty of discussing the cases with him and he will be up to snuff on the day of the procedures. Please just give him a call and supply him with the address and time he is to be there. His name is Allen Mitter."

This statement caused my emotions to yo-yo in the space of a few seconds. My state of shock turned immediately to calm and then to joy. My life was still on the track for which it seemed to be destined! I got Dr. Mitter's phone number from Dr. Pratt before hanging up. My spirits were lifted and I proceeded with my mundane chores preparing for my trip to the airport.

At 11:00, I met our Texas researcher at the gate. On the way home, we discussed the particulars of the upcoming event. Since one of the patients, Doris, was allergic to all local anesthetics, he would need to work with her extensively before surgery for the hypnoanesthesia to be successful. The other two cases would only require his presence just before and during the surgery. The abduction work-ups had been completed. He explained there was only a minimum of details to which he personally had to attend. In turn I advised him of the latest plans pertaining to the surgical facility and the change of general surgeons. He took this in stride and let out a hearty laugh when I related the story of the surgical change. I told him I had met the new surgeon, who seemed very nice and willing to work with us. I also explained he didn't want to appear on camera with a full face shot and I really didn't consider this much of a problem.

Over dinner at my house, he quizzed me about the medical aspects of the surgical candidates. I brought him up to date with the results of the x-rays and laboratory tests. There was nothing in the lab reports which would preclude them from having the surgery performed. I told him the first case was going to be Annie. She had no allergies to anesthesia and showed a healthy physiological and psychological profile. The x-rays showed a small round opaque foreign body in the superficial layers below the skin. The surface of the skin at this site demonstrated one of the typical abduction scoop-type lesions. I described my plan to remove the entire portion of superficial skin as well as to carry the wound deeply and remove the small round object below. This could be done by obtaining the tissue in one elliptical slice. He listened carefully as I explained the procedure.

The second case was to be Doris. She would require his direct attention before the surgery because of her allergy to local anesthesia. He told me he had made arrangements to begin her hypnotic sessions the next day, May 17. He also thought making her the second case would provide enough time for him to induce a deep hypnotic state prior to the time she entered the surgery room.

The third case would be the male patient, his x-rays revealed a small triangular, radio-dense foreign body in the left lower jaw. His physiological health was good but there was some question as to his psychological profile. For example the event itself could result in the subject becoming an alcoholic, lead to behavior problems or even outright psychosis. The important factor was that Don did meet all our medical criteria.

I showed the my Texas colleague the latest x-rays on Don. He held the film up to the light. The foreign body was visible just below the left lower jaw. He had seen this before and was not surprised at what he was viewing. Next I pulled out another x-ray of Don's shoulder.

"Take a look at this and see if you seen anything strange here." He took the x-ray and held it up to the light. A puzzled expression came over his face and he turned to me.

"Is this some sort of a joke or what?" he asked. I was grinning from ear to ear and told him there was no joke intended. He pointed to an area adjacent to the left clavicle. "What in the hell is that?"

I said, "It appears to be some sort of screw. Sometimes screws are used in cases of bone fracture repair. He could have had a clavicular separation. I questioned him about this and he swears he never had a fractured shoulder or a surgery on this area."

This was just one of the mysteries we would have to contend with. He asked me if I had plans to remove the screw and I told him no. I said I thought it would be a good idea to follow this patient for some time post-operatively and perhaps get another x-ray at a later date to see if the screw was still visible.

Suddenly fatigue engulfed my mind and body. We had our dessert and turned in for the evening.

On the morning of May 18, 1996, we awoke early. I gulped down glasses of orange juice my wife had prepared and I took my coffee cup with me in the car. We arrived at the medical facility at 8:05 a.m. and noticed that we seemed to be the only ones there from our group.

"Come on, let's grab our stuff and I'll show you the lay of the land," I said excitedly. Soon we were standing before the big wooden double doors of the surgical complex. I reached for the knob and swung the door open wide. We stepped into the waiting room and dragged in some of our equipment. We were greeted by a friendly voice.

"Good morning, Dr. Leir, You remember me, don't you? I'm Dr. Miller." I looked up into the eyes of a familiar face I had not seen for many years.

"Bill, my gosh, what are you doing here?" I asked.

"Well, Rog, I'm working with the group now and they asked me to be here so that I could give you any help you needed with the surgeries. I also know how to operate the Fluoroscan."

I was glad to see a familiar face, and pleased to find there would be a separate operator for the x-ray unit we needed to use. He immediately offered to give us a tour of the facility. We were shown the entire complex from the operating rooms to the kitchen.

I took Bill aside and explained the proposed surgeries to him. I also instructed him regarding the supplies we needed and the approximate time it would take to do each case. In addition, it was necessary for me to explain about the large number of participants and observers who were due to descend upon us soon. Just as I was making my final comment, Alice and the first contingent arrived. Introductions were made all around.

Because of our rehearsal, the team already knew where to go and the individual tasks they had to perform. Soon the area abounded with activity. Cables were being connected between the surgery room and the waiting room to a huge large-screen TV. One of the cameras was mounted on its tripod and lined up with a view of the surgical table. Our professional videographer and his colleague had not yet arrived and that was beginning to disturb me. Alice, Peggy and other members of MUFON brought up huge trays of food they prepared for lunch and placed them in the kitchen. Still other members of the team were arranging the furniture in the waiting room so the TV screen could be viewed by the maximum number of people.

Next to arrive were our patients, who had been transported by another MUFON member of our team. We greeted them warmly and escorted them to separate rooms which would serve as a waiting area for each patient. The plan was to have our psychologist give them a brief examination and then have Mike Evans draw their blood to prepare the solutions which would ultimately carry the specimens.

Suddenly I heard a burst of laughter emanating from the waiting area and I knew our invited guests had begun to arrive. It seemed as if my presence was required in a thousand places all at the same time and I couldn't get there fast enough. I made my way to the waiting area and greeted the arriving guests. So far so good, I thought to myself. No one had attempted entry without my letter of admission and no one had to be turned away. One of our guests had asked me if it was okay to invite Gordon Cooper, the astronaut. I told him I thought it would be just fine, but I had heard his health was not good. Perhaps he would not come for that reason.

Within fifteen minutes the room began to swarm with guests. Bob and Cecelia Dean were among the first to arrive. They were followed by Anne and Whitley Streiber. We busied ourselves greeting everyone. Just as I turned to say hello to one of the guests, I heard a voice calling me from somewhere in the depths of the office complex. It was Dr. Miller. I followed the sound of his voice and found him in the supply room. He was inquiring about a particular item we requested for the surgery. No sooner had I solved this problem, than someone came up behind me to remind me that Jerry was not there yet with the video team. I rushed to the phone, hastily called his numbers and left messages. Next I dialed his beeper number and left the number of the surgical center. I advised the reception area personnel I was expecting a call and to please put it through as soon as it came in. The time was now 9:45 a.m. and the first surgery was to start at 10:00. We could not begin without the correct video equipment in place.

The next person I heard calling me was Jack Carlson, who was assisting in the operation of the video feed to the waiting room. He told me there was a problem getting the signal to the TV set and he didn't know why.

"Please get it fixed," I barked at him. "There is only a certain amount of time allotted for this. We are paying $1,000.00 per hour for just this room alone."

My mood didn't improve when I looked at my watch and found it to be 10:05 a.m. Not only was Jerry not there yet but our general surgeon was also late. Seconds later a voice called my name from the front office reception area. There stood a man in surgical greens. Relieved, I reached out to shake his hand.

"Allen, nice to see you again. Come on in and let me show you the facility."

Yes, my panic was premature. Our surgeon was now present and ready to start. I took him on a tour through the office and introduced him to the principals. I also explained to him about the videotaping and offered him all the anonymity he wanted. He seemed satisfied with my assurances.

By 10:30 a.m. there was still no word from Jerry. At that juncture I had to make up my mind about what to do. I decided that at $1,000.00 per hour I was not going to wait any longer. We had one camera in operation and whatever happened we would still have an adequate recording of the event on tape. I raced back to the doctor's lounge and quickly donned my surgical scrub suit. I spread the word to all concerned that the first surgery was about to begin. With that the back office came alive. The patient was brought into the operating room and immediately Mike started the surgical prep. I took a last opportunity to walk up to the front office and announce to our waiting audience that it was time to start paying attention to the TV screen.

Our first patient, Annie, was in excellent spirits, appearing calm and unconcerned about the procedure which was about to be performed on her. She hadn't met Dr. Mitter previously. He introduced himself and asked some of the routine medical history questions. I asked Mike for the local anesthetic mixture and handed the filled syringe to Dr. Mitter.

He said to Annie, "You're going to feel a little pinch now. Let me know when it feels better." I steadied her leg with both hands and Dr. Mitter plunged the needle into the spot adjoining the surgical target. He pushed in the plunger of the syringe and I felt the skin and surrounding tissue swell with its burden of new fluid. I also felt the muscles tighten in Annie's leg and advised her to tell us if she felt discomfort. She responded by saying she had felt a little pain but it didn't last long.

Soon, the area was fully anesthetized. Allen took a needle and tapped it over the surface of the skin.

"Do you feel anything, when I touch you here?" he asked.

Annie quickly responded, "No I don't feel a thing."

I asked Mike to start handing us the sterile drapes. He reached over to the back table and handed us the first sterile covering. Dr. Mitter took one end and I held the other. We stretched it over the area above the surgical site. The second drape cover was placed below the surgical site. Next we applied a drape which had a manufactured hole in the center. The portion with the hole was placed directly over the operative site and sealed in place with adhesive gum.

We were ready to begin the surgery. The surgical Mayo tray containing all the instruments was rolled over to adjoin the surgical site. Dr. Mitter was about to reach for the surgical blade. Suddenly, we were aware of some activity at the entrance to the operating room. I looked up and saw a heavy-set gentleman wearing a green scrub suit and surgical mask standing in the doorway with a very large video camera in one hand and a tripod in the other. It was Jerry.

"Doc, I am so sorry we're late," he said apologetically.

I was in no mood to hear his excuses, no matter how valid they might be. I noticed he had brought his associate, Sharon. She was also dressed in surgical greens and holding another type of video camera.

"Jerry, can you just go ahead and get things set up without screwing anything up in the room? We are ready to cut the skin open at this moment. We can stop for a minute or two until you get the camera situated but you better get it done post-haste," I directed.

I then reflected that my words had been carried to the audience in the waiting room because the sound feed was live at that moment. I told Bert to shut down the live feed for a minute or two until Jerry got his equipment set up. Bert did as he was instructed and shut the camera off. Jerry and Sharon quickly set up the tripod and plugged in the myriad of cables and power supply units. In just a few minutes Jerry told us their equipment was operational. I instructed Bert to fire up the live feed again and apologized for the delay.

I picked up the Bard Parker handle containing a number 10 surgical blade and handed it to Dr. Mitter. After instructing the patient to tell us if she felt anything uncomfortable, he made the first incision. I reached over with a gauze sponge and dabbed blood from the surgical site. He completed the first incision and quickly turned the blade in the opposite direction, cutting through the skin on the other side of the section we were removing. This was a routine type of elliptical incision with the portion of tissue we intended to remove in the center of the ellipse. I took the blade from Dr. Mitter and passed him the second blade and a forcep. He looked up at me with a smile on his face. This was apparent approval from the surgeon.

We had never worked together before and my function was that of an ordinary surgical nurse. I was glad we were off to such a fine start. It wasn't long before he lifted out the segment of flesh containing both the superficial and deep aspects of the tissue. I took the specimen and began to probe it. Dr. Mitter proceeded with closure of the wound. It seemed most of our attention was drawn to the specimen and less was paid to the completion of the operation. The close-up camera was focused on the bloody tissue resting on the sponge. I took a sharp instrument and began to probe the deeper tissue. Suddenly I heard and felt a little clicking sound. My instrument had touched something solid. There it was: a small, round, greyish-white ball which glistened under the powerful surgical light. A feeling of excitement washed throughout the room and I heard a cheer from the folks in the viewing room. Annie responded to our excitement by asking what we had found. I took the gauze sponge and brought it over where she could see it.

"My heavens, did that come out of me?" she asked excitedly.

"It sure did," I answered.

Our abduction researcher stood by Annie's head and leaned over so he could get a better look at the contents of the sponge.

"That doesn't look like the others," he said in his Texas drawl. "Is that what we saw on the x-ray?"

I told him it appeared similar to what we had seen on the film and was surprised to see it was such a hard substance. I also told him it was similar to the object removed in a previous case I had done with a dermatologist. That doctor had diagnosed it as a calcifying epithilioma; however, it did not conform to the clinical history of that type of lesion and, in fact, its formation was totally reversed from what it should have been. I told him it would be very interesting to compare the analysis of both specimens.

Our attention centered on finishing the surgery, applying a bandage and moving the patient to the recovery area. Our personnel functioned as a well-oiled machine. The room was cleaned and prepared for the next case.

I made a brief appearance in the viewing area and answered a few questions before returning to my post at the side of candidate number two.

I saw Doris walking down the hall. The patient appeared as if she had been on an all-night binge. She was totally unsteady and I wondered if she was going to make it into the surgery room. I didn't know what hypnotic procedure was used but it was obviously effective. This was the patient who had allergies to all local anesthetics and was going to have hypnoanesthesia only. I looked at her lying on the table. Her eyes were glassy. I asked if we could talk with her.

"Doris, how do you feel?" I asked.

"Doc, this is the greatest. I could have this kind of surgery all the time and learn to love it," she answered with a big smile on her face.

The procedures were going to be similar to the first case, without the injection of an anesthetic. Mike performed a sterile prep as he had done on the first patient and then surrounded the area with sterile drapes. Dr. Mitter had never performed a surgery before which used only hypnosis as the anesthetic. He was cautious in his approach and kept asking the patient if she felt anything when he pinched the surgical area with a forcep. She strongly denied any discomfort. Finally he seemed satisfied and gingerly made the first incision.

The procedure progressed similarly to the first case in which the superficial skin lesion was contained within the ellipse of skin being removed. Then, a terrible mistake occurred. Dr. Mitter, who had performed numerous surgeries under typical local anesthetic, picked up a forcep and gently grasped the segment of tissue to be cut free from the underlying anatomy. He looked directly at Doris and said, without thinking, "This may hurt just a little now, dear."

With that, the patient screamed in pain and tried to remove her leg from the surgical area. I didn't know if any of us knew what happened except our hypnotherapist, who quickly took hold of the patient's head, looked directly into her eyes and stated in a loud voice, "Doris, listen to me. Your entire leg is frozen. It is a block of ice and you feel nothing. It is absolutely numb. It is numb and cold just like ice."

Dr. Mitter, Mike and I were holding on to her leg, trying to keep it in the surgical field. We could feel the tension drain from the muscles and slowly she lowered her leg back onto the table. A bead of sweat formed on Dr. Mitter's brow. Mike noticed its progress and used a sterile towel to pat the area dry. This was a good lesson to all of us. When a patient is undergoing surgery under hypnoanesthesia we would have to be very careful about the spoken word.

The tissue specimen was again placed on a surgical sponge. I probed it just as I had done previously. The tension in the room mounted. Again, an audible click was heard and there it was-another small, greyish-white, shiny ball.

An announcement of our findings was made over the audio system of the camera. We could hear the excitement of those in the viewing room. Our attention was directed to the surgical closure of the patient's wound. Mike had taken my place during the time I was probing the specimen. The wound was neatly sewn closed with nylon suture material and a simple dry sterile dressing was applied. Our hypnotist was still actively talking to the patient. He told her that she was going to get up and come with him into another room where she would go into a deep sleep and remain sleeping until he awakened her. He also suggested she felt no discomfort and would be completely healed in a very few days. She followed his commands like a robot and accompanied him to the recovery room.

The room was readied for the next patient by the surgical crew. I took the opportunity to grab a quick cup of coffee with Dr. Mitter. I asked him how he thought things were going so far. He seemed satisfied with everything we had done. I noticed he kept looking at his watch and asked him if he had a pressing engagement. He told me he had promised his wife he would be home at 4:00 p.m. I promised he could leave promptly following the next case. We were two down and one to go.

Don was on the operating table when we entered the operating room. Mike had performed the surgical prep and was standing ready to proceed with the surgery. The cameras were repositioned to focus on the jaw area and Dr. Miller had positioned the Fluoroscan unit. Dr. Mitter and I were both scrubbed and ready. We donned our surgical gloves and approached the table. Mike, without being instructed, passed the sterile syringe filled with the anesthetic mixture to Dr. Mitter. Without being asked, the patient informed us that his jaw area was numb with anesthesia. The drape material covered not only the patient's upper torso but also his head and face. When the patient was asked a question, his answer sounded as if his response came from somewhere other than his mouth.

The initial incision into the skin would be the only one made. There was nothing to remove from the superficial tissue. I helped retract the wound, holding it open so the deep tissues could be seen. The foreign body was triangular and small. Again, it was like looking for a needle in a haystack.

Dr. Mitter looked up and said "I think we are ready for the Fluoroscan." Dr. Miller moved the arm of the unit over to encompass the jaw area. He stepped on the pedal to activate the machine. We quickly moved our eyes to the TV monitor and watched as the tissues of the jaw became visible. Suddenly there it was.

"Hold it!" we all chimed in at once.

The small triangular metallic object was visible on the screen. I picked up a hypodermic needle and handed it to Dr. Mitter.

"Why don't we place this marker inside the tissue and watch it on the screen? Go ahead and try to touch the object with the end of the needle. That way We'll visualize it and know precisely where to probe," I suggested.

He concurred and quickly but carefully placed the needle in the deep tissue. Slowly and cautiously, he began to push the needle deeper a little at a time. He had to be very cautious in this area because of the possibility of hitting a facial nerve. If this happened it could result in permanent damage with numbness or paralysis. We held our breath and watched the TV monitor. Soon the tip of the needle was at its mark. I reached over and steadied the needle. Dr. Mitter took the surgical blade and cut deeply into the tissues, using the needle as a guide until he had reached the object. As usual, Mike was right there with the correct instrument, holding an Allis clamp in his outstretched hand.

Dr. Mitter took the instrument and directed it toward the area of tissue we were viewing on the TV screen. He carefully closed the jaws and slowly withdrew the clamp from the depths of the wound. A pool of blood welled in the area which obscured our view of all the deep tissues. I applied a surgical sponge with direct pressure to the wound and soon it soaked up the blood. Dr. Mitter removed the clamp and placed it directly between jaws of the Fluoroscan. We turned and looked at the screen. Much to our relief, contained within the tissue was the triangular metallic foreign body.

We let out a shout of excitement and instantly heard a number of jubilant yells emanating from the adjoining room. I immediately took the specimen and placed it on a surgical sponge. I took a surgical blade and began to dissect the soft tissue away from the metal portion. It appeared to be triangular in shape and was definitely metal. Slowly I removed the clinging surrounding tissue until more detail could be seen. It was then I noticed it: the metallic portion was covered with the same dark gray, well-organized membrane we had seen covering the metallic specimens we had removed in August of 1995. I couldn't believe my eyes. I picked up the blade again and tried to cut through the membrane. The harder I tried, the more frustrated I became. It would not open, just like the other specimens from the previous year.

Dr. Mitter finished closing the wound and applied a sterile dressing. The patient was asked if he was hearing voices as he did previously. He said the voices were gone. We told him we didn't know if they would come back or not but we would watch him carefully and monitor his progress. We helped him off the table and walked with him down the hall to the recovery room. He was placed on another table where the process to monitor his vital signs began.

We took this opportunity to greet our waiting guests. Their spirits were high and they hailed us as the heroes of the day. We asked everyone to join us in the kitchen area for a luncheon. From the expression on most of their faces, our invitation was somewhat of a surprise. We asked our guests to follow us to the kitchen area. Peggy had done a wonderful job with the preparation of the food. The display was fit for the finest of hotel banquets. The moment she saw us coming, she came forward with a plate in each hand and offer to fill them with food.

We grabbed a few bites of our food, set the plates aside and returned to the laboratory. The day's tasks were not yet over. There was more minor dissecting of the specimens to be done and we had not done the black light examination either. Jerry and Sharon were on hand to do some close-up photography. I carefully laid the specimens on white gauze sponges. The overhead light in the room was turned off and the room plunged into darkness. I reached over and turned on the ultraviolet light and held up the first specimen; there it was, a greenish glow in the light of the ultraviolet lamp. The cameras were positioned close to the object and a recording was made of the fluorescence.

One by one we performed the same procedure on all the specimens. Each one fluoresced but not all were the same greenish color. There was a variance of green to pink in color. We did not have an explanation for this. It was just another one of those mysteries which would have to be solved. Following the black light examination, each of the specimens was placed in containers of the blood transport solution. This time all the specimens would be kept by me. My plan was to parcel out generous portions of the soft tissue to at least three bio-logical laboratories. This would mean we would have three different pathology reports for each specimen. The metallic and dense portions of the specimens would be held by me until we knew where their analysis would take place.

The day was almost over. We bowed to the Japanese and shook hands with the remaining guests who were our casual acquaintances. Then came the more emotional good-byes. Among these were the Streibers. We hugged Anne and Whitley warmly. It wasn't until some days later that we heard of Whitley's overwhelming emotional behav-ior during the surgery. It seems he felt a personal responsibility for all those undergoing the surgical procedures and started to cry. Whitley is a very emotional man and through his vast experience in the field of alien abduction has an innate empathy for those who are victims of the phenomenon.

Photo Gallery

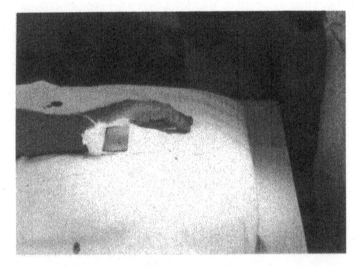

1. Implant removed from thumb.

2. Whitley Streiber & Dr. Leir

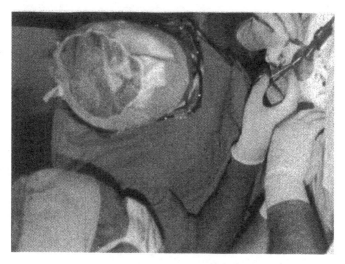

3. Surgeons Removing Suspected Implant

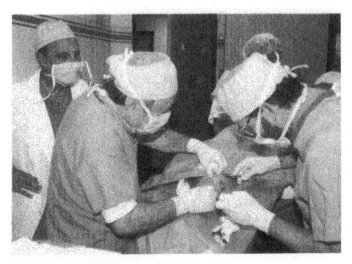

4. Surgical Scene

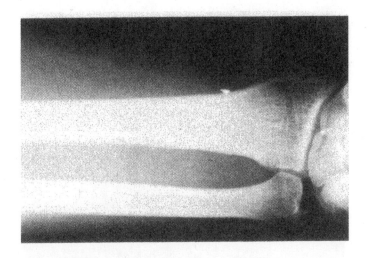

5. Implant X-ray - object next to bone

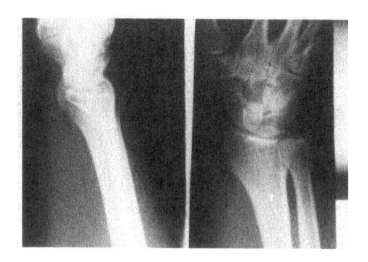

6. X-Rays of Object in Wrist

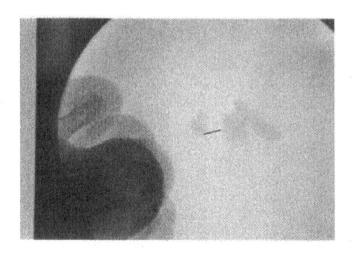

7. Object appears on x-ray scanner

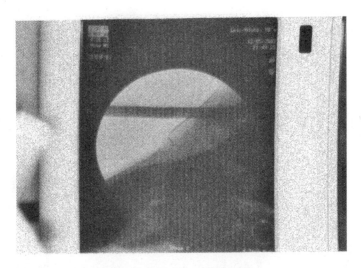

8. View of object on X-ray scanner

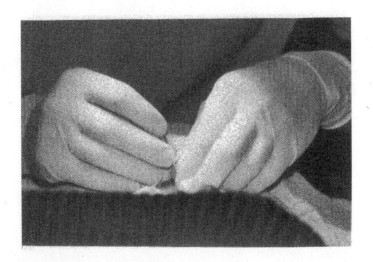

9. Surgery in progress

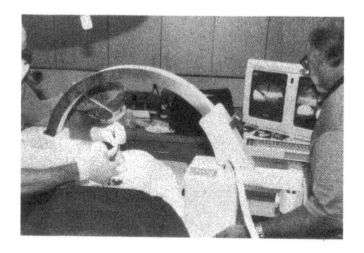

10. C-Arm X-ray device with T.V. View Screen

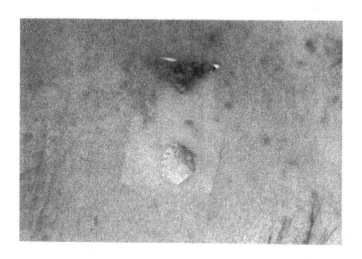

11. Markers indicating where objects located

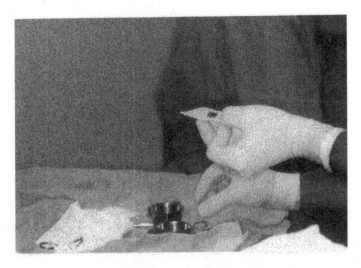

12. Specimen being transferred to container.

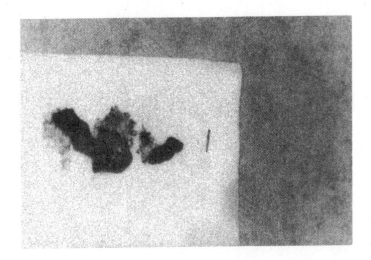

13. Metallic implant with soft tissue specimens

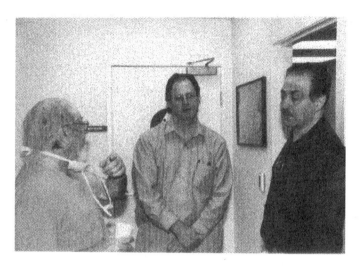

14. Dr Leir, "Coast to Coast" producer and George Noory - all present in the surgery

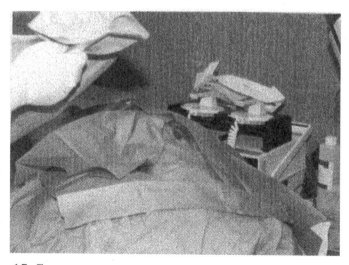

15. Surgery scene

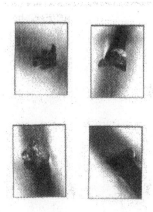

16. High magnification views of metallic rod end

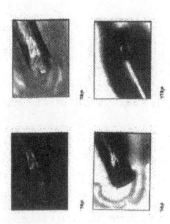

17. High magnification views of flat end of metallic rod implant

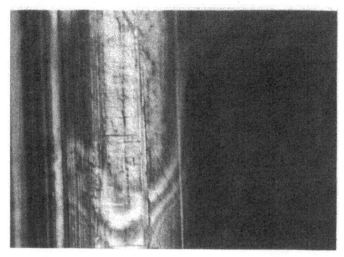

18. Optical medium power view of metallic rod implant

19. High optical photo of implant rod show biological tissue attached

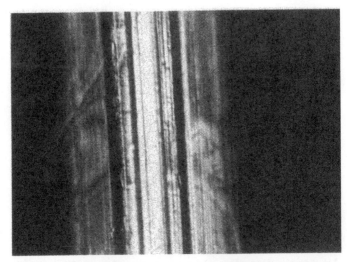

20. Medium magnification of metallic implant

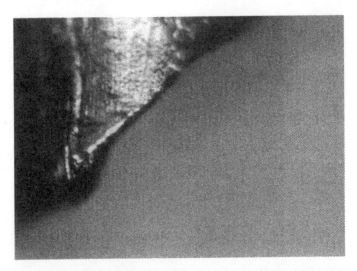

21. Medium magnification of oblique metallic rod end

Chapter 9

THE ABDUCTION HISTORIES

One of the criteria we established for removal of alleged alien implants was an abduction history of the proposed surgical candidates. I knew it was important to have a detailed abduction history for each potential candidate.

Critics and debunkers of the alien abduction phenomenon point disapprovingly to the retrieval methods of investigators. Their number one criticism focuses on the use of regressive hypnosis. Derrel and I acknowledge that in some instances, their criticism has merit. This is because there has never been a methodology universally adapted by the researchers. Although there are many well-qualified individuals performing hypnosis, there has never been a professional standard developed for the best method of memory retrieval. In a world full of complexities such as false memory syndromes, childhood abuse memories, and past life regressions, we must adopt research criteria that are beyond reproach. Therefore after careful consideration, I decided to forego the use of regressive hypnosis altogether. It was also decided to only use hypnotic regression techniques post-operatively, if necessary.

The abduction histories which follow will be presented partly in the verbatim words of the experiencers. As stated previously, their names will be altered to protect their anonymity. Although all our surgical patients had abduction histories, I have chosen just two of the cases for illustration, but they are typical cases. They are based on as many details as we could recover through waking recall by the candidates. In other words, since hypnotic regression was not used, the basis of these case histories is conscious memories.

PATRICIA'S ABDUCTION HISTORY

In 1969, Patricia and her family lived in a small rural area of the state of Texas. She was 23 years old and married to John, a caring man with a very strong personality. They were the parents of two young boys, Michael, 6 years old, and Billy, 5. John had been hard at work for months without a break and Pat felt they were soon due for time away from the daily routine. She was also considering the amount of time she had left to pursue a vacation, due to the fact she was eight months pregnant.

One evening in October, while Pat bustled about the kitchen preparing the evening meal, John came in, smiling. "Honey, how would you like to take a little vacation break?" he asked.

Pat spun around and stared at her husband with a surprised expression on her face. "How did you happen to come up with that idea?"

"Well, I had some free time today," John answered, "and started thinking that we haven't had any time off together for quite a while now. With the new baby coming, it might be a good time to get away."

Looking John in the eyes, she said, "Hey, that really sounds good to me. Let's go for it."

Several days went by before the subject came up again. John began by telling Pat that he had discussed the vacation with a couple of his buddies and they suggested an excellent place to go fishing. Pat considered the idea for a few moments and said, "You know, honey, that really sounds like a great idea. I'm sure the boys would just love it. We could get all the camping gear out and really have a great time. How do we get to this place?"

Clearing a spot on the kitchen table, John said, "Please hand me the old map in the top drawer."

Pat opened one of the kitchen drawers, riffled through a bunch of papers and pulled out an old crumpled map of Texas. The edges were frayed and the paper yellowed with age. She handed the map to her husband and he spread it out on the table, then traced a route on one of the major highways with his finger. "Pat, take a look. I think I know where this place is."

Pat peered intently at the map while John indicated the route, tracing along an easily visible major route as it branched off onto what appeared to be some minor roads. "I think it's right here," he said, pointing. "Honey, would you hand me that pencil over there, please?" Pat reached across the counter and picked up a worn yellow pencil with half of the eraser missing. She handed it to John and he traced a circle around the area.

Pat looked again and asked, "Are you sure you can find that spot? It looks a little desolate to me."

"You're such a worry wart," John teased, grinning. "You know I can find anything, anywhere!"

"How long do you think it would take to get there?"

John glanced at the map and said, "I think about two and a half hours."

Pat retorted, "Is that with or without a potty break? Remember my condition."

John laughed. "I think we can work that out when the time comes. Are you going to tell the boys or shall I do it?"

"Go ahead dear, you can have the pleasure, "Pat said. With that, John left the room. A few moments later, two bright-eyed boys burst into the kitchen, shouting. "Mom! Are we really going on a camping trip?" Pat assured them they were.

The next evening, plans were finalized. It was decided that if they took the boys out of school for only two days, they wouldn't miss much work. This would get them on the road the following Thursday.

At noon on the day of departure, John rushed into the kitchen and asked, "How are we doing? All set to go? I have the car all gassed up and she's ready and waiting." Pat was too busy dashing about the room and placing items in boxes to answer. The table was piled with pots and pans, food, and camping gear.

"John," she finally replied, "you can start packing this stuff in the car now, while I go and get the boys dressed."

John nodded and began carrying the boxes out to the awaiting car. He arranged the items so that they would all fit into the trunk. After a few trips John announced he was ready. Soon Pat and the two boys appeared in the doorway. Within a few moments they were all seated in the car and ready to begin their adventure. As John turned the key, the car started with a loud bang.

"What was that?" Pat asked.

"Oh, don't worry about it. I just had a tune-up and there was probably some raw gas still left in the carburetor," John answered. He was just about to depress the accelerator when Pat suddenly asked, "Did you take the map off the table?"

John looked at her in amazement and said, "No, didn't you get it?"

Pat jumped out and raced back to the house. Within moments she was back with the tattered map in her hand. "Okay, can we get started now?" she asked, with excitement in her voice. John put the car into gear, stepped on the gas, and it lurched onto the highway.

****

Pat looked at her watch. The trip was taking longer than expected; it was now almost 4:30 p.m. and they had not arrived at their destination. Some of the roads were not clearly marked and it had become increasingly evident that the map they were using was not up to date. "John, how much longer until we get there?"

John took a quick glance at the map and said, "We should just about be there."

Billy had his face pressed against the car window and was drawing figures in the steam created from his hot breath. Michael, seemingly oblivious to his surroundings, flipped through the pages of an old comic book.

Pat peered intently into the distance and noticed a structure ahead. "Is that the old iron bridge you were talking about?" she asked.

Sitting upright, John stared ahead, then slowed down, and said, "It sure is, honey."

This was the spot John's friend had talked about to him. It was an old wrought iron bridge which crossed a beautiful stream, and was endowed with a rich civil war history. The Confederate Army had built it as part of their supply route for the shipment of arms by horse-drawn military vehicles.

John slowed to a snail's pace as he approached the old bridge. A creaking and thumping sound replaced the customary noise of the tires contacting a paved road as they began to cross the old wood planking. Pat rolled down the window and stuck her head outside. "Do you think this bridge is safe?" she asked.

"My friend told me it was built to last forever," John replied.

Pat thought to herself, I wonder when forever stops? Soon they were on the other side. There was a clearing to the left and a small trail which led down to the river. Billy and Michael were jumping up and down on the back seat.

"Hold on guys, were almost there," John said. He stopped the car at a small section of the clearing just after they passed the far end of the bridge. It was an ideal campsite, close to the river and below the level of the bridge, where they would be protected fromthe wind and dust. The area had a few sparse trees, with numerous bushes and spaces that had once been the home of some rather large trees. Many branches and logs were strewn over the area. The family scrambled from the car.

"Let's start unloading before it gets dark or we won't be able to see what we're doing," John commanded.

Everyone dashed for the car and began to grab various articles. It only took about an hour to prepare the camp. John erected the tent while the boys laid out their sleeping bags. Pat was busy with pots and pans, preparing for their first outdoor feast. John and the boys went in search of firewood. He had a good deal of experience in making outdoor fires and knew what kind of wood it took.

Darkness slowly began to consume the campsite. A few stars were clearly visible in the sky overhead. The boys went back to the car and brought out two small flashlights. They found a comfortable log to sit on and began flashing their lights at the sky.

"Hey, mom, come on over here! I want to show you something," Michael yelled. Pat walked over to where the boys were sitting, with John on her heels.

"Hey, look at this! It's really neat." Michael pointed his flashlight skyward toward a brighter than usual star, and made two short flashes. Pat and her husband watched with amazement as the two flashes were returned!

"Pat, did you see that?" John shouted.

"I sure did!"

John ran back to the tent and got two larger, more powerful flashlights. He gave one to Pat and aimed his upward at the bright star, flashing two short and one long flashes. Within a few seconds, the very same sequence of flashes was returned.

"Pat! For God's sake, did you see that?" he asked excitedly.

She didn't answer, but instead held up her light and flashed a different series. These were also returned. Soon the single bright star was joined by a few friends. The whole family was having a great time, flashing away and getting their answers back, just as they had sent them.

****

The fire was bright and the air was filled with the scent of burning logs. The only sounds beside the crackle of the fire were night sounds of the open country. Both Billy and Michael were tucked securely into their sleeping bags. Pat cleaned up the dinner remnants as John found a comfortable spot adjacent to a log and sipped a cup of hot coffee. He slid his hand into his inside vest pocket and withdrew a dark, hand-carved pipe. Filling the bowl, he carefully packed it with his thumb. He placed the pipe between his teeth, struck a match, held it above the bowl and took a long puff. A plume of white smoke ushered forth from his mouth. Pat came over, nestled beside him.

"How're you doin', darlin'?" she asked.

John put his arm around her and gave her a big hug. He looked deep into her eyes and asked seriously, "What do you think was going on before with that weird light show?"

Pat gazed back intently, and said, "I bet they were a bunch of helicopters from the air base. Probably some hot shot military air jocks out to have fun with the citizens. Well, what the heck! We had as much fun as the kids did!"

****

The following morning was filled with excitement as the fishing lines hit the stream and the boys started to catch fish. The weather cooperated nicely, with the temperature staying in the mid-seventies. By noon, the family had caught its limit.

With the sun bright overhead, the boys were put down for a nap. It was time to enjoy the outdoors and just lay about, reading a book and relaxing. John never thought about turning on the radio. Late that afternoon they all went for a hike, and on the way back gathered firewood for the coming night's fire. John gave instructions about the type and dryness of the wood he wanted. He planned to build a fire that would last the night through, and needed wood with a high moisture content.

Pat had always thought that one of the fun parts of a combined camping and fishing trip was the pleasure of not only catching the fish, but also being able to cook them on the spot. So the family was treated to a feast that evening. She had prepared the day's catch using a recipe which had been handed down to her from her mother, along with hearth-baked biscuits and other good tasting goodies with a wonderful aroma.

With all the after-dinner chores completed, it was time to relax again. The little family played games and sang songs until Pat escorted the boys to the tent and tucked them in for the night. John puffed on his pipe and talked about his plan for the next day, which was to get up early and hike downstream to a spot where his friend said some of the biggest fish ever caught in that region had been taken. For that reason they had decided to retire early. John checked the fire one last time. It was well stocked with wood and should still be burning when they arose in the morning.

****

Suddenly, at about 1:00 a.m., Pat was awakened by her terror-stricken husband, who appeared looming over her like a huge giant silhouetted in the reflection of the firelight. He pointed a finger directly in front of her nose and said, "Get up right now and throw the kids in the car!" His voice was gruff and demanding. Frightened, Pat's heart pounded and her mind raced. She thought to herself, what could possibly be so wrong to cause her husband to act like this? She quickly extricated herself from the sleeping bag and put on her shoes.

John was now outside the tent and she couldn't see what he was doing. A few moments later he stuck his head in the tent opening and bellowed, "Hurry up! Come on! Come on!" Pat jumped to her feet and grabbed Billy. She dragged him rather violently out of the sleeping bag, the sudden movement waking him. He started to cry, so Pat gently soothed him in a quieting mother's voice. "It's all right dear, we're just going for a little ride." She rushed out of the tent and gently placed him on the rear seat of the car. "You go back to sleep now," she said softly. John appeared, carrying Michael, who was still sound asleep.

"John, please tell me what is going on," she pleaded.

His answer was a curt, "Never mind now! Just get in the car!" She did as she was told. John immediately followed. He started the motor, put the car in gear, and they quickly began to move down the desolate, dark road, leaving the campsite with all elements intact.

As they raced down the deserted path, Pat, becoming hysterical, pleaded with her husband to tell her what was happening.

He turned toward her with a look of terror on his face. "Something was under the bridge!"

"What are you talking about? Deer? People? Other animals?"

Her husband merely turned his head and said loudly, "No!"

John was concentrating on the narrow road ahead. All he could see was what the narrow beam of the headlights illuminated in front of the car. They were heading back the way they had come, toward the old iron bridge.

He suddenly turned to Pat and said, "Look behind us! Do you see that bright light following us?"

She turned and peered out the rear window. "Yes, I do see a light."

John glanced at her and said, "Don't be frightened. I'll protect you. Maybe it's just a truck. Try and see."

Pat strained her eyes to see what was following them. "Yes, yes, I think it is a truck," she stammered, turning about for a second time to stare at the rapidly gaining light. It was getting brighter and brighter, matching the speed of the car. She was gripped with cold terror as they approached the old iron bridge, a dimly lit silhouette in the darkness.

It was becoming apparent that the brightly lit object behind them was not a truck, and in fact was of such a gigantic size that it would never fit on the tiny bridge. They were now almost across the bridge, just a short distance from the other side.

Pat's attention was suddenly drawn to the front of the car. John appeared as if he was a zombie. "John! John!" Pat yelled, poking her husband on the arm. "Stop the car right now," she commanded. John quickly stopped. There they sat, dumbfounded.

"What just happened?" asked Pat after a moment.

"Honest to God, honey, I don't know," John replied. Together, they stared through the windshield in amazement. The car was now pointed in the opposite direction from the way that they had just been heading. The road before them led back toward the campsite, not away from it!

John stepped on the gas and the car once again clattered across the old, tired bridge, which groaned and creaked under the weight of the car. As they approached the campsite, Pat was aware that something was wrong with the entire scene. he first thing she noticed was that the campfire was out. There was nothing left to burn, just the red glow of the ashes. She thought to herself, This is impossible, John made that fire to last all night. We've only been gone a few minutes. I don't get it! It was as if hours of time had just vanished. She looked at John, trying to read his thoughts. He was extremely agitated and afraid. Pat considered her husband's personality; he was a man afraid of no person, nor anything. Just what had happened to him: that was a question which began to eat away at her very soul.

They stood and stared at each other. Sharing one mental thought, they both blurted out, "Let's go home!"

****

The boys appeared to be sleeping comfortably on the back seat of the car. John was driving too fast for the road conditions. Pat was concerned, but kept silent. She turned and shifted her gaze to the road behind them, noticing a greenish light following them. She was afraid to say anything to John, but from the look on his face she realized he must have seen it in the rear view mirror. The object continued to follow them for several more miles and did not vary from its path of pursuit. Pat looked over at her husband and noticed a tear running down his cheek.

He suddenly began to vocalize his fears and said in a loud voice, "Please, don't hurt us!"

The children were beginning to stir and seemed agitated and restless. Pat turned and gently pushed them down on the seat. John continued to panic. He threatened to stop the car, allowing their pursuers to catch up. Pat pleaded with him not to do so.

It was almost a miracle, as far as she was concerned but for some reason he followed her advice and did not stop.

During their long trip home, the fear was with them constantly. Time dragged as the greenish light constantly kept pace behind them. Finally, they turned onto the main highway and John pushed the car to its maximum speed. Eventually, the light disappeared. Pat snuggled close to John. It was almost 7:00 a.m. Soon they were looking at the most welcome sight they had ever seen—their home. This ended the couple's strange camping adventure, but it was not the last of Pat's experiences.

****

The day following their return, Pat was due for a check-up by her obstetrician. She was examined in the usual manner for that stage of pregnancy. She was told that the course of her pregnancy was proceeding normally and that she was going to have a healthy baby. As it turned out, her daughter Sonya was born on schedule.

Pat has always been concerned about the health and welfare of her daughter because of her experience on the camping trip. Pat states that her daughter has grown into a marvelous type of human being. She is extremely intuitive and has an uncanny sort of wisdom. She has a high IQ and has become a skilled writer. Pat also states that Sonya expresses many premonitions and has a very instinctive nature. She is extremely unpretentious and has other sorts of vague uncanny abilities. Pat also states that she is much different than her other two children.

When I questioned her about how the camping trip might have influenced her unborn child, she simply said that she did not know.

Some years later, Pat and her husband did return to the campsite but saw no more lights. Some friends they took to the area were never told what had happened to them that night. The geographical area of their encounter was later flooded by the Army Corps of Engineers, and a lake now exists at that spot. Their encounter occurred at what is now the south side of the lake.

PATRICIA'S SECOND EPISODE

It was 1970, a year later. It was a cold, damp night, and both Pat and her husband decided to turn in early. There were numerous chores they had planned to do the next day and both decided to get some extra rest.

The small bedroom night stand lamps produced a dim and relaxing glow. John was comfortable with his head sunk deeply in the feather pillow. A fluffy home-made quilt covered the king-sized bed.

Pat decided to read for a little while before going to sleep. She had only read a few pages when she began to become drowsy. Pat placed the book with its bookmark flat on the night stand, reached over and turned off the light. The room was totally dark except for the alarm clock's luminescent glow, which indicated 12:05 a.m. Pat drifted off into a light sleep.

****

The clock read 3:00 a.m. when Pat became aware of a strange greenish light bathing the bed. She turned her head and looked around. The light pervaded every part of the room; its source was outside the bedroom window. Her free will seemed to disappear, and her body would not respond to commands originating in her brain. She thought to herself, What in heaven's name is happening to me? She tried to turn and wake up her sleeping husband but found that she could not move her body. "John...John...Wake up! Something weird is happening here and I'm scared," she shouted. John didn't stir.

****

After some time, Pat was relieved to regain her voluntary body movements. She was once again in control, and turned her head to the side, noticing that somehow she was in a gigantic room. The surroundings appeared to be glistening chrome. She was sitting on some sort of table and all around her were strange beings. (Pat could not remember what the beings which surrounded her looked like.) She gazed about the room. Her only restriction of movement was her hands, which were being held by the beings standing beside her. As she looked ahead, her eyes became fixed on three huge transparent cylinders, apparently composed of clear glass, which she estimated to be about 18 feet tall. She describes these tubes as "the infinity type." Contained in each of these cylinders was a basketball-sized object similar to a ball bearing, which she heard making a strange motion-like noise, and each tube had what appeared to be a huge fan belt which was twisted on itself to form a continuously moving mobius strip. The objects looked as if they were in perpetual motion. This apparatus was making a sound, like the roar of the wind, which seemed to be coming from inside the cylinders.

Looking about the room, Pat noticed that she was on what appeared to be an upper landing or balcony, about thirty feet above the origin of the cylinders below. She thought to herself, If I were to fall, I'd be killed instantly. She stared once again at the area below, taking notice of apparatus which looked like large gears, other working parts, and equipment.

****

The next thing she recalled was being back in her bedroom, lying next to her husband. Pat called out once again, "John, John, please wake up!"

John sat up straight with a horrified expression on his face. He turned to Pat and said, "What's going on here, and where is that green light coming from?" Before Pat had a chance to respond, the room was filled with a humming sound which seemed to come from outside and above their house. The greenish light began to fade, and then the room was again dark, with only the faint glow of the alarm clock remaining.

PAUL'S ABDUCTION HISTORY

In 1954, Paul lived with his family in the small Louisiana rural town of Dubberly, a few miles east of Minden and 100 miles from Shreveport. He was six years old, and lived the very simple life of a typical farm boy. Paul went to a rural school and was responsible for certain chores about the farm. He was an only child and had a very close relationship with his mother, Virginia, and father, nicknamed "Doc." Since it was customary for his family to get up early in the morning, they usually retired early, at about 9:00 p.m.

The spring season was in full bloom and the crops were growing according to schedule. Paul's father had been plowing the field adjacent to their house. A small amount of dirt had piled up around the window sills and his mother removed the excess dirt with a damp sponge.

Paul spent a typical day at school, arriving home about 3:00 in the afternoon. He rushed into the house, grabbed a couple of cookies from the jar in the kitchen, and sat down at the table.

Virginia entered and asked Paul if he wanted a glass of milk to go with the cookies.

He replied quickly, "Okay, Mom."

She filled a glass with cold milk and placed it in front of Paul.

"Thanks," he said and took a big gulp.

"Don't fill yourself up on too many goodies or you won't be able to eat dinner," his mother said in a firm voice.

Paul spent the rest of the afternoon in his room making an effort to do the primary reading that was required of him in the first grade. He was more at ease leafing through a comic book and looking at the pictures than trying to read his primer. Soon he heard his mother's voice calling, and went back downstairs. Paul helped set the table while his mother bustled about the kitchen. The entire room was filled with the heavy aroma of cooking meat and freshly baked pie.

"Hey, Mom, that sure smells good!" Paul said enthusiastically.

Without missing a beat, his mother replied, "I'm glad you have a good appetite, dear. You're growing, and you need all the nourishment you can take in."

Paul's father entered the room, went to the kitchen sink, and started to wash his hands. Virginia turned and said, "Doc, how many times have I asked you to wash your hands in the bathroom?"

"Aw, come on...this is much easier for me than dragging myself all the way to the bathroom and back," Paul's father responded. "I'm tired and hungry. Let's eat!" He dried his hands on a kitchen towel and sat down at the table.

"Paul, did you wash your hands?" his mother asked. Paul got up and went to the bathroom to wash.

Once the after-dinner chores were done, Paul prepared for bed in his room. His mother stuck her head in the doorway. "Make sure you say your prayers and I'll be back to tuck you in."

Paul did as he was told and climbed into the soft bed. It always felt good to sink down into the covers. It made him feel secure. Wearing a flannel nightgown, his mother entered the room, bent over the bed, and tightened the covers around her son. She leaned over, gave him a kiss and said, "Good night, son."

****

Paul awoke from a sound sleep immediately alert. He seemed to lose control of his body; as if it wanted to do things on its own without him telling it to. He got out of bed and walked toward the door of the bedroom, continuing down the short hall until he reached the back door of their little house. He reached for the doorknob, opened the door, and peered into the blackness of the night beyond. He stepped out onto the porch. The old wooden panels creaked beneath him.

The young boy didn't notice the cold outside temperature, nor did he feel his bare feet touching the cold ground. Guided by some inexplicable force, he proceeded around the back of the house, then crossed a small empty lot. Passing by a barbed wire fence, he walked out to a field which had been plowed earlier that morning. He recalled that his father had just planted a new crop of sweet potatoes.

Paul looked up at the night sky and was surprised to see it filled with a spectacular array of beautiful lights, moving back and forth, to and fro. His eyes fixed on one very special light, which came slowly toward him. He stood very still as the ball of light approached...slowly... slowly...closer and closer. Paul's heart began to race! Fear welled up within him. The object stopped about 18 feet from him. As he stared at the sphere, it suddenly began to spin and make a hissing sound. He stood frozen, an unseen force holding him. Fear overwhelmed every inch of his physical body. He became so scared that he was able to overcome the strange force immobilizing him. He turned and ran back to the house. He heard the sound of an explosion and instantly felt a sharp pain in the back of his left hand. Blackness surrounded him and time evaporated. His next conscious recollection was that of his mother's warm arms holding him tightly.

PAUL'S SECOND EPISODE

In 1960, Paul and his friends were involved in some childish pranks. They teased each other. No one was spared from becoming a potential victim. One subject of choice was UFOs. They would tell stories about seeing strange craft hovering in the sky and coax their unsuspecting prey outside to gaze upward for hours on end. Their pranks amused only the participants, leading to a number of return pranks and physical battles. A few years later, all that changed dramatically.

Late one summer day in 1965, Paul and a close friend embarked on a fishing trip to one of the local lakes. The trip was uneventful and they wound up with their limit of fish. It was nighttime when they made their return trip home; Paul was driving, with his friend in the front seat next to him. The mood was relaxed as the radio blasted country-western music. Only a few miles from their destination, Paul's friend peered upward through the windshield and said, "Paul, look at that airplane up there."

Paul slowed the car and looked up. "Hey, yeah, look at that!" They had arrived back in their own neighborhood and Paul guided the car into the driveway and stopped. They jumped out and immediately noticed a group of people standing in the street.

"Lets go over there and see what this is all about," Paul said hurriedly. They broke into a quick pace and approached the group. "What's happening, folks?"

A heavyset, gruff-looking man turned and pointed skyward. "Do you see that damn plane? It's been doing that kind of stuff for almost two hours now. I can't imagine what the hell is going on!"

Paul and his friend sensed the excitement. This was no prank. There was some weird kind of a flying object cavorting above them. Paul turned to his friend and said, "Come on, let's grab the car and find a better place to watch."

They both hopped into the car and headed for the open highway. Paul's friend rolled down the side window and pushed his head outside so that he would not lose sight of the aircraft. Soon they found a good vantage point and pulled off the highway onto a dirt clearing. Paul jumped out of the car, his friend close behind. They ran to the front of the car and looked skyward. Both quickly realized this was no ordinary aircraft.

Paul reached into the car and withdrew a long black flashlight. It was the type capable of focusing the beam. He adjusted the handle, pointed it toward the strange flying craft, and sent up a couple of quick light pulsations. He was amazed when he received a signal back!

He called out to his friend, "Pete, come here and take a look at this." His friend rushed over to see what was happening. "Watch this!" Pointing the flashlight up again, he began signaling. There were return signals from the craft! He flashed another round of signals and suddenly the object began to descend. It came toward them slowly and stopped almost directly over them. Paul was excited but not afraid. He signaled with the flashlight and the craft responded in a like fashion. Paul thought to himself, Whatever is controlling that ship is obviously intelligent.

Both boys stood transfixed, scrutinizing the under-surface of the object above them. The craft was circular and appeared to be made from a shiny metallic substance. In the center appeared a large circle which contained three smaller circles within it. Coming from each of these circles was a bluish-green glow. They observed a small opening in the exact center of the craft where the return flashing seemed to come from. This light was red in color. Paul began to doubt his sanity and had to fixate on something that he knew was real. Looking up at the star-riddled sky, he noticed that his field of view of the stars overhead was blocked, and knew instantly that the craft above him was indeed a solid object.

The encounter lasted for about ten minutes. Paul was aware of the silence surrounding him as the object slowly began to drift off. It was a strange, eerie silence. The air did not stir.

From that moment on, Paul knew for sure that the object was not from this world.

Both teenagers, their curiosity still aroused, rushed to climb back in the car. Paul started the engine, put the car in gear, and accelerated out onto the highway. He was bound and determined to follow the flying object for as long as he could. They noted the craft was headed toward the city of Freeport.

Without warning, it turned 180 degrees and began to head back toward them. Again, they pulled off the road and stopped the car. The object paused for a brief moment, then, with a lightning burst of speed, disappeared into the night sky. Paul turned and looked at his friend, who sat motionless in the seat next to him. They both knew that they had just witnessed something they could neither laugh off, nor forget.

****

In 1971, Paul was living in the small town of Punto Filo, Venezuela. He had just been the victim of an auto accident, injuring his left arm. The physician who examined him suggested that an x-ray be taken of both his arm and hand. He agreed to this and soon the doctor held a freshly taken x-ray film in front of him.

The doctor asked, "Paul, did you ever injure your hand or have surgery performed on it?" Paul told him that, to his knowledge, there was no history of an injury, and he certainly hadn't ever had surgery.

Pointing to a small bright spot on the x-ray, the physician said, "Do you see this, right here?" Paul nodded. The doctor told him that it looked like a surgical clip. He insisted that it was a solid metal piece of some kind, and asked if it caused him any pain. Paul denied any discomfort whatsoever. The doctor, taking one last glance at the film, stated it was probably nothing to be concerned about; probably an old cyst of some kind.

The entire episode seemed to jar an early childhood memory having to do with a strange night in a plowed sweet potato field.

PAUL'S THIRD EXPERIENCE

Three years later, in 1974, Paul had occasion to visit his parents who continued to live in rural Texas. His life had become quite settled and he had asked Laura, his girlfriend, to marry him. The announcement to his parents was made during the visit. Laura accompanied him and he was extremely happy and proud that his fiancee was so well accepted into the family. They had not set a date for the wedding yet, but planned to do so in the very near future.

Paul opened the car door, and Laura climbed into the front seat. She straightened her dress and reached over to unlock the door for Paul, who jumped in and started the engine. Laura scooted over in the seat so she could be close to him. She gave him a peck on the cheek and asked, "Well, how do you think it went?"

Paul turned to her, placed his strong arm around her and said, "Honey, they loved you." He backed the car onto the street and started their journey home.

Almost immediately, Laura looked through the upper part of the windshield, pointed at the sky and asked inquisitively, "Paul, what is that thing up there?"

Paul slowed the vehicle, leaned toward Laura, and looked up into the sky. To his amazement, he saw a craft much the same as the one he and his friend had seen in the 1960's. Immediately, he stopped the car. He was surprised to see the ship begin descending directly toward them. Laura's face turned ashen and she began to scream, gripped with terror. He reached out with both arms and held her tightly to him. "It's okay, darling, everything will be just fine," he whispered in her ear.

His mind raced with thoughts. If only I could get some more witnesses to see this. He removed his right arm from around Laura's shoulders and pressed firmly on the horn, hoping this might rouse the neighbors so that they could witness this phenomenon. He continued to pump the horn button as he rolled down the driver's window and started waving and pointing to the craft. Suddenly, it seemed the pilot of the strange craft was able to understand the stress he was causing. The object came to a dead halt. With an incredible burst of speed, it ascended and disappeared into a darkening sky.

****

Paul's experiences have been ongoing, even since the surgery. He seems happy to point out that he and his wife Laura recently celebrated their 22nd wedding anniversary.

Chapter 10

PUBLIC DEMAND

I had hoped that once the second set of surgeries was completed, there would be time to relax and ponder what we had done, so I prepared to take a few days off with my family. Sharon and I had some very close friends who lived in Visalia, California, a relatively small town in the Central Valley about 70 miles north of Bakersfield. Phil is an optometrist I have known for many years and his wife, Virginia, is a very beautiful lady from the heart of Alabama. We had traveled many times with them all over the world.

Every Friday I saw patients in my Camarillo office and was usually able to leave soon after 3:00 p.m. We planned to leave for Visalia as early as possible when I completed my day. This particular Friday was exceptionally busy and I ran late all day. Consequently we did not leave town until approximately 6:30. Each time we had made this journey it always took the same amount of time to get there: two-and-a-half hours.

Since Phil's residence was some distance from town, when we paid him a visit he would usually stay in town with us. This time he had made a reservation at the Holiday Inn in Visalia. About 20 minutes outside of Visalia, I called his room from the cell phone to alert Phil and his wife of our estimated arrival time.

Our daughter, Shaina, became excited with the news we were going to arrive shortly. She was always a good traveler and never seemed to get bored. Perhaps Sharon's constant attention provided her with enough diversions to keep her occupied.

We pulled into the parking lot of the hotel knowing that our room would be right next door to Phil's. Soon we were knocking on Phil's door and when it opened, a gust of smoke poured out. Both Phil and Virginia were chain smokers. The room looked as if we were about to enter a cloud. We took a few moments to hug and kiss before making humorous comments about the smoke. Then Phil handed us our card key and I opened the door to the adjoining room. I glanced at the telephone and noticed the message light blinking. I thought that was strange since the only person who knew where I was staying was Janet, my office manager.

"Hey, Phil," I said, "look at the message light on the phone. Is that one of your little jokes?"

He smiled. "Hell no, why would I do something like that? I'm hungry too and don't want to delay our meal."

I picked up the phone and pushed the button to claim my message. In utter amazement I listened to the voice on the line telling me that I had to call them back immediately as they wanted to do an interview with me in regard to the implant surgeries. I related this message to my wife and friends, and asked them what they thought I should do. The consensus was that I should call back and see what this was all about. I dialed the number I had written down and when a female voice answered, I identified myself.

"Hi, Doc," she said, "I'm Vicki from UFO Magazine. We heard all about the surgeries you performed and I wanted to do an interview with you for the magazine. We have a deadline and I would like to get it done right away."

Astounded, I replied, "Vicki, I'm flattered you want to write an article about this. How soon do you want to do the interview?"

"I need it ASAP. Could we do it right now? It won't take very long."

I asked her to hold on for a moment and then advised the group as to what was going on. They were not overjoyed about the idea of having to sit around and wait while someone asked me questions on the phone. I suggested they go on ahead and I would meet them in the restaurant. That seemed to satisfy everyone.

I however, was ready to eat the pillow. I explained to Vicki that I was out of town and was a bit pressed for time. I hoped she would take that into consideration and make the interview as short as possible. As it turned out we were on the phone for over an hour, which ended with more questions yet to be answered at a later date. She wanted to meet me at the office and asked for some pictures of the surgery. I told her that no pictures would be available without Derrel's consent. I hung up and looked at my watch. I knew I was in trouble with the group and hurried downstairs to meet them.

Our dinner was a late one and I was the first to point out that consumption of food not only appeased the appetite but also soothed the soul. Phil and Virginia asked if I had done many interviews about to my work with the abduction victims. I said this was the first formal interview and since it was for a publication in the field of ufology, I did not find it surprising. After the meal, we left the restaurant and headed straight to our rooms. It was almost 2:00 a.m.

In a deep sleep I dreamt that a telephone was ringing. With each ring I became more awake until I realized the sound I was hearing was, in reality, the phone. I reached over to the night stand and groped for the receiver. I couldn't imagine who would be calling. I glanced at my watch—it was almost 9:00a.m.

"Hello," I mumbled into the mouthpiece.

"Hey buddy, aren't you up yet?" I heard Phil say, as if he had been up for hours.

"Oh, sure, I've been up for at least 60 seconds now," I responded sarcastically. "What's on your mind so early in the day?"

"Hey, I just thought you'd like to know some guy is looking for you and I guess you're some famous person now."

"What in heaven's name are your talking about? Is this one of your jokes?" I asked

He started laughing hysterically and I thought for sure he found some excuse to wake me up for no good reason. Suddenly he became quite serious and told me a man had called who was with a radio broadcast service and wanted to talk with me about the abduction phenomenon. He was put through to Phil's room by the operator by mistake since the reservation for both rooms were in Phil's name. He told me he had taken the number and I was to call back around 2:00 that afternoon.

I was still not quite awake and would need some time to digest what I had just heard. Sharon looked at me with a quizzical expression on her face. Shaina heard all the commotion and was also awake. She reached for the TV remote and tuned into a children's program. I tried to explain to Sharon what had just taken place and she was of the opinion the entire episode was a dream.

The morning passed quickly and I prepared myself for the phone call. At this point I still was not convinced anyone would be calling me regarding the surgeries who was not either intimately involved with the UFO field. I asked myself why anybody outside the UFO field itself would be interested in what I had done. What I was about to find came as a shocking surprise. I called the number and asked for the person who had called me. I was put on hold for a few moments and then a man came on the line and asked if I was the person who performed surgeries on patients for the purposes of removing alien implants. I didn't know how to answer him as I was still trying to conceal my identity. I asked him how he found me. His explanation was less than satisfying.

I explained to him I was the person he was looking for but I wanted to keep my identity concealed from the public. He told me that I was "hot news" His service was a radio news hotline service and with my permission he would have me on radio stations all over the world, telling my story. If I wanted to remain anonymous, I could use any name I chose. I told him I would consider his offer but would have to consult my partner first. He seemed satisfied and told me to contact him again within 24 hours. I told my wife and friends what was going on and they encouraged me to go through with it.

Thoughts about my anonymity became paramount and I called UFO Magazine and told Vicki she must give me an alias. I did not realize at the time this was only the beginning of a long chain of events which would ultimately result in my name being heard around the world.

My next phone call was to the radio service. I advised them of my decision to go forward with their plan but I would be known as Dr. X. They agreed and explained that within a short time I would start to get calls from various radio stations around the globe. I thanked him for his efforts and concluded the call.

The remainder of our trip was quite ordinary. We enjoyed our visit with our dear friends and on Monday morning said our good-byes and headed for home.

The very first thing Sharon would always do when we returned home was to check the messages on our answering machine. This time was no different. I handed some small items to my daughter and proceeded to empty the car of its contents from the trip. Once all the baggage was inside and my wife finished with the phone, I asked her if there were any messages for me.

She looked at me with a half-smile, pencil still in hand, and said, "I think you better have a look at this. There is an entire page of phone calls for you to return including two calls from KNBC TV and FOX TV. I don't understand why they're calling you."

I was also in a state of disbelief. The truth had not penetrated. I still did not understand the importance of what I had done but evidently someone out there did.

I took the list from her outstretched hand and began to read the messages. Some were from local radio stations and a few were from out-of-state stations, along with the calls Sharon had referred to. I thought of calling my cousin Ken and seeking his guidance. I finally decided I would wait until the next day before getting in touch with anyone.

The following day I made the call to Ken. His advice was to take the ball and run with it, which I did.

In the months which followed I began to feel like I was back in school again, starting the first grade...my education was just beginning. By January, 1996, I had been interviewed on more than 50 radio programs worldwide. I was just starting to get the hang of it. Some of the shows were obvious set-ups, supposedly with me as the dupe and the show host out to get the most from the entertainment value of the segment. I was a fast learner and it didn't take long to get a feeling for what was about to happen.

Sometimes a talk show host began to make comments such as, "Well doctor, so you went poking around in a toe for these alien implants? Did you expect you were going to be taken up in a space ship?" This kind of a question would tell me he was a host who needed to be carefully controlled or I would be removing myself from the show rapidly.

In order to handle a question such as this I would usually come back with something like, "Well, John, let me ask you this. When you were on your way to work this morning to do this show with me, did you think you might be taken up in a space ship?" This type of comment would usually stun the host for a moment and place his control of the show in jeopardy. At that point, I would not let him answer, but continue on in a very scientific manner, which usually left the host in silence until I was ready to stop talking. I found a radio show host will usually let the guest continue to talk endlessly unless there is a commercial break coming up.

It was not just radio I began to become familiar with, but also print and television. I had almost stopped my writing for the Vortex altogether. There were just not enough hours in the day. I continued my practice full-time and tried to find time to fit it all in. There was a continuous stream of reporters calling me. They wanted to do a story for this paper or that magazine. Some of these were domestic and some were foreign. I never knew who was going to call next.

One night I was attending a Los Angeles Chapter MUFON meeting. During the proceedings my beeper went off. I left the room to find out who needed me. It turned out to be a radio station in South Africa. They wanted to do a show via telephone in a half hour and asked me for a number where they could call me. I told them there was only a pay phone and gave them the phone number. At exactly 9:30 p.m. I was on the air via telephone from Burbank, California, broadcasting to a South African audience.

About a month went by and I received a call from Walt Andrus, the International Director of MUFON. I had talked with Walt several times over the years and had developed a good relationship with him. To say the least, I was flabbergasted when he asked me to do a presentation at the upcoming MUFON annual Symposium. I considered it an honor to be asked and told him I would think it over and call him back. I immediately called Walt and told him I would appear. He explained the fine points of the symposium and said I would receive all the particulars in the mail.

The date for the conference in Greensboro, North Carolina, was July 5-7. I had to write out my talk so it could be published in the symposium proceedings. I knew this was going to occupy a major portion of my time.

I don't know whether the prestige of being invited to the MUFON Symposium triggered other invitations, but they started to come in like a high tide. I was invited to present at conferences in Florida, Illinois, Texas, California, Oregon, Washington and other states. The more conferences at which I presented, the more I was invited to.

Soon television programs started calling, so I sought the services of a professional agent who would handle all the details of our affairs with the entertainment industry. I appeared on numerous television programs including "Paranormal Borderline," "Strange Universe," "Fox News," "CBS News" and a six-part program on Persian Television.

I began to receive phone calls from programs such as "Hard Copy," "Sightings," "48 Hours" and dozens of other shows. We learned to be careful and never to make any kind of a deal with the show representatives. They all wanted to do the so-called "balanced piece," which meant they could bring on skeptics and debunkers. We wanted to make sure any information presented was in a clear-cut scientific manner. At this point we decided it was necessary for us to sign a contract with a CBS contract producer, Chris Wyatt. He was going to investigate the possibility of creating a one-hour television special and/or series depicting our work. His job also was to advise us on other offers from rival stations and other facets of the television media such as home video.

In July, 1996, I left for the MUFON symposium in Greensboro. I expected the weather to be hot and humid and was pleasantly surprised to find the temperature quite mild. The hotel was full and I recognized many familiar faces. A good number of the major researchers in the UFO field were there and many of them knew me personally or knew who I was. At his conference, I learned what it felt like to be in the "inner circle" of the UFO field. I also learned a few other things, such as the meaning of the words rivalry, greed and petty jealousy. I met people who were there only to represent themselves or their cause.

My education continued. The more I became a public figure, the more criticism I received. I learned there were a certain number of armchair experts in every field of science or pseudoscience relating to this field. Each one of these individuals had access to the Internet. They used this medium to gossip, dissect and comment on whatever type of research they could get their monitor to focus on. Some of these armchair experts had a little knowledge in one field and some had knowledge in another but all seemed experts in our field.

There were also moments of sheer joy, pleasure and adulation. One shining example occurred when I arrived in Tampa, Florida, for a conference. I had just disembarked my flight and entered the terminal. As I walked through the gate, I heard my name called.

"Dr. Leir?"

I looked up and a saw a small crowd of people up ahead. A short, trim, pretty lady in a green dress stood there waving frantically. I didn't know her at all. As I approached, she darted forward and said, "Hi, my name is Anne. I was on the flight with you and thought I recognized you. I am so happy to see you. Would you please give me your autograph? Also I would like to introduce you to my friends. They will be attending the conference and would be thrilled if you would give them your autograph."

It is difficult to describe my feelings at that occasion. There was a bit of non-reality involved. I couldn't believe this was happening to me. My thoughts raced. How in the world did I get to a point where anyone would want my autograph?

I did as the group requested and told them all I would look for them at the conference. When I arrived at the hotel there was more of the same. One of the moments which sticks in my mind was when I was standing at the registration desk waiting for the clerk. There were numerous people milling about, including a young man who seemed to be inquiring about something from various individuals. Soon he was headed my way. He walked directly up to me and asked, "Dr. Leir?"

"Yes, that's me."

He pulled a Federal Express envelope up from a bag he was carrying. "This just arrived for you. If you would just sign right here, please."

He leaned over, showed me where to sign and handed me the pen. I did as he asked and thanked him. Suddenly a voice behind me called my name. It was the desk clerk. I turned back around to confront the man who had just handed me the envelope. My hand held his monetary reward. To my amazement he had faded into the woodwork and was nowhere to be seen.

I could not help but muse and reminisce after this conference. I thought of the trip to Visalia my wife and I took shortly after the August 19th surgeries. I also recalled the phone conversation with Vicki from UFO Magazine and how I insisted in remaining anonymous. This certainly was a far cry from what I had just been through.

The year 1997 was spent traveling to numerous countries presenting our work with our findings to date. The results came in continuously a little at a time, slowly providing new clues to the puzzle.

I was invited to present our work at the opening of the new Cosmo Isle UFO Aero Space Museum in Hakui, Japan. It was a great honor. We were two of the seven researchers invited to represent the United States. The others included Dr. Bruce Maccabee, Dr. Jesse Marcel, Jr., Dr. Richard Haines, Dr. Leo Sprinkle and Colin Andrews. We found the Japanese people to be very ceremonial, polite and extremely respectful of the work we all were doing in the field of ufology. The museum itself is a brand new edifice devoted entirely to the subject. There's nothing like it in the entire world and I believe it will become a world center for UFO research.

One of the most phenomenal countries we visited was Brazil. The people there were plain simple folk. Anyone who is not convinced the abduction phenomena has a basis in reality should visit this country.

I stood outside of the auditorium where the conference was held from about 9:00 a.m. until 9:00 p.m. talking with alleged abductees. Although most did not speak English and had to use an interpreter, they told us their stories. I watched the expression on their faces. In their eyes I saw sheer terror. Their faces would turn upward, mouths taut with lips that trembled and eyes filled with tears. These are some of the reactions they displayed while relating their stories. Most were similar to what we heard in the United States. The beings they described were the same. There were some extreme cases we heard about, however, which were much different than we had heard in our country. Some involved human mutilations which never seemed to get reported in any news media, mainstream or otherwise.

I have come to the conclusion that the alien abduction phenomenon is happening worldwide. There seems to be no limit in the number of alleged abductions or the extent of what the abductors do to their human captives.

During these trips we have been given many different specimens from either UFO crash sites or material which has come from the bodies of abductee victims. We will continue to process these specimens and the results will belong to all mankind.

Chapter 11

F.I.R.S.T. FORMS

The sun was beginning to set. Cool, crisp air swirled around us as we walked. The smell of honeysuckle permeated it. Although the day had been long and tiring, I was left with a feeling of sheer ecstasy.

Robert Bigelow was a star in his world and that day I began to find out why. We had spent most of the afternoon in the dining room facility of his splendid office. He had welcomed us with food and offered as much as we could consume during our wait. The entire time was spent with his many interrupted visits in which he explained the progress the board was making toward acceptance of our material for analysis.

It was not until the very last meeting with him that we finalized the agreement. I decided we needed to have an agreement in writing and a release for the specimens we were about to turn over to him. During our final get-together we realized this was not going to happen. Bob was so congenial and seemed so sincere in his attitude that he convinced us a handshake agreement would suffice. A few years prior I would have continued to argue against this, but I had learned from one of my very close friends, who frequently closed deals with millionaires, a hand shake meant the man's word and the attorneys representing each side would later handle the details. In considering our deal with Robert, I came to the conclusion we should behave in the same fashion. At that point we did not know if we were turning over anything of value, monetary or otherwise. Moreover we were in no position to refuse his offer if we wanted to continue our work.

Again I found myself strolling through the magnificent gardens behind Bigelow's office complex. Both the pace of our walk and the pace of the conversation was set by Bigelow. He would ask a question or make a statement and then we would stop dead in our tracks to consider both his statement and our answer. We also took this opportunity to ask questions of him.

"Bob, after all is said and done and the board has decided which way to go with the analysis, how are we going to handle the mechanics of getting the actual funds for our continued investigations and surgeries?" I asked.

He didn't smile, but just began strolling ahead once more at a very slow pace. Suddenly he stopped, turned in my direction and said, "What will happen, is that N.I.D.S. will issue a check payable to you and then you'll deposit it into an account. By doing it that way you will be able to keep track of the money you spend. Of course, you will be responsible for any tax liability."

I listened intently to what he said and answered, "Bob, my suggestion would be to make the check payable to the non-profit corporation I have set up, called 'The Fund For Interactive Research in Space Technology' or F.I.R.S.T. In this way we can keep better track of the funds and our accountant would make sure it was all handled properly and in keeping with the tax laws governing a non-profit entity." He seemed to be satisfied with that arrangement.

We resumed our pace again and when we had almost arrived back at the main building Bigelow stopped, turned and said, "I want you to understand we have many things to do before we actually send the specimens out for the first set of tests and this will take some time. Please be patient. We will stay in touch with you."

The truth of the matter was that our organization was not yet fully formed. We had been slowed by our financial situation. Some of the documentation was in place but we still needed the funds to pay the attorneys. We agreed this was going to become a priority issue.

The thought of forming our organization occurred within a few months of the first set of surgeries and during the period of our initial "backdoor research," when we had our first experience in attempting to obtain satisfactory results from those who volunteered their research facilities. It didn't take us long to learn this was not the way to make progress. We came to the conclusion that appropriate tests had to be performed by qualified persons who would be able to generate a report on the letterhead of the institution where the tests were being performed. The only way to accomplish this task was to pay for them. It was just that simple. To do so we needed a mechanism to raise the funds for our research. We could not continue to pay for the surgeries and all the incidentals which went along with them. We decided that the solution was to form a non-profit organization which could raise funds and distribute them in a manner which was legal and would satisfy any accrued tax liability.

We mapped out our plan and established a set of specific goals for the organization which were:

1. To collect funds from outside sources.

2. To act as an intermediary between other research organizations and ourselves as individual researchers.

3. To legitimately advertise for the needed funds.

4. To provide information to the public about the work we were doing.

5. To release the results of our research in an orderly and scientific fashion.

6. To publish the results of our work in scientific publications.

7. To provide legitimate scientific information to the UFO community.

8. To guarantee privacy and security to people who provided our organization with physical evidence for analysis or safekeeping.

9. To coordinate public and entertainment events for the purposes of raising funds.

10. To establish a new standard where hard science would become involved with the UFO subject.

Once we had set the criteria, we realized it was going to take some actual funds to get the necessary documentation and tax status filed. Among my contacts were two barter exchange companies in which I participated through my podiatry practice. I suggested I give them a call and see if they had someone who did this type of organizing. The following morning I made a series of telephone calls to both the barter companies and the attorneys they recommended. One individual sounded just right for the job. He was located in the city of Ventura, which was only about 30 minutes from the Thousand Oaks area. I called and made an appointment for the following day.

Ventura was very close to the ocean and that morning the sky was, as usual, obscured by a thick marine cloud layer. When I parked and stepped outside, there was a cold breeze which would have been chilling had I not worn my suit coat. The smell of the damp, salty ocean air permeated my nostrils.

I entered the restored 1920s-style building and took the old wooden elevator to the third floor. There were a number of plaques and pictures depicting some of the original old city, hanging both on the elevator walls and in the hallways. The hallway was dimly lit and there was a smell of age that added to the nostalgic ambiance of the building. I found an office door with Howard Sale-Attorney at Law lettered on the stippled glass. As I pushed the door open I heard the sound of a bell. The room was decorated in a type of period furniture in keeping with the age of the building. I thought for a moment I had stepped through a time portal and fully expected to find a quaint female receptionist sitting behind a desk to greet me. Instead there was absolutely no one. I wandered about the room peering at the antiquated books in the wooden bookcases. I wondered if Mr. Sale had a more recent library he used for his practice. I sat down in one of the armchairs, crossed my legs and picked up a magazine to read. I did have an appointment and was on time. I was sure the attorney would pop his head out at any time and greet me.

After waiting for about 15 minutes I decided I would venture out in the hall and look for a restroom. Just as I reached for the door handle, I heard footsteps approaching. I stood back and watched the door swing open. Standing there was an older gray-haired gentleman clutching an unlit pipe. The smell of burnt tobacco followed him as he entered the room. There wasn't time for me to say anything. He stuck out his hand.

"Hello there, I'm Mr. Sale. You must be Dr. Leir. I am sorry if you had to wait but I was just down the hall gabbing with the fella in the adjoining office. You see, he's going to move and I was thinking, well maybe, I'll make my office bigger."

I listened to him rattle on. He gestured for me to follow him into the inner sanctum. The decor of his private office was similar to the trappings of the outside office. It was filled with antiques. I didn't know whether I should mention them. Perhaps he didn't consider them antiques since they were from his era. He offered me a seat in front of his desk in a wooden chair that was less than comfortable, settled back in his oversized desk chair and lit his pipe. A puff of smoke billowed.

"Okay, young feller, let's take a look at the papers you've got there."

I reached into my briefcase for the documents Derrel and I had filled out. I put them in his outstretched hand. He leaned back in the chair and started thumbing through the papers. It only took him a few moments until he looked up at me again.

"Well, okay. So you want to form this non-profit corporation, eh? Well, it all looks pretty above-board to me. I don't see any problem."

I took that as good news but thought I had better clarify some of the most important details, namely, money. I asked him to give me some idea of the costs involved.

He grinned widely and said in a low voice, "You know, you're through the barter aren't you?" I nodded and before I had a chance to comment he peered directly into my eyes and stated, "My fee will be on the barter but you guys have to come up with the filing costs and the initial tax amount. The filing fees are nominal but the initial tax deposit in this state may run you as high as a thousand dollars."

It was a shock. We didn't have that amount of money and I thought to myself that the barter was of no use whatsoever, in this instance. I told him we did not have that much. He took a long drag on his pipe, reached over and opened a very thick book.

"There is another way we can do this and that's by registering your corporation in a state that requires less money. After it is registered there we can come back to California and register it as a foreign corporation."

I asked him to explain the particulars. He did just that and I made up my mind to have him go ahead with the process. Then I asked him how much time it would take to perform his magic. He surprised me by telling me if he used the state of Delaware, the turnaround time would be about 30 days. That sounded fine to me. I shook hands with our new corporate attorney and departed the premises with a smile.

Within the next two months, all the necessary items fell into place. We had our Corporate Seal, articles of incorporation, bylaws and all the other numerous pieces of legal and tax paperwork. Our non-profit status was approved and we opened an account at a local bank. I felt it was akin to a mother giving birth. F.I.R.S.T. was born.

Chapter 12

SECRET ANALYSIS

Webster's Dictionary defines the word secret as "something kept in concealment; anything unrevealed or kept from the knowledge of others; a hidden cause; a mystery."

At this time I can reveal that such were the practices in which I was forced to participate. Some of our efforts were hamstrung by the necessity to procure results without having the necessary funds to do entirely as we wished. This put us into a position where we had to comply with the will of others. We had originally decided that all information collected by us would ultimately be communicated directly to the world. So far we have been able to keep that commitment. However, it has taken much longer to acquire this information than we thought it would, primarily due to the agreements we were compelled to make along the way.

During our initial experiences with so-called "backdoor research," we realized the monetary factor would become most important in our future quest for analysis. It was several months before we realized there were sacrifices we would be required to make in order to achieve our goals.

Our first exposure to secret agreements came about at our meeting with Robert Bigelow. It didn't take him long to make it clear that we would have to fulfill certain requirements before N.I.D.S. would agree to any type of funding. One of the most important of these was a request from him not to divulge who was working on these implant specimens. In the beginning, he emphasized that not even N.I.D.S. was to be mentioned. In addition, he requested that the names of the laboratories they were using for the tests also be kept confidential. This turned out to be one of the easier parts of the bargain to keep since they did not inform us who they sent the samples to. The third part of our arrangement was a request for us not to release or publish any analysis results until we received clearance from N.I.D.S. At that point they would also advise us as to where they thought it should be published.

These points were difficult to agree to but I carefully weighed them against the benefits Bigelow offered:

An unlimited supply of funds for the project at hand.

The use of the worlds finest laboratory facilities

A quality of testing which could not be surpassed

Peer review by the N.I.D.S. board, which included some of the finest scientific minds in the United States.

The possibility of having an article published in a scientific journal.

When I considered the benefits and the sacrifices, we came to the conclusion that we had no choice but to carry on with the proposed plan. It wasn't until we were well into the investigative process that we really began to feel the effect of our agreement. Perhaps I was the first victim.

I was overjoyed and honored to be asked by the National Director of MUFON, Walter Andrus, to do a presentation at the National MUFON Symposium in July, 1996. I felt as if I were the "new kid on the block" and was being treated in the same manner as major researchers in the field of ufology who had been doing investigative work for many years. I couldn't conceive how he placed me in the same category. I thought to myself, What have I really done that warrants me standing on a stage presenting material to hundreds of people from all over the world?

In numerous conversations with my close friends and colleagues, they seemed to grasp an aspect of the situation which I could not clearly see. They told me there was no need to wonder what I had done, because it was obvious. They said I had put my career on the line for a surgical endeavor which could lead to the discovery of information which would effect the entire world. Slowly I realized that what they were telling me was true.

I went to bed that night with the day's events weighing heavily on my mind. Sharon had retired early and I tried not to disturb her as I fluffed my pillow. The warmth and security of the surrounding blanket made me feel peaceful and calm. I reached over and shut off the light, plunging the room into darkness. All that I could see was the pulsing of the digital clock on the video recorder. I took a couple of deep breaths and tried to clear my mind. As much as I tried, all I could think about was the word secrets. It pulsed in my mind over and over...secrets...secrets...secrets. I had the sense that this was going to be a strange night.

Suddenly I found myself in a deep trance-like sleep. Perhaps I was drawn into some weird altered state. For the first time in my entire life, I could not discern physical reality. Without warning I found myself standing in what appeared to be a court-like setting. Before me was an elevated platform upon which was standing a wooden lectern. The room was filled with the aroma of freshly finished wood, much like one would experience in a furniture store. I looked about the room and noticed I was standing directly behind a large wooden table which appeared to be the only one in the room. There were wooden chairs both to my right and left. Lying on the table was a withered brown book covered with a thick layer of silvery dust. I reached down and touched the decomposing cover. It felt as old as it looked. As I withdrew my hand I noticed some light silvery powder clinging to my fingers from where I touched the ancient text. The dim light in the room seemed to be coming from everywhere rather than a single source.

Suddenly I heard a noise behind me. I was terrified and confused. My mind raced. What kind of a crazy dream am I having? Come on Rog, wake up, wake up, I thought over and over again.

Finally I summoned the courage to raise my eyes, turn my head and look behind me. The reality I was trying to comprehend became almost too much for me to handle emotionally. I yelled, "Hey, somebody wake me and take me the hell out of here!"

Behind me were about a dozen shadowy figures slowly entering the room. One by one they began to take seats in what appeared to be a gallery. I couldn't make out much detail other than they were all about the same size, under four feet tall, and were wearing shiny, silk-like garments which seemed to wrap around their bodies. There was a sash belted about the waist and a hood thrown over the head and draped over the shoulders. As they slowly shuffled to their seats, the room fell into a complete and deafening silence.

I turned back to face the lectern and was startled to see a figure standing behind it. One of the most interesting and illogical aspects of my vision was that there was absolutely nothing supporting the platform. It appeared to be suspended in mid-air. I looked up and tried to see if I could find wires that were supporting it. There were none to be found. How could this possibly be? I thought. The entire structural configuration defied not only reason but sanity.

I was sure that at any moment I would awake with Sharon telling me I was talking in my sleep and complaining about how I was keeping her awake. I had talked in my sleep many times before which was usually due to something I had eaten to close to bedtime.

All at once the sound of a deep, booming voice resonated through my entire being. I listened intently. The words repeated and over again.

"Secrets...secrets...secrets...look, listen and learn."

The voice was commanding, and its repetition was like the beating of a bass drum. A strange and weird rhythm pulsed through the very depths of my consciousness. I asked myself, Is this an outgrowth of today's events? Is there a lesson for me to learn?

Whatever this experience was, I could not seem to escape. I was stuck and would have to see it through to the end. As that thought coursed through my mind, the voice suddenly stopped.

The figure behind the lectern became easier to discern. It was taller than the beings who had seated themselves in the gallery and wore a similar garment, although the material did not appear shiny as did the others. I strained to make out a face. The hood which covered its head was a lighter color than those worn by the mysterious audience. There seemed to be a silvery light emanating from within the confines of the hood where a face should have been. A cold chill ran through my body.

I tried to compose myself and bring my scientific training into play. I attempted to use all of my senses to observe. At that point that I noticed two pairs of ancient, withered white fingers clutching the front of the podium along the top. Their clutching grasp seemed desperate, almost as if they sought to crush the wood into splinters. My mental investigation was interrupted by the mysterious booming voice.

"So, you want to know the secrets. Who do you think you are to ask this of us? Why do you persist in your quest?"

I couldn't believe my ears. Was he addressing me or was there somebody else in the room? I turned my head quickly to find an answer to my own question. No, there was no one else present except the silent gallery. Suddenly, I felt a cold wind cut through me like a spear made of ice. My head snapped forward again.

"I AM WAITING FOR YOU TO ANSWER MY QUESTIONS," The voice boomed again louder than before.

"Hey, wait just a damn minute, I didn't ask to be here and who in the hell are you, anyway?" I bellowed.

The icy wind coursed through my body again. I saw the hooded figure lean forward and speak. This time its tone was softer, almost a harsh whisper. "Answer my-y-y-y questions."

"What is it you want me to answer?" I queried, chuckling to myself with the thought that this mysterious fellow was really going to answer my question. To my surprise, my ears were instantly filled with a chorus of voices. I strained to listen to what they were saying. Even with concerted effort it was difficult to comprehend their words. I was able to make out a few distinct words such as science, learn, seek, care, love, watch, listen.

Within moments everything began to sound like a whirring, blurring hum. The pitch was rising higher and higher. The voices were louder and louder and my head began to swim. I felt dizzy and slightly nauseated. Suddenly the scene began to blend into a whirlpool of visual and auditory smears. Round and round, over and over, in and out.

My next conscious thought was that of being back in my room, in bed and lying next to my wife. My daughter had climbed into bed with us and was sitting straight up staring at me. I must have had a surprised expression on my face. She leaned over and whispered in my ear, "Daddy, where were you?"

I thought I was going to have an instant heart attack. What in the world did she mean? I looked at the clock. It indicated almost 4:00

a.m. I had no intention of quizzing her at that hour of the morning so I let her remark pass and said, "Lie back down and go to sleep, sweetheart. It's late and we'll talk in the morning."

No conversation occurred with Shaina that morning or any other morning. In fact, I have never discussed her remark with a single solitary soul.

I thought deeply about my night-time adventure and wondered if it was to serve as a profound learning experience. It would take some very deep and prolonged thought to come up with the answers. At least it changed the way I felt about keeping secrets. Perhaps the lesson I was to learn was that secrets are just part of our very existence and was given the knowledge that our spirituality was also cloaked in secrets.

My next exposure to the realm of secrets came some months later. I was entrusted with a piece of material which was touted as originating from the Roswell crash site. It seemed as though our reputation for using the scientific method had gained some prominence. Many people began to contact us who had materials which they had acquired from a variety of sources having to do with the UFO phenomenon. Some of these individuals feared for their lives. This was the case of the Roswell specimen. We agreed to make no disclosure or reference of who supplied the material to us and were to report the results only to the owner.

We realized that this was a digression from our implant research but decided it could serve as a valid tool to open doors that perhaps were not previously available to us.

We proceeded with the analysis and at a certain point decided the results should be made public. We contacted the owner of the object and asked his permission to divulge the metallurgical composition of the sample. He seemed duly impressed with our performance thus far and surprised us by giving his approval.

July 4, 1997, was the date chosen for the release of this information. We involved an independent producer, Chris Wyatt, formally with the CBS television network, who decided to hold a press conference in Roswell, New Mexico. His decision was based on the fact that there would be a huge celebration of the fiftieth anniversary of the Roswell UFO crash and this would attract news media from all over the world. Until this time, we had kept all the analytical information secret. We were convinced that we would be making a statement that would shock the world.

One of the scientists involved with the analysis was Dr. Russell Vernon Clark of the University of California, San Diego. It took a great deal of courage for Dr. Vernon-Clark to come forward and put his reputation on the line. The purpose for the event was to announce to the world that we had a piece of material believed to be from the

Roswell crash site and that it had undergone scientific analysis and was found to contain extraterrestrial isotopes. In other words, material that was not made on this earth.

Our press conference took place on schedule but the results were less than satisfying. This was the same day that the Mars Pathfinder was scheduled to land on the red planet. Every TV and radio station was covering that extraordinary event, allowing little time for our very significant finding, which was considered by us to be just as earth- shaking. We also learned that the AP news service had been less than kind to us. They took the effort to verify employment of our spokesperson scientist, Dr. Vernon-Clark, at the University of California, San Diego. In doing so they supplied the university with the wrong name and consequently were told that no such individual worked there. As soon as we became aware of the situation, we contacted the wire service and advised them of their mistake. They apologized and said they would print a retraction. Technically, they did as they promised. Their original statement appeared in over 60 newspapers; however, their retraction appeared in only two. This was another eye-opening experience and gave me instant insight into the workings of the print media. I had grave doubts about the whole affair being just a simple mistake.

This would become for me, a classic example of the lessons I had to learn. The reality of the situation was that not only were we working in a field which never had been seriously scrutinized by the scientific establishment, but also was apparently at the mercy of the media's unwritten instruction to debunk UFOs.

There were numerous times when I recalled my strange dream. The experiences we were going through all pertained in some way to secretive material. Was this past experience just another example?

In early 1997, I was in the United Kingdom to present our material in two cities Andover and Bornemouth. We were guests of a noted rock-and-roll star, Reg Presley. His world famous group, the Troggs, was extremely popular in Europe. They rose to fame during the 1960s and in the past few years found themselves again in the limelight. Presley was extremely interested in the field of ufology and was quite generous in his financial support of UFO events. He was responsible for masterminding and subsidizing the two conferences in which I had participated.

During our stay in England, we were treated to numerous and interesting tours of the English countryside, as well as a memorable trip to London. During this excursion we were introduced to Ray Santilli, the owner of the famous "Alien Autopsy" film.

Presley had arranged a meeting with Santilli which culminated with a luncheon at a wonderful Chinese restaurant. During the meal, I offered Santilli some assistance with regard to authenticating the mysterious autopsy film. My proposition was simple. If he would give us a few frames of the original film, we would have the chemistry analyzed at a credible laboratory. By using this method we would establish, once and for all, the accurate date of the film's manufacture. We knew that Santilli had been previously criticized for the way in which he had gone about authenticating the film. We proposed to him that the results of the analysis would initially be sent to us at F.I.R.S.T. and we in turn would send them directly to him. It would then be up to him to treat them in any way he saw fit. It would become Santilli's decision to either keep the results of the analysis private or release them to whomever he pleased.

We did not get a definitive answer to our proposal at that meeting and left London empty-handed.

Some months later, a colleague was back in the U.K. for another conference. During this visit he was given a package by Presley which contained pieces of film from Santilli. In addition, the package contained a letter from Santilli explaining the nature of the film scraps.

After he arrived home he told me about the package of film. I hadn't expected Santilli to accept our offer of help. We proceeded to find the proper facilities to have the tests performed and have turned over the samples. No results have been obtained yet.

It came as a big surprise when I was asked during a radio interview about the autopsy film sample. This was supposed to be confidential information. How could anyone have known? Suddenly this closely guarded secret was being broadcast to the entire radio audience. Dumbfounded, I called my colleague immediately after the program was over. He denied any knowledge of how the information was leaked to the radio host. We concluded that the information must have come from England. We certain that someone there had leaked it and now our endeavors were no longer a secret.

Soon after the program aired, the Internet was filled with comments and criticisms of the entire event. During the broadcast I mentioned our luncheon with Santilli, and explained that we had celebrated his birthday. I was shocked when I received an e-mail message containing a forwarded letter from one of Santilli's close friends in England. The letter contained a severe rebuke of me and stated that my entire story was not true based on the fact that Santilli's birthday did not occur during that time.

I asked the English ufologist, Philip Mantle for his help in the matter, as he was a party to most of the happenings and knew all the principals involved. Since Reg Presley was present at the luncheon, Philip was going to call him and see what his recollection was. He did and was told by Reg that he had no memory of celebrating Santilli's birthday. When Mantle e-mailed me with this information, I began to doubt my sanity.

I told Phillip again about my recollection of the event such as details of a champagne toast and singing happy birthday. Perhaps it was my insistence that made him call Presley again. During this call, Presley was on the speaker phone. Phillip asked him the question again.

"Reg, are you absolutely certain that during your luncheon with Santilli you never celebrated his birthday? Roger insists this happened and describe you all singing 'Happy Birthday' and toasting with champagne."

Presley answered by saying, "Phillip, I am sorry, but I don't recall any birthday celebration for Ray."

Phillip went on to tell me that suddenly there was a burst of laughter and Reg excused himself for a moment. Phillip said he could hear a female voice shouting in background, "Reg, what's the matter with you? That was your birthday!"

The voice was Presley's wife. She reminded him about how he celebrated his birthday on Sunday and how he must have had an earlier celebration at the Santilli luncheon on the Saturday before.

The matter was instantly cleared up and our sanity restored. I wasted no time in sending an e-mail to the originator of the critical letter and in a very short time, received an apology.

I considered this another lesson in the subject of secrets. As trivial as it was, this was a powerful example of what could happen when secret information is leaked to the general public.

Chapter 13

THE FINAL WORD

One of the most exciting aspects of research is the initial quest for new knowledge. However, reward begins with the actual collection of raw data. Once the data has been received and categorized, it is time to begin the process of formulating theories. The scientific method then calls for these theories to be taken back into the laboratory setting and either proved or disproved.

In this chapter I will present the raw data and start to lay the foundation for our theories. It will be some time in the future before we will be able to say with any certainty that these theories are scientific fact or not.

I'll present this material in a reader-friendly manner not found in scientific papers or technical texts. I'll describe the findings and in a following parentheses show where they can be found, e.g.(Appendix) This will enable all who wish to obtain further details to readily find it.

****

THE BIOLOGICAL FINDINGS

The first specimens sent for analysis were the soft tissues which surrounded the objects. When the surgeries were performed, we took care to remove all the tissue that visibly surrounded the foreign objects. Some of these appeared abnormal in color or presented other specific reasons for dissecting them free from the adjacent areas.

All soft tissue specimens were prepared for laboratory analysis as we would with any of our other surgical specimens. They were placed into a formalin solution for preservation and transportation to the laboratory. Each specimen was identified by the patient's name, date of the surgery, procedure performed, attending surgeon and pre-operative diagnosis. The laboratory forms were completed by my office staff and the only diagnosis presented to the laboratory was: Soft tissue, adjacent to foreign body. Since we wanted all laboratories to perform blind or double blind studies, we did not want to supply them with anything but the most basic of information.

The initial samples sent were obtained from the surgeries performed on May 18, 1995. The first sample came from the great toe of our female patient, Patricia and the second specimen from the hand of the male patient, Pat.

When I received the first reports of these two cases, I was absolutely stunned. One of the most shocking findings was the large amount of nerve proprioceptors found within the tissue sample (See appendix). There was no anatomical need for these specialized nerve cells to be clustered about a foreign body which is housed deep within the confines of a toe and adjacent to a bone. Usually these little tiny specialized nerve cells are found in areas such as the fingertips. They serve to conduct sensations such as pressure, temperature, or fine touch. Another area where proprioceptors are found is the bottom of the foot. These serve to send messages through the spinal cord to the muscles in the lower extremities which results in our ability to walk in a smooth and flowing manner. What purpose would they serve, deep within the soft tissues of toe and adjacent to the bone?

Recently scientists at UCLA have been working with neurological tissue and have produced a hormonal substance which can increase such tissues growth rate. In addition their Biomechanics Department has been working with a device which converts bioenergy to a useful electrical output. This converted electrical energy can then be used to drive servo-motors in artificial limbs. With this in mind it would be safe to say that all nerve tissue serves as a conductor of bioenergy and perhaps this energy can be tapped and used for purposes not yet discovered.

Another astonishing finding was the complete lack of visible microscopic inflammation in the tissue samples. Seeing this in the pathology reports forced me to look into the possibility that the human body had changed since I graduated from medical school. I spent hours sitting at my computer, searching the medical literature on-line. I used the internet to sift through the latest medical journals housed in medical school libraries such as Harvard Medical School, George Washington University and Stanford Medical School. At the end of my search I felt gratified as I found no change had occurred in the human body since I went through my medical school training in the 1960's. There were additions and refinements pertaining to the inflammatory process which included more minute details of the microscopic reaction. These included hormonal influences and bio-molecular changes. Basically, it was more of the same. All in all I found that it is impossible to have a foreign substance enter the human body without having the body react to that substance. Our system of defense, called the reticuloendothelial system, comes into play the very moment a foreign object enters our body. This system of defense is designed to ward off any invading substance, providing the body with the protection it needs.

The transplantation of donor organs is a prime example of how our body rejects even the smallest differences in human tissue. If it were not for drugs which suppress the effects of our immune system, no transplant would be possible. The question for me was: Why did the body not produce an inflammatory reaction against the foreign bodies which we removed? A possible answer to this question made itself apparent after I had acquired the results of the next set of specimens analyzed.

My colleague taken the foreign objects which we had removed surgically back to Houston with him. Once they arrived there he began the process to determine what they were. Working with a chemist, they subjected all three specimens to ultraviolet black light and found they fluoresced a brilliant green color. He was amazed because we had discovered that in a small percentage of abductees there was also a similar colored fluorescence present on their skin.

One such case was a lady we were investigating who came to my office. We examined the patient. I was interested in the medical aspects of the case. During her visit she was taken into an examination room and we dimmed the lights. I used the ultraviolet black light to examine portions of her skin. Suddenly I observed a pink fluorescence in the palms of her hands. I asked the patient if she had touched anything with her hands which could account for the pink stain. She told us perhaps she had gotten it from the steering wheel in her car. I would remove it from her skin with alcohol. With that, I picked up a gauze sponge, wet it with alcohol and proceeded to scrub her palms. Again I dimmed the room light and turned on the ultraviolet. The pink stain was gone.

The patient was then taken back into the consultation room where we proceeded to ask her a myriad of questions pertinent to her experiences. We watched her carefully while she answered his questions and made notes of her very minute gestures, movements, and reactions. This contributed greatly to my ability to understand both the medical and psychological aspects of the phenomenon.

I left the patient in the exam room while I attended to some office chores. By the time I got back almost two hours had passed. The patient was preparing to leave. On the spur of the moment I turned to the patient and said,

"Oh, just a moment before you leave, could you just give me one more moment of your time? I would like to check your hands one more time."

My colleague looked at me rather strangely and followed as I took the patient once again into the examining room, dimmed the room light and turned on the ultraviolet. I asked the patient to hold up her palms and keep her fingers outstretched. I moved the black light over the area and much to our surprise, her palms were once again glowing a brilliant pink.

In Texas, the chemist dried the specimens and found the membrane surrounding the objects had become brittle and could be scraped away from the metal object it surrounded. He sent the pieces of the membrane back to me and I sent them for analysis. I separated the specimens so that each portion could be easily related to the metallic object it encased. The only diagnosis submitted on the laboratory form was again: Soft tissue surrounding foreign body.

About a week went by before the lab reports began to come in. I was again astounded to see the results of the analysis. (see appendix 1) It seems as though the membrane was only composed of just three biological elements:

1. A Protein Coagulum
2. Hemosiderin
3. Keratin

PROTEIN COAGULUM

This substance is derived from clotted blood and consists of pure protein.

HEMOSIDERIN

This substance is an oxygen-carrying iron pigment and is related to its close cousin, hemoglobin. Hemoglobin is found in our red cells and serves to bind with oxygen in the lungs. It is then circulated to all portions of the bodies tissues where it gives up its oxygen and takes on carbon dioxide. It is then transported back to the lungs for expiration and the process begins over again. This is the mechanism for total tissue respiration. Hemosiderin also has the same oxygen-binding potential.

KERATIN

Keratin comprises the outermost covering of our bodies. It is the most superficial layer of the skin. It also is contained in our finger and toe nails as well as our hair. This substance is probably the most cared for substance in our bodies. About ninety percent of the cosmetic industry depends on our treatment of this outer keratin layer.   I asked myself how this strange concoction of natural biological material could have come about. In order to answer this question I once again used the internet to search for the answers. I researched as many texts as I could find that pertained to this subject. I also purchased a new addition of Robbins' Textbook of Pathology. This book is considered by many to be the bible of pathological studies. It did not show any similar pathology occurring anywhere in the body.

****

My next step was to consult the pathologists who had performed the analysis. My phone conversations were interesting but did not bear fruit. One such example of a conversation went as follows:

"Hello, this is Dr. Wong. Did you have some question on the sample I reported on?"

"Yes, I'm the surgeon who removed this sample and I had a few question about your report." I told the pathologist.

"Sure, go ahead and ask."

"To start with, how do you think the protein coagulum was formed?" I asked

There was a moment of silence.

"Most probably there was some internal bleeding which became organized over the past weeks. What we are seeing is the remaining portion of the organized clot that has not been carried away by the body." He rattled off in one breath.

"The only problem I have with that, is this object has been in the patient's body for 41 years. Don't you think that after this period of time the body would have had enough time to remove this debris or wall it off with fibrous tissue?" I fired back.

Again there was dead silence and finally he began to speak.

"Well, Dr. Leir I didn't know those facts but you know the human body is not always predictable."

I thought to myself, What kind of a line is he handing me? Certainly nothing that is helpful.

"Dr. Wong, could you possibly help me understand how the keratin could be part of this, since the specimen was removed from the deep tissues adjacent to the bone?"

His answer was quick. "Most probably, you dragged in some skin when your made your initial incision and this became involved with the deeper mass."

"Dr. Wong, let me make this very apparent. I am a very careful surgeon and I can assure you I did not drag superficial tissue into the depths of the wound. In addition, even if that was done, how would it be possible for the keratin strands to become actually part of the tissue we are analyzing? Since the object had been in the body for many years, I would think that the structure of this organic tissue would be stable and not allow for penetration of substances like keratin."

He answered quickly.

"Perhaps the original penetration brought keratin into the wound."

"Dr. Wong, that is the most plausible answer. However, there is one small problem. There is absolutely no evidence of an obvious penetration wound. We searched the extremity with a loupe and could not find even a hair or pore that appeared out of place," I quickly added.

"Well, my friend, as I told you a moment ago, the body works in very mysterious ways and sometimes we just don't understand enough to come up with all the answers."

With that our conversation came to an abrupt end and I sat staring at the wall in front of me with what probably was a blank expression on my face.

This was typical of the way my conversations went with other pathologists in reference to this same subject.

In considering all the factors pertaining to this membrane, I reluctantly came to some far-out conclusions. We knew these objects did not cause the body to react to them with an inflammatory or rejection response. The reason for this might have to do with the membrane. I discussed this possibility with a couple of bioscientists and they concluded that, if this were true we would have just discovered something that could revolutionize medical science. We also realized, if this membrane could be duplicated, we could wrap anything we wanted to instill into the body and the body would not reject or react to it. Even transplant organs could be wrapped in this substance and as a result the patient would not have to take anti-rejection medication for the remainder if his life. This is an avenue we are pursuing at this time.

Although the biological findings presented numerous mysteries in general, I felt there was something specific about the keratin which I couldn't get out of my mind. I began to wonder if the keratin was responsible for the tensile strength of the membrane. I remembered that I could not cut through it with the surgical scalpel. I began to think about the possibilities of how such a strange brew of ingredients could be made and suddenly the proverbial light bulb turned on.

I thought about one of the most common marks found on the bodies of alleged abductees and that was the scoop mark. When the scoop mark is visualized, it appears as if someone had taken a tiny little teaspoon and scooped some of the most superficial skin away. I had seen many of these during the previous few years. They also healed in a peculiar fashion. Most superficial abrasions usually healed in a week and demonstrated typical healing with the formation of a scab that later peeled off, leaving only a red mark on the underlying skin. These scoop marks did not heal in that fashion. They had a very shiny base which appeared moist but if the lesion was touched there was no moisture. This condition lasted for only a few days and after that time only a perfectly formed depression was left in the skin. I began to wonder if there was a device that could scoop keratin from the surface skin. Perhaps keratin obtained in this manner could be incorporated into a gel like mixture which would then become a membrane.

I had to stop and collect my thoughts. I had no proof of this and was straying from pure scientific thought. This was not what I was trying to accomplish with our research. I felt it was probably okay to have such thoughts pop into my head but I could not permit myself to dwell on them.

The next set of biological findings I acquired were from the soft tissue specimens sent to the laboratory following the May 18, 1996 surgeries. Those specimens would be more complicated because of the additional analysis that had been done. Since we had more funds I felt we could get a better and more accurate result if I divided the specimens into three portions and sent them to three separate laboratories. This was done. As with the previous specimens, each laboratory was only given the bare minimum of data so that the studies performed continued to be blind.

Of the three surgeries performed that day, one had a metallic foreign body. This was a triangular object also covered with the dark gray, dense membrane. The result of the surrounding tissue analysis was about the same as with the first two surgeries showing a lack of an inflammatory response and accumulations of nerve cells (see appendix).

The results of the other two were somewhat different. There was a little round ball of greyish-white material found deep within the tissues but attached to the underside of the skin. The superficial portion contained a skin lesion that appeared suddenly on the left legs of the two female abductees. When we performed the surgery we basically ellipsed the superficial skin lesion and extended the wound deeply to encompass all the tissue below. This provided us with a good cross section of the entire segment. The results of the microscopic examination on these two subjects demonstrated the following:

1. Focal blood vessel lumen obliteration and chronic perivascular inflammation.
2. Collections of nerve tissue
3. No foreign body reaction
4. Solar elastosis

These findings presented a familiar pattern, when compared to the pathology results from the first set of surgeries. However, there was some new surprising information. One of the new findings referenced the blood vessels in the area. The obliteration of the lumen of these vessels meant that essentially the interior cavity of the blood vessels had been destroyed. This was coupled with another effect on the vessel called perivascular inflammation. Although there was little or no evidence of inflammatory changes in the surrounding tissue, something had caused a great deal of inflammation surrounding the vessels themselves.

The next and probably most surprising finding was that of solar elastosis. This meant that the deeper layer of the skin (the dermis) had been subjected to a large and intense amount of ultraviolet light. This seemed like an impossibility when we consider that the two female individuals were housewives with no histories of extended exposure to sunlight or sunburns of the lower extremities. Even if their memories were incorrect, it would not explain why only one tiny section of their skin would show overexposure to ultraviolet radiation. There were no other marks on either leg.

Once again I took an intuitive leap toward a solution. I flashed back to my previous thoughts having to do with the keratin portion of the membrane. I began to wonder if an instrument existed that was spoon shaped, sharp and contained an ultraviolet light source. If there were such a device it would explain both the presence of keratin and scoop marks. It would also explain the pathological findings. I asked myself. Was there somewhere a being who possessed an instrument which could scoop keratin out of the superficial skin and then seal the wound with ultraviolet light? After all, I thought, perhaps there was secret research of an earthly origin which possessed an instrument capable of doing this type of procedure.

I knew that Whitley Strieber would be extremely interested in my findings, so I gave him a call and explained my idea to him. He complimented me on my original thought and told me he considered it to be in the realm of possibility. He encouraged me to proceed with all aspects of this investigation. One of the avenues he thought to look into was that of veterinary medicine. At this time our investigation is ongoing.

Another one of the cases involved soft tissue findings more difficult to assess. This case was an alleged abductee with a painful, pinpoint-small, raised area on the back of the left neck-shoulder region. She had noticed a dime-sized, raised, red lesion on the skin the morning after a possible abduction experience. She stated it was extremely painful to the touch and thought she might have been bitten by a bug or stung by a bee. After about two weeks the lesion shrunk to a small pin point area but was still painful to the touch. I considered her symptoms and in light of our previous soft tissue analysis thought they might contradict our findings of absent inflammatory responses. However when I considered all the microscopic analysis, I recalled they contained large amounts of aberrant nerve cells. This would justify the pain response without having inflammation. The initial redness could have been merely do to a histamine response in the local tissues. This would be temporary and normally disappear within a few days. At that point she contacted me and asked if I would evaluate her case. I agreed and interviewed her in my office where she was subjected to the tests which Derrel and I had devised. These tests were later evaluated and scored. She scored high on the probability scale. Because of these factors I decided to take an x-ray. It showed a small shadow below the area of the skin lesion.

I called a colleague of mine who was a dermatologist and pathologist. He agreed to see the patient without charge and I arranged a mutual time for us to meet at his office. He examined the patient and came up with the diagnosis of a calcifying epithelioma. I asked him how he arrived at this conclusion and he explained that it was his clinical opinion based on many years of experience. I thanked him for his help and asked if he would consider removing the entire area surgically. He thought it was a good idea and suggested he do the pathological analysis himself. I advised him that his offer would be okay with me but I would be responsible for the analysis of any solid object we removed. He agreed and a date was set for the surgery.

The surgery went smoothly and we removed not only the skin lesion itself but also a little greyish-white ball attached to the superficial tissue. My colleague smiled and told me that the object was most probably a calcium deposit. I asked him what color the calcium deposits were in the other patients he had operated. He told me they were a bright white in color. I then asked him why he considered this object to be calcium. His answer was, "What else could it be?"

I felt is was my duty to learn as much about calcifying epitheliomas as possible. I researched the dermatology books as well as the pathology texts. I found that in general, these lesions usually started small, sometimes as big as a pin head and after some weeks or months slowly grew to that of the size of a dime and were painful to the touch. This was not the clinical picture presented in this case. In fact it was the exact opposite of what I found in the medical texts. Later analysis of the greyish white ball would prove this lesion was not a calcifying epithelioma. (See appendix).

To date, seven surgeries have been performed. The last case in the series was that of a female patient with an object in her left heel. X-rays revealed a radiodense shadow which was approximately mid-heel and superficial. The surgery consisted of a simple procedure using a small amount of anesthetic instilled into the superficial tissue, followed by a small incision. I probed the wound for a few minutes until I heard an audible click. This sound indicated I had touched something solid. I proceeded to expand the wound slightly until I could see a shiny object. I clamped it with an instrument and withdrew it from the wound. After placing it on a gauze sponge, I began to examine it with a strong light and magnification. The object was narrow and elongated, measuring less than one-half a centimeter. It had the appearance of glass or crystal. There was no soft tissue attached to the object and no noted membrane surrounding it. I did not excise the adjacent soft tissues as they appeared normal in color and texture. At this time the object is still undergoing analysis.

BIOLOGICAL SUMMARY

We have performed a total of seven surgeries to date, (January 1998). Of the seven cases, three consisted of metallic objects covered by a dark, gray, shiny membrane which could not be opened with a surgical blade. This membrane was shown to consist of a protein coagulum, hemosiderin, and keratin. All three of these substances are naturally occurring in the body but investigation has shown no record of this combination in the medical literature.

The soft tissues adjacent to the objects underwent analysis and the findings demonstrated conglomerations of nerve cells and a total lack of inflammatory response.

Three of the surgeries consisted of the removal of a skin lesion with an attached small bb-sized, greyish white round ball in the underlying soft tissue. The pathological findings were similar in all three cases. There was solar elastosis, either minimal or no inflammation present and clusters of nerve cells.

The seventh case was totally devoid of biological findings but did produce a crystal or glass-like object.

Other factors found to be significant were:

1. All objects were obtained from the left side of the body. There has been a significant number of other cases investigated by us which show the suspect object is in the left side of the body.

2. Almost all of the specimens fluoresced under ultraviolet black light. This is another area of current investigation. We have experts in the field of biofluorescence studying this phenomenon.

3. All subjects in our study showed abnormal reactions to procaine local anesthetics. Either the normal amount of anesthetic was not sufficient to produce the required anesthesia or there was frank outright allergic reactions to these compounds.

4. All subjects had a compulsion to consume salty substances and found it difficult to refuse food items such as potato chips, pretzels and other salty food. When consuming their ordinary meal they needed to apply large amounts of common table salt.

5. About 50% of the subjects suffered from xeropthalmia, (night blindness). The incidence is even higher when sex is considered. About 90% of the female portion of the study suffer from this condition.

6. Only one person with an object in the body, stated prior to surgery that he was able to hear voices and attributed this to the foreign object. After the surgery was performed the voices stopped for a short time but then returned.

7. One hundred percent of the patients in the study appeared normal on their psychological profiles. According to our Ph.D. psychologist they were all well adjusted and showed no indications of psychotic behavior.

8. The preoperative laboratory tests performed on the surgical candidates were all within normal limits.

9. The two patients who underwent hypnoanesthesia showed approximately a 50% more rapid healing process and took 90% less postoperative pain medication.

10. The psychological postoperative adjustment period was wide and varied for all the patients in the study. One patient stated he had initially lost his psychic abilities but as time went on felt they were returning. One of the other patients became completely divorced from the subject of ufology and wanted no further involvement. Three of the others continued to have additional abduction experiences following the surgeries. One of the patients is suspicious that he might have another implant in his body that was not removed at the time of surgery. All of the patients continue to live what appear to be normal, well adjusted lives. Each has his or her own opinion regarding whether the surgeries should have been performed at all. About 90% of the sample stated they would have the same thing done again if given the opportunity. All are concerned about the scientific findings and wish the results were already available.

THE METALLURGICAL FINDINGS

"What's in it?"

"What's it made of?"

"What's it do?" These are three of the most commonly asked questions. It should be remembered that although the questions are simple, the answers are not.

Our endeavors to fully answer these questions have cost us dearly in time and money. The answers have come slowly and at this time are still incomplete. We continue to wait for the results of complex testing. I am not a metallurgical scientist and therefore must rely on experts in that field to find and present the answers. Once the information is properly presented to the scientific community, then it is time for scientific thinkers to debate the issues.

What I will do here is introduce the material in the order that it was presented to us. Then I'll comment on the substance of the analysis.

The first metallurgical results came from the analysis performed by Los Alamos National Laboratories. These tests were done on the samples removed during the first two surgeries as well as the little greyish-white ball removed from the neck and shoulder area of the third case.

They have been designated the (T) group, e.g.. T-1, T-2, etc. The first test performed is called Laser Induced Breakdown Spectroscopy (LIBS)

LIBS was used to determine the elemental composition of the samples. The samples were small rod-like materials 1-2mm in diameter and less than one cm in length. Because of the small size of the sample surfaces when observed under a microscope, it was decided that LIBS was a suitable method to determine elemental composition because of its microsampling ability and relatively nondestructive analysis capabilities. Under microscopic examination, some of the samples appeared to be metallic and all but one sample (T-4) were observed to have areas of visually different appearance (See appendix).

The method of analysis is as follows: LIBS is an elemental analysis technique in which powerful laser pulses are focused on the sample to generate a hot microplasma (10,000 degrees K). Because the laser beam can be focused to a small area, this method has microsampling capabilities. The microplasma vaporizes a small amount of the sample (less than 50 nanograms), and excites the resulting atoms to emit light. The light is then collected, spectrally dispersed, and the resulting spectrum is recorded to determine the elemental composition.. Because each element has a unique spectral signature, the elements can be identified by analysis of the spectrum. The intensity of the emission lines can be used to determine the concentrations of elements if the sample has uniform composition.

The following is the result of this elemental analysis:

T-1 Scaled Portion: Al, Ca, Fe, Ba, Cu, Mg, Mn,Na,Ni,Pb, Zn.
　　　Black Portion　　Ca, Cu,Fe, Al, Ba, Mn, Na, Ni

T-2 Black Portion　　Ca, Cu, Fe Al, Ba, Mg, Mn, Na, Ni
　　　Brown Portion　　Ca, Fe, Ba, Cu, Mg, Mn, Na, Ni, Si

T-3 Black Portion　　Ca, Cu, Fe, Ba, Mn, Na
　　　White Portion　　Al, Ca, Cu, Fe,Ba, Mg, Mn, Na, Si
　　　Rust Portion　　Ca, Cu, Fe, Ba, Mn, Na

T-4 Black Portion　　Ca, Cu,Fe, Al,Ba,Mn,Na,Ni,

T-6 Brown Portion　　Al,Ca, Cu, Ti, Mg, Na, Si, Zn
　　　White Portion　　Al, Ca, Cu, Fe, Mg, Mn, Na, Si, Zn
　　　Beads on White　　Ca, Cu, Fe, Al

These are the chemical symbols. Their meaning is as follows:
Al=aluminum, Ba=barium, Ca=calcium, Cu=copper, Fe=iron, Mg=magnesium, Mn=manganese, Na=sodium, Ni=nickel, Pb=lead, Si=silicon, Ti=tin, Zn=zinc

Under microscopic examination, some of the samples appeared visually to have areas of different color. These areas were analyzed separately. Different elemental compositions were found for the different areas. These are listed above. The area indicated as scaled was a larger diameter than the main rod. This area appeared glassy-like and scaled (See appendix).

The report and summary included the following recommendations:

"Additional tests not performed by us [Los Alamos National Laboratories] may indicate some unusual properties. These tests should include x-ray crystallographic and metallographic analysis to elucidate the sample structure(grain boundary structure, unusual metal phases, preferential grain growth)."

When these results were received we immediately contacted N.I.D.S. and asked their recommendations. It was decided that further testing should be performed. We were informed their board would make a decision as to who should perform the next set of tests.

It took several weeks before we heard from N.I.D.S. again. They informed us that another world class laboratory had been chosen for the next batch of testing. This laboratory was New Mexico Tech.

We received this information in a letter from N.I.D.S. which stated the following:

"One purpose for N.I.D.S.' involvement was to establish some appropriate standards for initial testing of materials samples. A number of experts were consulted to determine what non-destructive tests were appropriate at this stage of the investigation. The battery of tests for structural, chemical and electromagnetic analysis recommended and conducted include:

Density immersion technique in toluene

Mechanical properties analysis including hardness and elastic modulus

X-ray energy-dispersive spectroscopy

Scanning electron microscopy

X-ray diffraction pattern analysis

Electro/magnetic properties analysis

All analysis were double blinded

(See appendix)

We all waited with bated breath for the results from New Mexico Tech laboratory. In a telephone conversation with John Alexander, who was directing the research at N.I.D.S., I learned there was a problem pertaining to reporting the results of the extensive examination performed by New Mexico Tech. It seems the contract signed by them did not include the terminology which would allow them to render an opinion pertaining to the test results. John told me they were working on the problem and it would be resolved soon. At that point I really began to understand the politics involved in scientific testing.

Finally in September of 1996 the results were released to me from N.I.D.S..

They had resolved their problems with the laboratory and faxed me the letter of opinion containing the results. My secretary handed it to me. I then sat alone in the confines of my private office, turned on the desk-lamp and began to read the letter. On the top, in large black letters, it said,

"New Mexico Tech" Letter of Opinion (Samples T1,2 and T3). (See appendix)

The more I read, the more confused I became. I wondered what had happened to the other samples which Los Alamos had done. It took a phone call to N.I.D.S and a conversation with John Alexander to clarify the matter. New Mexico Tech had not used the same coding system which Los Alamos had used. Instead they had subdivided the samples into A and B portions. In addition the sample designated T-6 was not sent to the second laboratory at all.

The letter of opinion contained two major statements. The first one they indicated that the T-3 sample contained 11 different elements. Sample T1-2, contained an iron core. The tests also indicated that iron and phosphorus were major constituents of the cladding material surrounding the iron core.

The second statement had to do with a comparison to meteorites. They thought this was the most likely material for these fragments to have come from. On the other hand there was a problem with the nickel-iron ratio. It seems that most meteorites contain between 6 and 10 percent nickel. They also stated that no meteorites contain less than five percent nickel and to resolve this discrepancy they deduced that these specimens could be just fragments of meteorites.

I was astounded by this revelation and knew I had to do something to help clarify the issue. Both Derrel and I knew that our patients did not step on a meteorite or hit one with the back of their hand.

I called the lab and talked with the individual who wrote the report. I told him I was going to tell him something that he might find shocking. With that warning, I said that the samples were obtained from the human body through a surgical procedure.

As a result of that, the metallurgist rendered an additional opinion which would ultimately prove to have little merit. The final letter of opinion contained an additional general statement responding to the fact that I'd said these samples were obtained from the human body. It stated that an iron-silver mixture imbedded into the body could cause a calcification reaction. It also stated that medicine and dentistry has used ceramic materials for many years. Unfortunately, the metallurgist's biological opinions did not hold water. In actual fact, no ceramic materials at all are used today because of the tremendous inflammatory reaction which occurs when they are instilled into the body. There were many biological findings which the author of the report did not know about our cases. One was the complete lack of any inflammatory reaction. Also he did not know that the specimens were covered by a strange, gray, dense biological membrane. Last of all, there was no evidence of a portal of entry (See appendix).

In summary, the metallurgical analysis has illustrated the following points:

The T-shaped object is composed of two small metallic rods. The horizontal portion contains an iron core which is harder than the finest carbide steel. This rod is magnetic. The iron core is covered by a complex layer of elements which forms a cladding. One portion of this cladding has a crystalline band which circles the rod. When viewing this rod, as seen in the electronmicophotograph, it appears to be structured. One end is in the shape of a barb, while the opposite end is flat. In the center is a small depression. The shape of this depression conforms exactly to the shape of one end of the vertical rod. The vertical rod contains a similar cladding but the core is composed of carbon instead of iron and it is magnetoconductive, not magnetic (See appendix).

It would seem these are structured objects which serve a purpose. This purpose has not been determined yet. We hope that further study will provide answers regarding function. There have been numerous individuals who have expressed interest in studying or postulating the function of these objects. One such person who has been working with us is Robert Beckwith, an electrical engineer. He has put forth a theory of how these objects might work. He is currently working on a book which will include his findings about them. We have been asked many times to speculate as to function. I feel it is safe to put forth theories but these must be looked at scientifically and either proved or disproved.

One such theory pertains to their ability to act as a tracking device or transponder. This would enable someone or something to find their subject anywhere on the globe. Another possibility is that they may act as behavior controlling devices. We know that abductees seem to have compulsive behaviors. They may wake their families in the middle of the night, ask them to get dressed and get in the car. Then all drive out into the country where the abductee might have an encounter or perhaps nothing happens and they just return home. I believe a more plausible purpose might be a device for monitoring certain pollution levels or even genetic changes in the body. This may be similar to the way we monitor our astronauts when they are in space. Only more time, effort and study will answer these questions.

CONCLUSION—BUT NOT THE LAST WORD

Since not all our research data is in, what can we say at this point? Most of the metallurgy indicates that the structure of these objects has an extraterrestrial origin. If this is indeed the case, we will be able to conclude that some individuals with alien abduction histories have objects in their bodies of extraterrestrial origin. The composition of the objects includes metals whose isotopic ratios are clearly extraterrestrial. Moreover, the form of the objects is clearly engineered and manufactured with precision rather than being a naturally occurring form. In short, we now have the "smoking gun" of ufology: hard physical evidence of an alien presence on Earth!

Chapter 14

THE DATA SPRING

It didn't take us long to learn that it was one thing to gain knowledge but another matter altogether to disseminate that knowledge. I made a promise to our benefactors that I would present whatever knowledge we attained from our research to the entire world. We would try not to do what so many of the other researchers had done. In our opinion, many fine research projects had occurred before ours came to fruition. But in reading the literature we found that a great deal of the data seemed not to be available to the general public or, in some instances, not to even to other researchers.

We were unable to determine whether this occurred by accident or the information was being kept secret on purpose. One example of this was the abduction literature itself. I was amazed to find how little detail was available having to do with the driving mechanism of UFO craft. Where was all the information pertaining to the temperature of the floors and walls that abductees came into contact with during their experiences? Was it only Betty Hill who was able to identify a star map? It seemed to me a lot more individuals should have seen star maps or charts. I knew there was some information available; however, I thought that if I were to inquire of my fellow researchers they would surely be able to point to a shining example of what I was looking for in a book. I am not saying there is no information of this type, only that there should be a lot more than what you can find in print. When it comes to the description of alien captors, it is an entirely different matter. Everyone seemed to be writing about the Greys, the Nordics, the Reptilians etc. but where was the kind of informational detail I was looking for? It was just not there.

It was a different story, however, when you queried a colleague in person. When asked point blank about these details, they would answer by telling me there was a certain amount of information they had to restrict from the public purview. This was necessary, in their opinion, because it helped to determine who was telling the truth about their event.

We found there was another reason for restricting information. It had to do with personal and petty reasons. In order to get their material out first, researchers would restrict its dissemination so that no one else could steal their thunder.

When I learned these practices were rampant in the field of ufology it upset me deeply. I could not fathom the mentality of the individuals who withheld information for those purposes.

The initial information gleaned from our research pertained to the biological data. There were so many surprises I began to doubt my own knowledge. In order to assure that our investigation was heading toward scientific highways, I had to be certain the information we were receiving was accurate before we issued statements to the public or scientific community. I spent many an evening sitting at my computer and delving into the available texts of on-line medical libraries. This was followed by discussions with my medical colleagues.

After nearly a year had passed we began to release our findings. Suddenly we were besieged by numerous sources such as lecture promoters, magazines in the UFO field, radio programs, newspaper reporters and, finally, television offers. At the same time, some very reputable scientists approached us with offers to perform research if they would be allowed to share authorship of an article in a scientific journal. We readily agreed, as this was part of our original plan.

Within a few months, I had spoken on more than 100 radio programs. Surprisingly, I was never asked to be on one of the most popular radio programs, the Art Bell Show. Many members of his listening audience had requested us, but we never got a call. In a personal telephone conversation I had with Bell, he seemed to be extremely interested in our work and even commented he would have me on the show. I said it would be an honor. I was never contacted again. The only other time Art was mentioned was when I was presenting at a conference in Florida and was introduced to Linda Howe. She was also extremely interested in the scientific data we had accumulated and offered to present it on Bell's program. I never again heard from Linda.

Robert Bigelow had his own ideas about releasing our information. When we originally entered into the agreement with him, it was understood that an article would be written for publication in one of the nation's leading scientific journals. Thus, I was quite nonplused when he called to ask my permission to release some of the scientific data on the metallurgy we had just received from New Mexico Tech Labs to the Mufon UFO Journal. Apparently, Walt Andrus had asked him if he would be willing to release the information. He told Andrus he could not do that unless he had our permission. My positive feelings about the Mufon organization were well known, so he probably was not prepared when I told him not to proceed. The reasons for this decision were many. First and foremost was that the research was not complete and I did not want to be in a position of being forced into premature conclusions. Another reason was that I wanted to personally write an article for the journal which would not only present the findings but also the background on the research itself. This finally came to pass. The article appeared in the April 1996 issue, and was widely read and commented on.

After completion of the second set of surgeries, we had a large amount of surgical video material at our disposal. F.I.R.S.T. was still in need of funds to perform further surgeries and continue research on the metallic portions of the samples. It occurred to us that we could possibly use the entertainment industry, particularly television and motion pictures, to acquire funding for more of our projects.

At the time it seemed quite simple. All we had to do, it seemed was find a producer who would create a work about what we were doing and use some of our footage. So we set out to find the right individual. Our travels took us to some of the better parts of Hollywood. We had meeting after meeting. Some were a total waste of time and some were to eventually have a degree of success. There was a time when we felt we needed professional help to move forward. I had resided in southern California since 1948 and was at one time employed by the motion picture industry. The way it did business had not changed since then. There were deals made in studio offices, posh restaurants, hotel lavatories, parking lots and the back seats of cars. The common wisdom was that you could not trust anyone in the entertainment industry and if you did not get your money up front, you would never see a dime.

The William Morris agency, one of the most prestigious talent agencies, became our next target. I made a few telephone calls and cashed in a few favors. This netted us the name of someone I could talk to within the agency. The more famous Hollywood talent agencies were not places where someone can simply walk in off the street and have a interview. It all had to do with who you knew and who might owe you a favor.

I made the call and asked for the secretary of Steven Farnsworth.

"Mr. Farnsworth's office, may I help you?" a charming female voice asked.

"Yes, my name is Dr. Leir and I am a friend of Maxine Klein. Would it be possible for me to speak with Mr. Farnsworth?" I asked.

I patiently waited on the line tapping my finger nervously on the desk.

"Dr. Leir, Mr. Farnsworth is in a meeting. Can he call you back this afternoon?"

She asked.

"Yes, that will be just fine. Let me give you a number where I can be reached after two o'clock. It is 800-449-0676. Please make sure he calls me after two."

"I will put this on his desk and have him call after two o'clock as you requested."

I put the receiver back on its cradle and wondered if he would indeed call me back.

As it turned out, I did receive a call that afternoon from Mr. Farnsworth. He appeared to be interested in what I was telling him and indicated he would take the information to his superior, then get back in touch with me.

I was again surprised when a few days later I received a call from the William Morris Agency with Mr. Farnsworth on the line. This time he was even more enthused and asked if he could meet with me.

A few weeks later I found myself in one of the inner offices of the prestigious William Morris Agency. I couldn't believe we actually had gotten this far down the road to success. The surroundings were not really impressive. The office was probably at least ten years old and in a very high rent district. There was a multitude of pictures of famous screen personalities decorating the walls, but an obvious lack of frills. Plain desks, with wooden chairs. A rug ran the entire length of the long hall and crept its way into the individual offices, portraying a colorful roadway.

I was greeted by the receptionist. She asked who we wished to see and if I had an appointment. He then motioned to have a seat and told me that Mr. Farnsworth would be down shortly. I waited about ten minutes and noticed a gentlemen wearing a dark colored business suit approaching the lobby from one of the adjoining hallways. He came into the room and spoke with the receptionist. She turned and said,

"Dr. Leir, this is Steven Farnswaorth."

I shook his hand and stepped back out of the way.

Farnsworth politely asked me to follow him to his office, and indicated that we would wait there for I walked down the long hallway to the elevator and proceeded to the tenth floor where I exited and followed our guide to his office, a few feet down the hall.

As I entered the office I noted a much improved decor. I was impressed and thought that perhaps it was only some of the more favored executives who had more plush offices. This gave me confidence that our meeting was going to bear fruit. Farnsworth asked me to be seated. I lowered myself into one of the soft easy chairs which ringed the room. Farnsworth offer to bring coffee or other drinks of our choice. I opted for herb tea.

I sat quietly sipping drinks. Two more executive types entered the room. Farnsworth made the introductions. One of the men, Jack, was responsible for placing scientific programming and the other Glenn, was in charge of general productions, which included a variety of different motion picture and TV programs. They explained to us that the agency was so large and covered such a wide segment of the entertainment industry that their functions were divided into various categories and assigned to specific individuals in each category.

I made my presentation, telling the story of our research. I explained the formation of F.I.R.S.T. and how I needed to fund the research which was ongoing. I indicated my wish for a television special or other suitable vehicle by which I could raise funds. Everyone appeared to listen attentively. Farnsworth was the first to comment. "Well, I think that we might have something here. I am thinking about setting up an appointment with Lee and Joe over at Rhino Productions. They just finished the pilot on a TV production that will be shown in about three months. I think this is just their meat."

He turned and looked at both Jack and Glenn, who were already nodding their heads. Jack was the first to speak.

"Yeah, I think that's a good idea and maybe we should also call Art with DDIX,"

Farnsworth looked and Glen and asked, "What do you think, Glenn?"

Farnsworth sat forward in his chair and in a low tone of voice said, "I think you guys are right on the money. Let's go ahead and make the calls."

With that, both Jack and Glenn excused themselves. They told me how pleased they were to meet me and left the room. Steven Farnsworth crossed behind a rather large executive desk and eased himself into the high back chair. He looked up at us and said,

"Gentlemen, I am going to make a couple of quick calls and see if we can get some opinions for you."

Farnsworth spent about ten minutes on the phone, and then leaned across his desk and said, "I have made arrangements for you to talk with two producers who are clients of ours. If you are satisfied with what they come up with, we will meet again and talk about signing you up."

"I would like to know what your fees will be if I decide to go forward with the deal," I said bluntly.

Farnsworth sat back in his chair, smiled and said,

"We only charge 6% of the gross earnings per deal. It is pretty standard in the business."

With that we stood, shook hands with our host and told him I would get back in touch.

About two weeks passed between the time I made our appointments and the time I was physically able to get together with the producers Farnsworth had recommended. The meetings were less than satisfactory. They were both interested in doing a deal but would allow us next to nothing in the way of profit. When we asked them why we should proceed with a nonprofit deal, their answer was: "exposure was what we needed and this would eventually lead into some money-making deals for our organization."

I felt like I had been handed a real bill of goods from some sly con artists. I wondered where the money was going that the producers would make on the deal. I was beginning to get the drift of the situation. Profit for the big boys but none for us.

It was sheer coincidence that I received a call from Dr. Tal. He was interested in what was new and how things were going in general. I explained our situation and he told me that he still had many friends in the entertainment business and offered to help us. I thanked him for the offer and told him to proceed.

In just two hours I received another call from him. The Tuesday afternoon time was satisfactory for all parties and we were to meet in a small Italian restaurant in Encino. He gave me directions and told me the time was set for 2 p.m. He also advised me to bring any visual materials that I could show.

Although the traffic that afternoon was light, the short jaunt to the restaurant took slightly longer that I anticipated. I arrived at about five minutes after two.

The restaurant was small. The lights were dim and the aroma of fresh cooked pasta and oregano permeated the air. There were only about fifteen small, round tables covered with red tablecloths scattered about the room. Each table was covered additionally by a white paper tablecloth which was rectangular and the corners draped about five inches over the side of the table. On each table was a bottle of olive oil, salt and pepper shakers and two additional spice containers. Each place setting had the customary cloth napkin and silverware. I looked about the room and saw Dr. Tal sitting at a table over in the corner of the room. He had his hand raised and was gesturing for me to come over. With him were two gentlemen also seated at the table.

I approached and was introduced to Larry and Bob. They were both with a company called Apollo Productions. A waiter appeared shortly after I sat down and asked if I wanted a beverage. I ordered a glass of juice and wondered what our two producers had ordered. I know enough about Dr. Tal's eating habits to know that he did not consume any alcoholic beverages and loved bread. Therefore I was not surprised when the waiter returned with a tray full of drinks and a large basket of Italian sourdough bread. Dr. Tal started in on the bread. I asked if anyone intended to order other food, but just bread and drinks were the order of the day.

Dr. Tal broached the subject of the meeting and why I wanted to use the entertainment industry to fund the organization. As I finished my presentation, Dr. Tal got right to the point.

"How much money would a project like this take and much could we make up front?" he asked bluntly.

"Well, I think if we do this right we are talking about a five hundred thousand dollar budget." Larry answered.

Bon nodded his head in agreement and asked, "How much did you consider your share would be?"

Tal looked Larry squarely in the eye and without hesitation said, "We need at least two hundred and fifty thousand up front. In addition we want at least ten points on the back end for home video and offshore distribution. If that can't be done, we'll go elsewhere. Did I tell you boys that Scott Alexander is interested in writing a screenplay and doing a major motion picture on this deal?"

"Well, I think if we do this right we are talking about a five hundred thousand dollar budget," Larry answered.

Bob nodded in agreement and asked, "How much did you consider your share would be?"

I felt about two inches tall. The numbers these guys were talking about were staggering. I thought to myself, Could this actually be money they were talking about?

Before I had a chance to speak, Larry turned to me and said, "Doc, could you tell me about one of the abduction episodes your patients were involved in?"

"Larry, I'll be more than happy to tell you one." I answered. I spent the next few minutes relating Patricia's story about the camping trip and the old iron bridge. Larry sat listening intently. I noticed that while he was wrapped up in the story I was narrating, he was also doodling with a pencil on the white paper tablecloth. The more he became involved in the story, the faster he doodled. Finally at the conclusion of the story he slowed down and stopped altogether. During my deliverance of this abduction episode, I told him about the light in the sky and how Patricia's husband thought it was a truck. I explained how she finally realized it was a flying craft and was too big to fit onto the bridge. But at no time did I describe the craft itself.

Both Larry and Bob were left to come up with a treatment for our story and arrangements were made to meet again at their office. Dr. Tal and I accompanied them outside. I excused myself and ran back to the table where we were sitting. None of the bus boys had been there yet and everything was as we had left it. I rushed over to the side of the table where Larry was sitting and peered at his drawing. My mouth dropped open and my eyes opened wide in astonishment. I could not believe what I was seeing. The picture Larry had drawn was an exact replica of the craft that Patricia had seen. I asked myself how this was possible. I definitely had not mentioned anything that had to do with a description of the craft itself. I grasped the paper tablecloth and tore the entire section from the table and stuffed it into my pocket. I didn't care, whether anyone was watching me. I just had to have that drawing. When I showed it to Dr. Tal, he was in a total state of disbelief.

Several weeks went by before we heard from Larry again. He wanted to set up another meeting, this time to be held at the Apollo offices. Our research had begun to show that a large percentage of abductees have a constant psychological battle going on. In one instant they are convinced they have been a subject of this strange phenomenon and in the very next instant they deny all aspects of involvement and try to convince themselves and others that the subject is total nonsense.

I called Dr. Tal and Larry. A meeting was set for the next week. Larry's office was in a high-rise building on Ventura Blvd., one of the main streets in the San Fernando Valley which connected a chain of small municipalities. His office was in Encino, a more affluent area than some of the surrounding cities.

I arrived slightly early. Dr. Tal was to meet us there. We took the elevator to the 9th floor and when the door opened we found ourselves directly in offices of Apollo Productions. Evidently their offices occupied the entire floor. In the main lobby was a reception desk. We approached the pretty blonde receptionist and asked for Larry. She knew he was expecting us and asked us to have a seat. Within moments Larry came out. I followed him through a complex set of hallways. I noticed numerous small half glass enclosed rooms which were bustling with activity. He led us into a conference room with a large wooden conference table surrounded by chairs. On the walls hung several blackboards with information typical of production schedules, framed posters of older motion picture titles and loose papers covered with writing. The decor did not appear to be new and that, in my opinion, was a big plus. I came to the conclusion that a number of different producers in the entertainment business will have enough seed money to make a good impression on some prospective clients but really have no financial backing and basically no funds for the production. They can accomplish this by walking into a multi-storied office building, make a deal for a large office, pay no front money, sign a long lease, lease all the furniture and bingo, they have an office to entice their unsuspecting victims. This was certainly not the case here. This office appeared to be a working facility and showed all the signs it had been functional for some time.

Dr. Tal joined us within a few minutes and at that point we were introduced to several other men who were part of the production staff. The last to arrive was Bob. We all took seats at the conference table. Larry began the meeting by reviewing the material we had discussed with him at our last meeting. We presented the details. Then, suddenly, his personality changed. His demeanor became almost antagonistic. He went on to explain that the only way to properly document what we were doing was to do it all over again. The shocked expression on my face must told the others about my feelings. Larry carried on with his bizarre suggestions. He told us that most of the surgery could have been faked and that if he proceeded with this type of production, he would have to make sure that everything was provable. He suggested performing another surgery and stated that he and his crew would be there to film the entire procedure. In addition he was going to install metal detectors outside the surgery room so he could prove to the world that the surgeons and other personnel could not bring these foreign objects into the surgery room and fake their extraction. As Larry continued, I glanced at Dr. Tal.

Dr. Tal was the first to speak. He completely changing the subject and got right into the matter of money.

"What kind of budget do you have in mind for this type of a deal?" he asked.

Larry looked up from the table with a detached expression and mumbled, "Well, Tal, in order to do this right, we're going to have to have a fairly decent sized budget."

Dr. Tal immediately came back with, "Just about how much do you think that would be?"

"Oh, I would say in the neighborhood of about seven hundred grand. Do you think that's accurate, Bob?" He in turn asked his associate.

Bob was in agreement and brought the others into the conversation. "Yeah, Tal, I think we can get this done for about that figure. You know we have to have a good product that we can sell to the majors," Larry added.

Dr. Tal's large eyebrows seemed to turn downward at that moment. He stared directly at Larry and asked "Larry, how much would we get out of that figure?

"Well, you'll probably be entitled to a licensing fee and then we could give you a bit for other things such as talent and stills." was Larry's answer.

"Just what would that come to?" Tal barked back.

"We could probably squeak out a few thousand bucks for you guys. You have got to realize that you will be able to do a lot better on the next one and maybe there could be some back end spin-off. You know, maybe a home video or other video series."

I am sure that our thoughts at that point were the same. We politely excused ourselves and thanked Larry and Bob for their time. We have not heard from them since.

Sometime later we met a young man Chris Wyatt who was a CBS contract producer. He was extremely interested in the field of ufology and had produced a UFO documentary which was the best Derrel and I had ever seen. Chris took a deep look at our work and offered to try to get CBS to do an hour special. He made such a favorable impression on us that we signed a contract with him.

As it turned out a year passed since that contract was signed and there is still no television production. Chris left CBS and struck out on his own. We still have faith that he will be able to get the job done. Chris and I are in full agreement that our work should not only be placed before a very large audience but should be presented in a format which is credible.

I have appeared on several television programs since we decided to release the information to the general public. Some of these include the television series Strange Universe, Paranormal Borderline and Hard Copy. We have also done both Warner Bros. and NBC News. In addition, we appeared on the Persian Television Network with a three-part series of interviews. We also have presented our material on more than 250 radio programs around the entire world. Some of these include "Sightings on the Air with Jeff Rense," The Rob McConnell show" and 21st Century Radio's "Hieronymus & Co."

In 1997, I traveled to many countries lecturing on our material and interviewing abductee victims. In the early part of the year we made a presentation in Brazil. I will never forget that experience. For three days we were surrounded by hundreds of abductees who gathered outside the auditorium where we were speaking. All wanted desperately to talk with us and tell us their experiences. They had no relatives to talk with, no psychologists, no hypnotherapists to work with. They could not tell their friends, their employers or their co-workers. There were many times when I found myself torn into emotional shreds. I listened intently as they told of their experiences, usually through an interpreter. I watched as tears began to well in their eyes and spill over onto their cheeks. I saw their eyes gaze upward as they began to mentally relive their experiences. I looked into their faces and saw their lips begin to quiver as the look of terror crept from the faces to the very center of their being.

Was this phenomenon real? Could anyone who has witnessed these things I have seen have doubts? Perhaps only a small percentage of researchers in this field have seen what I had seen in Brazil.

The abduction phenomenon had a different connotation among some of the Brazilian Indians who live in the rural jungle areas. We witnessed cases which could be best termed human mutilations. Some of these were analogous to the better-known phenomenon of cattle mutilations. One such case was that of a poor farmer who had both his eyes surgically removed during an abduction experience. I am not referring to a gross gouging out of the eyeball but rather the delicate surgical excision and instant healing of the surrounding tissue. What purpose do these procedures serve? To date we do not have a clue but hope to gain a better understanding in the future. All this needs to be disseminated to the world. That is the purpose of this book. That is why we also hope for a major television special.

Chapter 15

INTO THE FUTURE

The future is unknown and many believe that it flows from the events of the present. Even the term future itself is undergoing scientific scrutiny. Questions are being posed about the exact nature of time. What is time and how does it function? What actually is the past, the present, or the future? Perhaps our concepts of time and our physical universe are going to take a major leap forward. We, as mortal beings can only continue to travel the timeline we are on. I have started my own time line with plans for our future endeavors and will see to it that these plans become a reality.

Our research project began in August, 1995. Since that time we have traveled a road filled with twists, turns, embankments, cliffs and ambushes. There were times when we were encouraged and uplifted and at other times discouraged. However, I did not give in to these feelings. This in part was due to my burning desire for knowledge and the encouragement of friends who urged me on. One of these was Whitley Strieber, who constantly pointed out the importance of the work we were engaged in. Another person who inspired me was my cousin Ken Ring.

The primary goal I pursued was to marry hard science to a subject regarded by many as a fringe area, to say the least and more often was regarded as pseudoscience. In looking back on our endeavors, I can say without reservation that in my opinion, this goal was accomplished.

However, because of unhelpful comments from the public at large and the armchair scientific community, it became necessary to restrict our communication on the internet. Many times, outside of public view, I found information exchanges occurring among scientists who were debating portions of the data we brought forward. One such debate took place after our July 1997 press conference in Roswell. Several of the scientists who saw the raw data supplied by Dr. VernonClark had questions about the actual mathematics involved in the Silicon isotopic ratios. As it turned out one of the people who made these calculations had erred. The net result was a new calculation which provided even a greater deviant from the terrestrial isotopes than previously recorded. Closing these debates to the general

173

public made this exchange between true scientists possible. The increasing interest generated by the scientific community is what we feel is needed to have our research published in a major scientific journal. We look forward to this occurring in the very near future.

Since our approach to ufology ultimately involves the scientific study of physical evidence, our ultimate goal seems possible to many of our colleagues: actually capturing one or more of the elusive beings which are entering our environment. I feel that any creature which operates in our three-dimensional world has habits. If this is correct, these habits can be recorded, correlated, studied and ultimately used to capture these beings.

Progress in our investigations is directly related to our ability to pay for the necessary work. Our efforts raise funding have been diverse. Among numerous avenues, we believe the entertainment industry may provide the much-needed capital to continue our endeavors. We are looking forward to a one-hour television production based on our work which we hope will be shown world-wide. If this comes about, the funds generated will go directly into our research and allow it to continue without interruption.

It has been made very clear to us that there is a large amount of physical evidence being kept secret. Many of the individuals with this evidence have deep fears of reprisal from government agencies. Because we have taken the scientific approach to this subject, we have been able to dampen some of their fears. In addition, our policy has always been to accommodate the requests of anyone who wishes to turn physical evidence over to us. If they request anonymity, we are always happy to comply.

One of the prime examples concerned the piece of material believed to be from the Roswell crash site. In dealing with the supplier of this material, we demonstrated that we would live up to the agreement we had made with him. We did not release one iota of information about him. Because we demonstrated our sincerity, he trusted us with additional information.

Another of our goals is to extend our research to an international level. We look forward to the time when we can arrange for the performance of surgical procedures in such countries as Brazil, England, Mexico, Japan, Ecuador, Australia and Puerto Rico. I would like to give assistance without charge to the people of these countries. We want to help with their physiological and emotional needs. During our travels we began to realize that the abduction phenomenon is a world-wide issue. Its effects seem to vary with respect to specific geographical areas. The effects on the individual are also varied. We feel that this is sometimes due to the lack of communication between the victim and their friends and relatives. Other psychological effects were also apparent, including memories of strange dreams, a host of sudden generated fears and phobias such as fear of animals with large eyes and clowns. I was a personal witness to one such case in Brazil where a young female abductee became hysterical when a person dressed in a clown costume jumped out into a street, crowded with people. It took several of us to calm her down. In addition to the psychological trauma produced by isolation there are a myriad of physical effects which go untreated. Many abductees suffer dermatological effects such as the sudden appearance of strange skin markings or changes in pigment or color. Other effects are the craving of salt substances, feelings of dehydration, and sometimes the generalized feelings of flu-like symptoms with muscle aches and pains.

Another one of our goals is to solidify abduction research. One of the most disconcerting trends in this regard has to do with the lack of uniform procedures among researchers. I look toward the day when there will be a standardization of investigation procedures and hypnotic regressions. If this is accomplished, the data could be placed in one common database and therefore the same information would be available to all researchers, no matter where they may be located. I believe the only way research should be done is to provide the means for all researchers to draw from a common database. It seems impossible for anyone to reach a valid conclusion unless the information is available to all parties having data which bear on the situation.

I believe also that it is imperative that this information be disseminated among medical professionals. I wonder how many abductees pass through the general medical community with no attention being paid to their specific needs. I have also have concerns as to the number of possible abductees who have been confined to mental hospitals with false diagnoses. Since I have surgically removed numerous foreign objects from feet during the past thirty years, I am acutely aware of how many objects were removed and probably thrown away having undergone little scrutiny or a vague diagnosis. All doctors performing these surgeries were only concerned about the entities being fully removed or whether the surrounding tissue was benign or malignant.

Another of our future efforts will be to hold an abduction conference where every researcher of merit will be able to bring their ideas and suggestions. I envision this as a high-powered event which will attract the best minds in this subject from all over the world. It would be also helpful to include representation from other segments of the scientific community such as psychology, psychiatry, physics and astronomy.

What does the future hold for the field of ufology in general? I believe that the complete picture is very complex. Public opinion polls in the United States, shows that the general public believes we are being visited by life forms from elsewhere. I think there is a government coverup in which a controlled dissemination of information about those entities is being made. The book The Day After Roswell written by now retired army Col. Phillip Corso is one of the prime examples. Since his book was released in June 1997, no government official has made an effort to refute his statements which claim that aliens crashed at Roswell and the army recovered them and their craft. He furthermore states that he himself had charge of crash debris and had it researched.

Another example of controlled information has to do with the recent deluge of television programming, demonstrated by individual one-hour shows and an onslaught of commercials having to do with alien visitation, not to mention the extraordinary number of major motion pictures dealing with this subject. It seems apparent that "the powers that be" are attempting to subtly inform the masses that we may have open contact with beings from elsewhere. I do not believe, however, that every source of information coming from the government is inaccurate or incorrect. I believe that many in our government do not have access to this knowledge. This is also true of the very laboratories we are working with on our research. How could we trust their findings if we did not have some trust in the institutions we are dealing with? We found there seems to be a pervasive paranoia amongst certain investigators within the field of ufology, believing they are constantly spied upon and can not trust even the slightest information presented by any laboratory that does government work. I have found it impossible to locate a good laboratory which does not have government contracts. I don't believe that our results have been interfered with or distorted in any way.

In another area, hard science itself seems to be providing information to the public which helps to shape public opinion about alien life. This includes the possibility of life on Mars and other planets as well as extraordinary life forms recently discovered on our world such as those micro-organisms which live in some of the hot water vents in the Pacific Ocean. The complexities of modern physics have yielded data recently released to the general public which is also mind-boggling. Subjects such as the possibility of time travel, faster-than-light travel, non-locality of the mind, universal consciousness and particle memory are currently being studied. It appears man's knowledge is undergoing a revolution.

Another pioneering area for exploration has to do with the expansion of human consciousness. If beings from elsewhere are engaged in some sort of program to expand human consciousness, they may have created a problem for not only us but also for themselves. If these entities have been continuously manipulating the human race for thousands of years, as the "ancient astronaut" hypothesis suggests, why do we suddenly recall the abduction process? The awareness of abduction seems to have occurred only within the recent past. Is it possible that our race is becoming more acutely aware of our environment and through this process we have also become aware we are being tampered with?

The Israeli-born scholar Zecharia Sitchin, in his multi volume work entitled, The Earth Chronicles, tells us that our planet has been continuously visited by extraterrestrials who came here from their planet, Niburu. The first visitation of these beings, called the Annunaki, was four hundred and thirty five thousand years ago. Sitchin's information has been mainly derived from the ancient Sumerian artifacts and inscriptions. He has also said the that planet Niburu has a 3600-year orbit around our sun and each time it approaches earth, there is an advanced team sent here for a particular purpose. He indicates that the human race has been genetically interfered with and this interference continues today. He has stated that he believes the grey aliens are part of this advanced team and they are clones or androids sent here for a specific purpose. He believes these beings are the ones responsible for abductions.

Another well known author, Alan Alford, in his latest book, Gods of the New Millennium, has stated his belief that the Annunaki, through gene splicing, have induced longevity and may be poised to make yet more genetic alterations to their wayward, earth-laboratory creations. In addition he has taken Sitchin's work one step further by stating that the recently found bible-code may predict world events simply due to the fact that our makers continue to manipulate the fate of mankind. What better way to make a book predict the future successfully than by actually manipulating events to conform to the text? Alford also states that according to his research, based on the Sumerian findings, 184,000 years ago homo sapiens suddenly emerged from homo erectus. He goes on to say that our species took a remarkable leap forward in a very short span of time. During this leap we acquired a 50% increase in brain size, language capability, and a completely changed modern anatomy.

It is not surprising then that Alford is receiving support from such notables as Dr. Johannes Fiebag, of Bad Neustadt, Germany credited with having coined the term "paleo-SETI studies". Fiebag drew attention in a recent paper to the early discovery, by scientists working on the Genome Project, that "the majority of human DNA appears to have no real function," but is, in the words of evolutionary biologist Robert Shapiro, "trash, nonsense, or litter". Fiebag contends that this "litter" could well be "important information about the structural code or a genetic language not yet recognized as such." He goes on to speculate, that "if extraterrestrial intelligences have carried out the manipulation of our DNA in the distant past hints of such an event would have to be found precisely here, in this so called 'litter". Could this be the purpose behind our modern abduction phenomenon? Is it possible that our consciousness is being expanded at such a phenomenal rate that now we are becoming aware of the abduction event itself?

I have been in private practice for over 33 years and during that time I have seen changes in the development of my child-patients that are rather astounding. It is my opinion that one of the primary examples of human change is illustrated by these children born within the last 10 years. I believe any mother who looks at her recently born child and compares it with children born over 20 years ago will testify that there is a tremendous difference. Today's babies are acutely aware of their surroundings the very second they are born. They instantly look about the delivery room and appear to be aware of those who are present. They instantly know and recognize their mother and in addition are acutely aware of others who are present. In recent years there has been a notable lack of medical discussion in reference to exactly what a baby is able to see at birth. Thirty years ago there was much discussion on this subject within the opthamological community. There were numerous diverse opinions. Some opted for them seeing only greyish figures; others thought they couldn't focus acutely enough to discern shapes or figures at all. Others held that newborn babies were able to see but could only discern back and white. This is a far cry from what we realize a newborn sees today. Recently there has been a great deal of attention drawn to communication with the baby. There also has been a system of sign language developed and it appears to prove that a baby can actually communicate.

There are those who look upon the great differences in the "new human" and say the reasons have to do with better prenatal care, improved health of the mother, communication between the mother and the fetus or what the mother was exposed to on TV. In my opinion this supposition is nonsense and in light of my recent studies and exposure to the alien abduction phenomenon, I have come to the conclusion the rapid advancement of the human species is due to alien intervention with our bodies and minds. UFO researcher Robert O. Dean has spoken many times of the development of a new humanity called Homo Noeticus. This was a term actually coined by the noted author, John White, who has been doing research in parapsychology and noetics, the study of consciousness for many years.

Another new fascinating aspect of this subject has to do with the ability of modern babies to actually read written print. This was the subject of a recent ABC television broadcast which demonstrated the associated techniques used to reach this conclusion. In another experiment, sign language was used to communicate with toddlers not old enough to speak. We may see this practice develop early reading skills of the child.

The expansion of the modern child's consciousness may be demonstrated in many ways. Quite often, a four- or five-year-old will seem to reach into what may be termed the universal pool of thought or knowledge and simply extract a sentence or phrase of the most prophetic nature. There has been numerous recent writings and discussions pertaining to a universal consciousness. Joseph Chilton Pierce, in his book, Evolution's End, talks about a universal thought stream, with reference to "idiot savants." He poses the possibility that these savants are able to tap into this pool of universal knowledge but only extract a tiny slice of a particular knowledge form. Therefore they may be able to perform astounding mathematical calculations of a complex nature in a lightning fraction of a second, faster than a computer, or play the piano to near perfection, all without the mental ability to actually learn anything. In addition, John White, in his book entitled The Meeting of Mind and Spirit also gives credence to the existence of a planetary "field of mind" which is analogous to Dr. Carl Jung's concept of the collective unconscious. Could this possibly be what is happening to our developing children?

In addition, if we scrutinize and compare the child's current development to the development of the same age child 20 years ago, we find some astonishing advancements such as the age of gait, the age of crawling, the age of stair climbing, and the age of speech. When I graduated from medical school in 1964, the statistics put forth by the American Podiatric Association showed that the average age of gait was thirteen and seven-tenths months. According to the statistics available today that age has been reduced to nine and eight-tenths months. I believe we can safely say that all the statistics in relation to child development has been greatly accelerated. The question is, why? I suggest that the answer involves alien manipulation of human genetics.

In general and in considering all the factors I have enumerated, I cannot avoid the conclusion that in the future the field of ufology will become more scientific, eventually taking its rightful place among the other hard sciences.

Chapter 16

Updates

Because my research is ongoing, many times I feel that it is necessary to review the data already existing before moving on to the new data. I believe that the reader of the book also deserves the same benefits, therefore let us just take a few moments and look at what we have uncovered so far.

My research into the possibility of alien implants started in 1995. The first two surgeries for removal of suspected objects were performed August 19, 1995. These carefully guarded specimens and their surrounding tissue were sent for analysis at some of the worlds most prestigious laboratories, such as Los Alamos National Labs and New Mexico Tech. Their findings, along with the biological findings propelled the research into high gear. We found ourselves surrounded and confounded by one technical mystery after the other and still, till this day that seems to be the case. It seems no sooner than we have one explanation for our examinations then another examination will reveal another unknown.

Today we have performed nine surgeries which has yielded ten objects. One of these objects was merely an expensive piece of bottle glass. The reason that I say expensive is that the research to prove it was glass and not a crystalline material turned into a nightmare of expenses. I believe that this is a good indication that our research is paralleling general trends in good scientific research. All the other nine objects presented findings that were of scientific interest. In order to summarize these findings I shall divide the objects into two groups, metallic and non-metallic.

NON METALLIC

The non metallic objects were three in number and appeared as little greyish-white, BB sized balls. These three objects also had attached skin lesions commonly called "Scoop Marks". The body tissues surrounding these objects showed similar findings to those found with the metallic objects in which there was no evidence of an inflammatory reaction as well as an abnormal amount of nerve fibers in the area immediately adjacent to the object. It was found these objects were solid when removed from the body but when preserved in serum solution began to change state to a gelatinous glob. This state could be reversed by evacuating all the serum and leaving the remaining contents exposed to the air. The appearance of a hard ball then again

181

became evident. It was believed by one of my colleagues, a board certified dermatologist, that these lesions were nothing more that a common skin lesion called a calcifying epithelioma. He was shocked when the analysis came back showing that there was no calcium in the sample but instead a complex containing 21 different elements. These elements were terrestrial but put together in a very strange fashion. As to what the cause is for their ability to change states of matter is not understood at this time.

METALLIC

The remaining six objects were all metallic in nature and consisted of an internal structure made of small pencil lead sized metallic rods covered with a very dense, well formed, dark, shiny metallic membrane that could not be severed or dented with a sharp instrument such as a surgical blade. These objects again can be artificially sub grouped by shape. Four objects were small cantaloupe seed shaped objects. These all appeared so identical that one could not determine one from the other if laid side by side. One of the other metallic objects was "T" shaped and about twice the size of the small cantaloupe seed shaped devices. The remaining object was triangular shaped. All these metallic objects were covered by the strange dark membrane.

The lack of inflammatory response to these metal objects by the body's system of defenses is now believed to be caused by the membrane. The membrane has been analyzed and is composed of a protein coagulum, hemosiderin granules and keratin. These substances are all normally present in the body but there is no historical record in the medical literature to suggest that such a combination has ever been seen previously. It is believed by many that this strange combination of natural biological ingredients may be responsible for preventing the body from reacting to these foreign objects. If this could be better understood, then it would seem possible that an artificial substance could be manufactured so that objects that needed to be medically implanted into the body could be wrapped with this substance and therefore relieve the patient from consuming those immunosuppressive agents that are necessary today for prevention of the rejection reaction.

1.

For those of you who are reading this book for the first time, I sincerely hope you enjoy it and for those who have read the original version, please be assured that this edition contains some of the latest information. It has always been my intent and promise to keep the public informed of the all the research data as soon as it makes itself available and to that end I am including it in this new chapter. In addition I will cover some of the events that have taken place since the last edition of my book, The Aliens and the Scalpel was published.

In late July of 1998, I received a telephone call from Whitley Strieber. This was not surprising since Whitley had become a good friend through the years. We were originally introduced to each other through my cousin Dr. Kenneth Ring, author of numerous books on The Near Death Experience. His book, *The Omega Project,* was his search for a common psychological profile that fit both Near-Death experiences and those who had UFO experiences. In doing research for that book he had made many friends in the UFO field. Whitley was one of these individuals. So, when I received his original phone call I automatically assumed it was another social event. Instead it turned out to be one development in my life that would add another synchronistic building block to the already growing mountain of episodes that apparently was there to rule my life's domain. The conversation went something like this:

"Roger, it's Whitley. How are you?"

"Just fine Whitley. How are you and Ann?" I asked.

"We are just great. I have something to tell you which is most important and would like your opinion and perhaps your participation if you are interested."

"Sure, let's hear it." I replied

"I have just arranged a television special that is going to be shown on NBC during prime time. It will be a two hour long program, the likes of which has never been shown on TV before pertaining to the physical evidence collected over the years in the field of Ufology. I would like to know if you are interested in participating in the program and if you are, I will tell you what I have in mind."

I stood there in a mild state of shock. I thought to myself about the opportunities this might bring. Without hesitation I answered,

"Please tell me the details. What part would I play in the entire event? I asked.

"Roger I think I can talk the production company into footing the bill for an entire surgery. In addition I believe we could get them to pay for the laboratory testing of the materials."

"Are you telling me this seriously or is this one of your little jokes?" I asked jokingly.

"Roger, I am dead serious and this is no joke."

It took just a few seconds for me to recover my composure and respond.

"I would be most happy to participate in this event with you and I am very appreciative of the offer. Please give me a few of the details. When are they planning to start filming and when would they like the surgery to be done?

Now let me tell you, his answer almost caused me shriek out loud.

"Well Rog, they want to start shooting right away and would like you to do the surgery in the next week or so." He answered softly.

"Whitley, do you realize what I have to do to get all this done on such short notice. I have to locate the right surgical candidate, make arrangements for rental of a surgical suite with the proper equipment, notify the surgical team, have the patient undergo a pre-surgical examination, have his labs done, arrange for the MUFON camera crew and a myriad of other details. How do you expect me to get all this done in such a short amount of time?"

"I know it is short notice, but I have faith in you and I know you can do it." was his reply.

"Let's take first things first. What I want you to do initially is to prepare a budget that would be all inclusive and submit it to me so I in turn can present it to the production company. How long would it take you to do that? Can you get it to me in the next few days?" Whitlely asked in a very persuasive manner.

"The best I can tell you Whit, is that I will try to get it finished as soon as conceivably possible." I replied.

"Okay then, see what you can do and let me know. I'll be talking with you again in a couple of days. Take care."

With that, we finished our conversation. I immediately turned to my wife and explained to her about my discussion with Whitley and what I had just tentatively agreed to. She stood there in a semi state of shock and severely reprimanded for biting off more than I could chew. I placated her be telling her I would have plenty of time to get it all done and for her not to be concerned. I had done many things like this in the past and asked her to remember they all came out okay.

The next morning I when I was in the office I called Dr. A and told him about the up and coming plan. I asked if he could help with any of the items I needed and obtained his assurances he would see what he could do. I followed this with phone calls to some of the perspective surgical candidates. One of them was very responsive but lived in Ohio. He had an object that was radio-opaque on x-ray and sometimes caused a spark when he talked on the telephone. He was quite willing and anxious to come to California to have the object surgically removed but I would have to foot his bill for the airfare. In addition it would take just the right surgeon to perform the surgery since it was difficult to determine whether the object was nearest to the inside or the outside of the jaw bone.

Some of the other tentative patients I could not reach at all or they had promised to call me back.

Two of the other cases had decided to wait for a protracted period of time to have the surgery done. I also contacted one other case. It was of a registered nurse who resided here in California with a radio-opaque object in her foot. She wanted to have the surgery done but upon reviewing the x-rays I noted the object was deep in the bottom of the foot and knew this would be a difficult extraction. Still, the best case was the jaw case. With x-rays in hand I left my office heading to my dental associates office to get his opinion. His name was Dr. David Schoenbaum, a professional dental colleague and friend for over thirty five years. He was aware of what I was doing with the implant surgeries and had consulted on a number of other cases involving the mouth. I showed him the films and he thought the job should be done by an oral surgeon. He gave me a business card with the name of his friend who he thought might be interested in doing the job. So, off I was again to see another doctor for consultation.

After a quick lunch, I took the elevator to the third floor office in an Encino, medical building. The elevator door opened and I began my quest for suite 343. I turned right and walked down the hall. I stopped and found myself standing before a door on which was written, Dr. Abraham Schlesinger-Oral Surgery. I went in and introduced myself to the receptionist who seemed to know who I was. She told me the doctor would be right with me. I stood at the reception window for just a few moments. Soon I heard my name called and the door opened to the inner office. A slight of build lady, pretty with thick, long blonde hair beckoned for me to follow her. She led me to a typical consultation room which was complete with a dental x-ray view box and asked me to have as seat. She advised me that the Dr. would be right in. Only a few minutes passed before the door opened and a tall greyish haired gentleman with dark rimmed glasses entered the room.

"Hi, I'm Abe. Dick Schoenbaum said you would be coming by. Let's take a look at the x-ray." He stood with his hand extended.

I handed him the film and he thrust it up on the dental view box.

"Wow, this is an interesting one." he offered.

I stood and watched as he carefully scrutinized the film. I thought for sure he was going to offer to become the surgeon who would extract this object and was a bit shocked when he told me this was not a job for an oral surgeon because it required an approach from the outer surface of the face and he would not be the one to perform this type of surgery. I was disappointed and considered myself back to square one again. I thanked him for his opinion and left to return to my office which by now had to be full of today's patients.

The following day I called my friend the dentist and asked him if he knew a surgeon that specialized in Maxillofacial surgery. He recommended a specialist in that field who just happened to be in my immediate area. I thanked him, made the call to the new surgeon and set up a time for a consultation.

The next afternoon, Dr. Fine, a Maxillofacial specialist reviewed the x-ray and told me that he would be able to do the surgery. I sighed with relief. I explained some of the details and circumstances, apprising him of the research project explaining there wasn't a large amount of capital to spend for this project. I asked him point blank, what he thought his fee was going to be. He looked at me with a strange expression and without a smile told be his fee would be $4000.00. I thanked him very much for his time and headed back to my own office. I knew at that point that this case was just not going to work. The budget would be too large and it would never be approved.

The phone calls I had made previously became productive. I was able to get a tentative agreement from the surgical team and other MUFON volunteers. My next stroke of luck came when I was able to nail down a surgical suite that would have the necessary x-ray equipment needed to do the surgery. This facility, for the time required would cost $2500.00. This was reasonable considering it came complete with equipment and staff. Also we could use it for the entire afternoon. A possible date for August the 17th was set. I told them I would let them know definitely in a few days. So as it were, I had everything all lined up accept I did not have the ideal patient.

The following day I placed another call to Whitley and advised him of the progress I was making. He told me he would be coming to California soon and would be staying here until the production was finished. I thought that was a great idea and it would make the co-ordination of events a lot easier. Somewhere down deep inside I knew my one remaining problem would be solved. I told myself, if it was meant to happen then it would happen.

I was in my office the next day seeing patients. At about eleven o'clock in the morning by secretary informed me I had a telephone call from someone that said they had talked with me at the last MUFON meeting. She told me his name was Paul. I don't usually take calls from strangers during my professional hours, but in this instance and for whatever the reason I decided to take the call.

Paul refreshed my memory immediately. I had met him at the last local MUFON meeting and I recalled he had told me he had a foreign object in his thumb and was concerned that it could possibly be an implant. I has asked him how he knew the object was there and he told me he had seen it on an x-ray. I asked him if he could obtain the film and he said,

"Sure, I have it right here with me."

I was startled. He produced the x-ray of his left hand and sure enough there was a bright shinny metallic object visible in the area of his thumb. I had asked him to contact me and to come to my office so that I could take another film and rule out the possibility of it being an artifact. He had agreed but had not called me until this day. I couldn't believe this strange set of events. I thought to myself, could this actually be the surgical candidate I was looking for? I asked him if he could come to my office ASAP and he agreed. I had my secretary set up and appointment for the following day. As it turned out he lived within a close proximity to my office and it was not a hassle for him to get there.

The next day, Paul came right on time. I reviewed his original x-ray and confirmed the presence of a foreign object for the second time. I immediately took another x-ray and developed it. Sure enough the film showed the object to still be present. I was now sure this was going to be our next surgical candidate and couldn't wait to tell Whitley the good news.

When the last patient of the day departed, I sat down at the computer and began mapping out the budget Whitley had requested. As soon as I had finished, I gave him a call. In the interim he had moved to California and his Texas number referred me to a number here. I called the new number and got him on the phone. I related the good news and at the same time told him I had just finished the budget. He advised me of his current fax number and told me to send it right away. He would go over it and then submit it to the production company for their approval. He indicated he would be back to me shortly and advised I not waste any time and continue preparing for the event. I agreed and left the office that day with new hopes and aspirations.

Past experience with the television industry had taught me a number of lessons. One of these was they never approved the initial budget. With this thought in mind I called Dr. A and filled him on the latest events. He told me I should have consulted him before submitting the budget. He was of the opinion they were going to tear the hell out of it and we would be left with expenses that could not be paid. He advised me he would come to the office tomorrow and review it with me so we could be prepared for their answer.

The next day at about 2:00pm he was in my office and reviewing the already submitted budget. He thought the only thing we could do is try to trim some of the expenses in preparation of the production company's forth coming rejection. It was his opinion by doing this we would be one step ahead of the game. Dr. A. knew the same individuals I knew in the medical profession. He spent the balance of the afternoon on the telephone discussing the surgery with everyone who was to be paid out of the budget. The results were agreements he made with the participants so that if their fee was rejected they would virtually accept what was proposed. This was good news. I felt as another giant weight had been lifted from my shoulders. Now all I had to wait for was Whitley's phone call.

At about 7:00pm that same evening Whitely called and told me he would put me directly in touch with the producer and that I should discuss the budget directly with him. I told him that would be satisfactory and would anticipate his call. About an hour later I received a call from a gentleman who introduced himself as Chad Finley (Name Changed) with Starfire Productions (Name Changed). He explained to me they were the company doing the production Confirmation for NBC. He seemed very congenial and told me he was looking forward to working with me and filming the surgery. He also wanted me to provide additional material such as photos, videos, past laboratory reports, as well as an interview with myself and the proposed patient. I told him I was sure all this could be arranged and asked him if had gone over the budget that was submitted. He advised me he had commenced with the process of chopping the amounts for each item down explaining that their budget was not big and they were limited in what they could afford. I was well aware that this was the stock line given by every production company in the industry I had ever worked with. We went over it point by point and I expressed my opinion as to what was feasible and what was not. I felt the most important thing on my side was I knew the medical business and he did not. Finally an agreement was reached that I could live with and I began to feel good about the entire deal. Even though I had some experience in the entertainment business I found after all was said and done I had not learned my lessons well and was given the royal shaft. As it turned out I wound up giving all my time spent being interviewed on camera away free. I also was not told the production company was going to produce a video which would be using all of my material and I would not receive one dime from all the money they would make.

When Whitley realized what had happened, he had me sit down and compose a letter explaining all the details. He told me that he felt terrible this happened and would try and have this rectified. I did as he asked but till this day have never received any further remuneration. In thinking of this episode with retrospective thought, I have now come to the conclusion I was fortunate enough to have the expenses paid and of course the surgery did get performed, in addition there was some scientific analysis of the object. At least our original goals were fulfilled.

2.

The time had literally flown by. Suddenly it was August 17th and the day of the surgery was upon us. I had loaded my car with several pounds of paperwork consisting of releases, consents and other medical forms needed for the performance of the surgery. I arrived at the surgical center early in order to prepare for what was about to happen. We had not invited as many witnesses to this event as the ones previous because of the small size of the waiting area which would house the closed circuit TV.

The first to arrive was the professional production crew with Chad Finley leading the parade. I counted approximately four members of this crew. I introduced myself to Chad and he told me the remaining crew would be here with more equipment in just a few minutes. He asked me to show him the facility so they could decide where the best vantage point would be for the television cameras. I gave him the requested tour and introduced him to the staff. I also advised him our own team would be filming the procedure strictly for the scientific record. He was less than happy with that knowledge and made me promise that the footage we shot would not be used for commercial purposes. I gave him my assurances.

Soon other members of the surgical team began to arrive. I was busy rushing from one spot to another trying desperately to coordinate the procedures. It wasn't long before problems began to arise. First we could not get the TV in the viewing area to work so another TV had to be moved from upstairs. Then there were technical problems with the size of the cable fittings and on top of this there were conflicts between the professional television crew and our MUFON volunteers regarding which camera was going to be broadcasting the feed through the closed circuit process to the waiting room. Finally it was decided that our own camera would function in this capacity. Next came a disagreement as to where our camera would be in the operating room so it did not interfere with the professional cameras. Another milestone agreement was made and our camera was placed in a corner high above the operating area. The view finder could only be reached by standing on a ladder.

Adding to the confusion were the requirements of the surgical facility and the enforcement by the operating room nurse who is essentially the boss and prime mover over everything that happens in her operating room. Her first duty was to perform what is called medically as an "In Service Review." In this meeting she informed all non professional personnel who would be present as to what they can and can not do in the operating room. This also included the number of individuals who could be actually present during the surgery. She informed everyone there were only six available sets of x-ray protective gear available and everyone in the room would be required to wear these special leaded garments. This presented another problem because the production crew exceeded their number by two. This included the producer, Chad. He made it crystal clear to our O.R. Supervisor that if he was not present in the room, no filming would occur. Fortunately the problem was solved when Mike, our MUFON surgical nurse suggested that Chad be allowed to stand behind a lead screen, which was already standing in one corner of the operating room. The O.R. Supervisor agreed and stated that when the x-ray equipment was in operation he would have to go behind the leaded screen. I sighed with relief; another problem solved however we still had too many people. There was the lighting technician and the sound man. It was decided that the lighting technician was to be ejected from the room after he was satisfied the lighting was satisfactory and the sound man was banished to a small supply closet with a glass door so he could observe the events in the operating room.

Elsewhere the beehive of activity began to grow with the arrival of the patient, Dr., our guests, our writers Jack and Ruth Carlson, Whitely and his wife Ann and other volunteers from MUFON. The most integral part of the team who had not arrived was the most key figure of all and that was the surgeon.

I made my way to the dressing room and changed from my street garb into the customary surgical greens. Most of the crew had already done this. It was at this point I heard Dr. Mitter's voice in the hallway. He was the same surgeon who had performed the procedures in May of 1996. I sighed with relief as another piece of the complex effort fell into place.

One final visit to the waiting area was in order and I proceeded there with vigor and haste as the time was passing rapidly. I had to make sure this procedure was finished in the agreed amount of time or the costs would rise considerably. Most individuals who had been invited were there and I welcomed them to another historic surgical event. It seemed there needs had been met and all the proper forms and documents signed. I excused myself and told them the next time they would see me would be when I appeared on the television screen.

I promptly went back to the operating room to assess the progress. I found that the patient had been brought into the room and was on the operating table getting prepped for the surgery. The x-ray equipment was ready and waiting to be used. In addition it was agreed we would have a standby anesthesiologist just in case it was necessary to induce more than a local anesthesia. My choice for this role was Dr. Muriel Kendred. She was someone who I had know for many years and had performed general anesthesia on many of my patients through the years. She greeted me with a friendly hello and I acknowledged by blowing her a kiss. Mike, our surgical nurse was preparing instruments on the back table and Dr. Mitter was preparing to give the patient his injection of local anesthetic. The professional film crew had found there niche in the room and seemed quite orderly and relaxed as if they had done this before. I turned to leave for the scrub area when something caught the corner of my eye. I suddenly turned around as was mortified to see our MUFON camera shoved way over in a corner and not pointing at anything in the surgical area. At this point I became very irritated and almost lost my composure.

"Who shoved our camera up there like that?" I shouted to anyone that happened to be listening.

The answer came quickly from Chad, the producer. He responded by saying, "Oh, we had to do that because there was no room to put our own camera."

His remark aroused my anger even more and I assailed him with, "I strongly suggest you get up there and move it so that it is focused in on the surgical field."

In addition I thought I would give him a taste of his own medicine and added, "If that camera isn't covering the surgical area, there will be no surgery done here today."

With that one of the technicians bolted over to the ladder, climbed it and tried desperately to peer through the viewfinder which was in a very awkward position. He then announced that everything looked okay. I was not sure of that so I decided to take a second look at the monitor that was displaying the surgery for our witnesses. It seemed to be just fine and I returned to the scrub area.

All the parts had finally come together and it was time for me to scrub and don the remainder of my surgical garb including the 6 pounds of protective lead shielding. Before the final covering the sound man placed several lapel microphones just under the front of my collar so that they could record my narration as well as having the audio feed go live to the viewing room. All the members of the team were now in place and I turned to place myself in the surgery field which was adjacent and slightly behind Dr. Mitter. Just as I was making the turn I felt a hand on my arm and my eyes almost bugged out of my head when I saw Chad standing there with his outstretched non gloved hand holding the sleeve of my sterile surgical gown. He was muttering something but I was in no mood to attempt to hear what he had to say. Almost at the same instant the operating room supervisor saw what was going on and shouted sharply,

"You there!! Touching Dr. Leir, get the hell away from him right now and get back to where you are supposed to be or you will have to leave the room immediately."

Poor Chad who finally realized what he had done quickly and sheepishly moved back behind the lead screen without uttering a word. Next I heard Mike shout,

"Someone get Dr. Leir a sterile cover sleeve."

With that, another package was handed to Mike. He opened it hastily and pulled forth a sterile sleeve. Another scrub nurse helped pull the sleeve over my existing gown sleeve and then helped me replace my corresponding surgical glove. Finally we were all set to go. I gave this indication to Dr. Mitter and he turned to the surgical tray, picked up the surgical scalpel and made his initial incision into Paul's thumb. With that I remarked to the viewing audience,

"The surgery has begun with the initial incision into the skin."

The time seemed to pass quickly after that. Soon the complex C Arm x-ray equipment had allowed us to visualize the foreign object on the television screen. The surgeon then penetrated the area with a sharp probe until he could see that it touched the foreign object. The patient was doing well. Periodic verbal checks with Dr. Kendred apprised us about the patient's vital signs and his general status. Next, the surgeon made a deep incision following the probe deeply into the flesh. We could see on the TV view screen he had touched the object with his blade. Next, Dr. Mitter asked for a surgical clamp. Mike handed him the requested instrument. He lowered it into the wound and announced to all concerned,

"I've got it."

With that he produced something from the wound area and placed it on a gauze surgical sponge. Dr. Mitter has always been a very conservative person and even though he is aware of what we were looking for remains pretty much of a non-believer. He looked at the object sitting on the white gauze square and said,

"My, that is unusual, isn't it?"

That was my first glimpse of what he had removed. He turned and handed me the gauze containing the object. I looked at it and the hair began to rise under my surgical cap. It was exactly the same as the other small cantaloupe seed shaped objects removed in previous surgeries. My gaze was affixed on the object and I heard someone say,

"What is it? What did he find? You had better tell the audience beside don't forget we are recording all this for the show."

"Yes, I stammered. It seems as if we have another one of those small cantaloupe seed shaped objects which appears to be covered by this very dark, gray, dense, well organized membrane. I am now taking a surgical blade and trying to cut it open. It seems as if it won't open. My word, it's just like the other ones."

The cameras began to close in around me. The specimen was the target. There was little more I could add verbally to the scenario being played out before the television cameras. I knew there would be one long giant leap from what was being filmed today to what actually would be shown to the public but kept the faith that enough would be shown to tell the story as it happened.

Within a matter of a few short minutes the operating room became calm again and devoid of people. The patient had been taken to the recovery area. The professional production crew had removed their equipment, cables, cameras, monitors and other items they had been using. The nursing personnel began to remove all the used linen and draping. It was at that point that Chad approached me and began giving me instructions on how they were going to set up the next scene. He told me I was to stay in the room wearing all my surgical garb and when given the signal I would walk through the surgical suite doors to where the cameras were set up and the pathologist would be waiting. I was to hand the surgical specimen to the pathologist and he would then have a short verbal interchange with me discussing what he intended to do with the specimen. Chad asked me if I understood and I nodded to the affirmative. What he failed to tell me was that they were going to shut the air-conditioning off during the time I was to wait in the operating room. They did exactly that and the temperature began to slowly rise. This may have not been that bad a thing except for the fact I was wearing all the surgical gear and the 6 pounds of lead. The longer I stood there the more uncomfortable I became. It seemed as if the time would never come when I would be given the cue to leave the room. All this time I was standing with the surgical specimen in my hand still on the original white gauze sponge. Suddenly I looked at the object and was shocked to notice it seemed to appear smaller than when it was removed. I thought perhaps the temperature was getting to me and my vision was somehow becoming distorted. I picked up one of the remaining clean surgical towels and wiped my eyes. I turned again to view the specimen and realized this was no optical aberration. The damn thing was shrinking right before my eyes. I thought to myself,

"What should I do? Perhaps if this continues I will finally pass through the doors and have no specimen to show or tell about."

I thought what ever I was going to I had better do it soon. It was at that moment I heard the pre-arranged knock on the surgical doors and I started by trek to the next scene.

Soon I was out in the next room. Dr. Roscher, the pathologist was standing there with a cart containing various vials and other medical supplies. I knew I had to do something fast and at that point decided to pay less attention to the prescribed Hollywood type scene and more attention to the ever decreasing sized specimen.

The first words out of my mouth were directed to the operating room nurse,

"Where are the tubes contain the serum solution that was removed from the patient?" I asked sharply.

The answer came swiftly from Dr. Roscher.

"They are right here." He said with a thick European accent.

I reached over and snatched them out of his hand.

"Please had me a pick-up." I demanded.

The operating room supervisor handed me a pair of surgical forceps and I used them to take the object off the surgical sponge and plunge it into the vial of waiting blood serum. I was not concerned with a myriad of smaller soft tissue specimens left clinging to the

gauze square. My primary concern was the solid object we had removed. I am sure no one knew the extent of urgency. Once the object was safely in the vial of serum I went on with the prescribed dialogue. No one seemed to comment on the sudden change of plans. Chad seemed well satisfied with the scene and the participation of the pathologist. The next thing I heard was,
    "CUT! THAT'S A WRAP."
    Even today very few people know the full story of what went on in that room during those minutes when I was standing there holding the surgical specimen. Fortunately with the object back in the patients own serum solution, the object began to return back to it's normal size. One might ask if I have an explanation for this. Perhaps the membrane surrounding the object just simply started to dehydrate and when placed back in the solution it re-hydrated. Then again there may be an explanation of a more complex nature. This was just one more event in the mystery surrounding the issue of implants and their removal. By this time I had learned there is no substitute for experience. It was also now apparent to me unless someone has had training in the removal of these objects, they should not attempt to do them.

3.
    Chris Wyatt and Productions
    I have previously written about my friend Chris Wyatt, formally a television producer with CBS. Chris has become an independent producer and is production with a number of new television video products. One of his newest projects is titled, Close Encounters. This video contains information on a huge amount of physical evidence pertaining to the field of Ufology. I am a featured segment in this production. It will be released soon or may become part of a larger project he is working on. If all goes according to plan, Chris will be introducing a brand new Internet UFO website, the likes of which have never been seen before. It will represent the activities of the world's top researchers, documented photos of the most prized UFO sightings, an entire documentary video library and a full compliment of the world's old science fiction movies. In addition it will be an interactive site with capabilities of real time video.
    Also I have just signed a contract to produce the first television news program that will dedicate all the news time to the subject of UFOLOGY. It is called The Mutual UFO Network News and will air initially on local cable stations in and around Southern California. To date we have filmed the first news show which is composed of a one half hour of the international, national and local news having to do with the UFO subject. The second half of the program is a one half hour interview with Jose Escamilla, the discoverer of a possible new

life form called Rods. It is hoped this will become a weekly show and in time expand to more than the cable networks. It is a new enterprise for me, as the program must be scripted and this is my first experience at script writing.

It is my sincere hope that the research in this field will continue with more individuals in hard science coming forth to take their rightful place in this magnificent adventure. I for one will be there for as long as I am able to donate my time and energies to this cause. All my work is for only one purpose and that is: To help the victims of the Alien Abduction Phenomena.

4.

IMPLANT UPDATE—-YEAR 2000

The ninth surgery was performed on February 5, 2000. The findings from this case have added a great deal to our general knowledge. It seems that more information has been derived from this last case than all the other's put together.

The surgery was performed on patient Tim Cullen, who resides in a small farming town in eastern Colorado. He is willing to talk with anyone about his experience and surgery and has given his consent to use his name freely. Tim has now undergone two hypnotic sessions to enhance his memory however these were not done prior to his surgical procedure in accordance with our protocols.

One of Tim's most significant events occurred in 1978 when he and his wife were returning to Yuma, Colorado from a trip to Denver. Both witnessed a flying craft which seemed to come out of nowhere, appearing as a very bright light. It was seen approaching him from the rear and then moved parallel his vehicle. They watched as it cross the road in front of them and came to rest out in a vacant field. Suddenly two very bright lights came on, one on top of the other. The lights were pointed in the direction of their vehicle and he and his wife were almost blinded by their brightness. The next thing they recalled is that Tim turned to his wife and made a statement that they should head for home now. Today he feels it was during this episode that he had an object implanted into his left wrist. Tim and his wife told no one of this experience for over twenty years. Tim told me that he had other experiences in the following years.

Tim originally contacted me about a year before we actually met and explained his suspicion that he might have an alien implant in his wrist. He was compliant with everything I asked him to do and ultimately sent me an x-ray which showed a definitive metallic foreign body in his left wrist area. Plans were made for him to come to California and undergo the removal procedure.

One of the many things we were interested in was to find out if there were any electromagnetic emanations coming from the area where the object was located. This was one of the first tests that he underwent upon arriving in California. First we used a simple Gaussmeter and found that it indicated about a 6 milligauss reading. In addition, Bob Beckwith of Beckwith Research in Florida who has become our consultant electrical engineer was able to construct a probe that could be used with a special oscilloscope to obtain and record the signal being generated by this object. Unfortunately this portion of the experiment was somewhat a failure because the scope we obtained was not the exact type Bob wanted. However, we were able to acquire a pulsed signal reading which he later indicated showed there was one signal being generated from the object as well as new being received. Of great help was the MUFON State Director for Louisiana, Greg Avery. Greg came here to California with some very sophisticated camera equipment and another electronic detection device called a Trimeter. When this instrument was placed over Tim's wrist it indicated a mid-band reading on the combination magnetic and electrical scales. We concluded from this reading that for the first time we were able to obtain solid scientific data indicating these objects do transmit and receive data. The nature of this data we were unable to determine. It is our hope in the future this question will be answered.

The surgery for removal of this object was performed on February 5th of the year 2000. Tim's specimen was the fourth in a series of small cantaloupe seed shaped devices. I was shocked to see another one of these objects that looked like an exact copy of the other three we had removed.

We were very impatient to begin the analysis of this specimen but wanted to try and get more data than we had gotten from the previous objects. We were fortunate in being guided to a company in Santa Barbara California named Digital Instruments Inc. They are the manufacturer of the world's most sensitive microscope. This instrument is capable of looking at the surface of an object a few microns at a time. The instrument is called an Atomic Force Microscope. In addition they manufacture another instrument which is similar and called an Atomic Field Microscope. This device is able to look at the magnetic fields surrounding an object. Both instruments are connected to cameras so that photos can be taken. These instruments showed the surface of Tim's object in detail. One of the other capabilities of this instrumentation was the ability to look at the biological covering. When this was done, we were astonished at what we saw. The process of looking at the biological surface of this object required that it be removed from the blood serum solution and placed in sterile distilled water. When this was done it was discovered that the membrane lost all of its coloring and turned clear to whitish in color. At that point we were able to see through the membrane and visualize the metallic rod inside. As we moved the object under the lens of the microscope we came to an area where there was an appearance of bubbles, eggs or small sacs never seen before. Later the mystery deepened when we found that the content of these eggs or sacs was filled with an oily substance.

Further studies were done on the metallic portion by another world lass laboratory in Texas. These studies revealed that the main elemental component was Iron. This was not surprising because the object was highly magnetic and spring toward a magnet held about an inch and a half above the object. The big surprise came when a test called x-ray diffraction was performed and we found that the Iron was amorphous. This means that it was without crystalline form.

The very big question arose as how it was able to be magnetic and at the same time have no specific atomic make up. At this point we learned one of our secret technical accomplishments was that certain Black Budget Scientists were now able to make amorphous metals. What amazed all the scientists was this amorphous iron was highly magnetic. They explained to me that we have no such process for accomplishing this feat. One can just imagine the scene of all these scientists crowded into one small laboratory room and looking in amazement at this new data.

We are still performing tests on Tim's object and will continue to do so for some time to come. The usual problems revolving around the financial support to do this research are the main factors that cause us to move so slowly.

5.

"WHY"

Why are abductions occurring and why are some of the abducted individuals apparently implanted with sophisticated nanotech devices? That is the question of the Millennium and I believe that my research has recently begun to show me the answer.

If we look at UFO visitation throughout history we find that these events have been occurring for thousands of years. If it is true and we accept the Sumerian record being accurate, such as described by Zacheria Sitchen, then we must accept that WE (The Human Race) are the result of a genetic manipulation which took place hundreds of thousands of years ago. If this hypothesis can be accepted then its next extension would be that we were not abandoned but have been continuously genetically manipulated though consciousness past history. There are many significant indications showing that human abductions have also taken place in the far past. Many abductees have been shown cataclysmic events taking place on this planet. In addition they have been shown how our own disregard for nature and each other continues to wreak havoc not only on the planet itself but also with possible extensions into space itself. Perhaps our counselors are continuing to genetically manipulate us in a manner that will expand our consciousness giving us abilities to survive not only our treatment of each other but coming earth changes. If that premise is true then what follows appears as a new problem for both the abductor and the abductee.

As our consciousness begins to expand, we then become more aware of all that is around us including our sensitivities. As this progresses we then begin to recognize that something is taking place which is not understood or accepted and that is the awareness of the abduction itself. Henceforth, a new problem arises for both the abductor and the abductee. This might also explain why so many abductees have screen memories, which are apparently artificially induced acceptable memories to mask the abduction itself. Perhaps this is the abductor's way of solving their new found problem of leak through memories in their victims.

But what has all this have to do with implantation? I would approximate only about 15% of the abductee population has some form of an implant. If these objects are a form of Nanotechnology that convey information from the abductee to the abductor then it is my opinion that only a small percentage is sufficient to allow a significant data sample that is collected to satisfy their needs. I have come to believe that the knowledge they are obtaining has to due with the progress of our genetic changes.

Now, the proof of the pudding is in the eating. I would like to suggest that this proof is easily demonstrated in the children born within the last forty to fifty years. I truly believe these are not the same children as those born over fifty years ago and represent a new race of human. My studies have shown that in the past forty years certain childhood developmental traits have had their clocks twisted far out of proportion to the evolutionary timetable. I will now present a few examples of statistics to prove the point:

Developmental Comparison Table

1947	1987
1. Sits with propping	
6 mo	5 mo
2. Turns head 45 Degrees	
6 m	2 mo
3. Responds to "NO"	
24 mo	8 mo
4. Obeys Commands	
60 mo	12 mo

Please note that over a forty year period the developing offspring in reference to number 1 had a reduced developmental time of 16.67%, number 2 66.67%, number 3 66.67%, and in number 4, 80.00%. These above figures only represent a small portion of the seventeen functional growth characteristics that if have graphed and studied. I have found that in my travels around the world that these figures remain constant. There is little doubt in my mind that this is a global condition which in many ways eliminates numbers of environmental factors and points to direct genetic intervention. Please remember that these figures are only the tip of the iceberg. Think about the children you know and try and recall what phenomenal things they can do or have done. Think about what statements they have articulated to you that made you stand with your mouth wide open, thinking, where did he or she get that from?

QUESTION: ARE OUR CHILDREN A DIFFERENT HUMAN SPECIES???????

6.

SURGERY NUMBER 10

Of the ten surgeries performed so far, I feel this one is probably the most unusual of them all. Even the circumstances surrounding this procedure were most unusual and thought provoking. When I began this research project I took great pains to originally establish a strict set of criteria and protocols. This would insure adherence to the scientific method of research. I found the scientific intrigue so compelling in this case, I literally through the established principals to the wind just to be able to perform this procedure.

The surgical procedure was performed on October 29, 2001. Our patient was a lady in her mid forties who was an airline stewardess working for a major U.S. airline. She made contact with me about three weeks before the surgery was performed.

I received a telephone call late one busy afternoon. The office was crowded with patients and I had little time for casual phone calls. In the midst this beehive of activity my secretary popped into the treatment room and informed me I had a lady by the name of Judy waiting on the line to talk with me. I asked, "Judy, who?" She informed me she didn't ask her last name because the lady had inferred she knew me. "Please ask her what her last name is and find out what this is in reference to." I barked, in a slightly less than patient manner. She shut the door and I continued on with my routine. Just as I was finishing up she opened the door and sheepishly volunteered the information pertaining to the waiting phone call. I didn't recognize the last name of the caller but my curiosity was peaked when I was told the call pertained to a possible alien implant. I glanced quickly at my secretary, grabbed the patient's chart, took leave and left the room. "Did she give you any details of what this thing is or any other information that might make me think this is a legitimate case?" I asked. "No, I really didn't feel it was my place to pry into her affairs. I thought she might want to talk only to you about it." She replied. I turned and walked toward my private office. "I will take the call in here. Please tell the next patient I will be with them shortly." I commanded. I approached my desk, sat down in the plush leather chair, picked up the receiver and spoke quietly into the phone, "This is Dr. Leir, can I help you?" A small but bold female voice answered, "Yes, my name is Judy Dench and I hope I am not bothering you. It took a great deal of courage for me to finally get in touch with you and now I have you on the phone I just don't know where to begin." I told her to please relax and take her time. She went on to explain she was suspicious she might have an alien implant in her right arm. I asked her about how long she thought it was there. She told me she guessed about 20 years. I asked her to describe it and was told it was about the size of a small pea and firm to the touch. At this point my scientific background took over and I began to picture this object in my minds eye. I came to the conclusion it was probably nothing more than some kind of cyst. I inquired about how much pain it was causing and was told it only hurt occasionally but just knowing it was there caused a great deal of psychological distress. At this point I had made up my mind this was not the type of case that fit any of my criteria or protocols and was about to gently discontinue the conversation. Fortunately I did not do this. Instead I asked if she had any UFO experiences. To this she replied there was only one experience that was possibly related but she was not sure it could even be classified as a genuine UFO experience. Suddenly, she told me something that sent an instant shock wave through my psyche. "Dr. Leir, did I tell you this thing bothers me the most when it moves around in my arm?" There was more than the proverbial pregnant pause. I almost dropped the phone. "What do you mean by that statement?" I asked. "Well, when I reach up with my finger and touch the object, it just scoots away. It looks really weird under the skin when it does that and I just can't stand it any more. I need it removed." She complained.

It took me a few seconds to compose myself and I asked Judy if she would be willing to come to my office and let me look at it. I also asked where she lived and to my surprise she was not far away from my office. I was pleased and excited when she agreed to come. I inquired if she had ever had an x-ray taken of it. She told me she had not. I advised her to hang on for just a moment and told her my secretary would make her an appointment. I scooted across the floor in my desk chair, opened the door and yelled for my secretary to come in. Judy was given an appointment, making sure we had obtained her contact information. There was no way I was going to lose this case. I did the utmost to compose myself and ran off to see the next patient and complete my day.

Almost a full week passed. I was engaged in the busy office routine. About two o'clock in the afternoon I was told by my back office assistant I had a patient waiting for me who was not a foot case. I knew immediately who she was referring to. "Please put her in treatment number one." I asked.

My secretary had made a file on this patient which was tailored toward an interview with an abductee. It was sitting in the chart holder outside the examining room door. Sitting on the treatment table was a blonde lady who appeared to be in her late forties. I walked over, stuck out my hand and said, "Hi Judy, I'm Dr. Leir. It's a real pleasure to meet you. How was your trip to Thousand Oaks? Did you have any trouble finding the office?" She looked at me with a smile and told me she had no problem with my directions and was happy to be there. I was so impatient to see the object in her arm I got right to the point. "Judy, which arm did you say the object was in?" I asked bluntly. With that, she reached over and rolled up her right sleeve. "Here it is, right here." she commented. I walked closer and held her arm up to the examination light so I could get a good view. About two inches above the elbow was a lump which stood out from the skin quite prominently. "Is this the object you are referring to?" I asked. "Yes, that's it all right. I am tired of looking at it. It has been there for about twenty years and it is time for it to come out." Her face was covered with a look of determination. I told her I was going to palpate the object and attempt to get it to move. She nodded with approval. I took the index finger of my right hand and slowly approached the object. I very gently touched the side of the nodule and suddenly it shot across the arm to another spot. I stood there frozen in shock and silence. My mind was racing for the most logical medical reason it would perform in this manner. "Perhaps this a cyst formed as the result of an old infection. Sometimes conditions like this can be caused by a canal that forms under the skin called a sinus tract. If this was the case and I stimulated it from the other direction, then it should move right back to where it was originally." My thought process concluded. I reached over again and touched the object. I soon found my original theory to be totally wrong. Instead of moving back to where the object started, it just slithered to a completely different spot. I soon found it moved anywhere it wanted to go within a 2-1/2 inch diameter circle. This was strangest subcutaneous lesion I had seen anywhere in the body during my 37 years of medical practice. It literally defied all logic and reason.

It was at this point I became convinced this object was certainly some kind of anomaly but was not sure it related to the alien abduction phenomena. I had remembered in our original conversation on the phone Judy had told me she only could recall one episode that might demonstrate a relationship.

I told Judy to just relax and advised her I was going to ask some questions. I began to ask her common abduction historical questions, much the same as I had done in the other cases. I kept a written note of her answers, tallying up the pluses and minuses. It seemed she might be an abductee after all. "Judy could you please relate to me the incident that gave you the impression you were involved with alien abduction?" I asked in a gentle manner. Her story was as follows:

JUDY'S EVENT

Judy explained she was engaged to be married about twenty years ago. Both she and her intended came home after an evening out on the town. They were both tired and proceeded directly to bed. She told me she was sound asleep when, for some unknown reason she suddenly awoke. Rubbing her sleep filled eyes she noted the room was filled with a very bright bluish-white light. It occupied the entire room and seemed to be coming from directly outside of her bedroom window. She reached across the covers and tried to wake her companion. She tried several times and told me he would not wake up. When she thought about this incident at a later date she had convinced herself he was the soundest sleeper she had ever seen. When she realized she could not wake him she decided to get out of bed and investigate the source of the bright light. She planted her feet firmly on the floor, stood up and slowly walked over to the bedroom window. Yes, she found the source of the light. It was coming from a hovering, circular craft that seemed to be just on the other side of her window. She told me the craft was about the size of a round school bus and seemed suspended in the sky. She observed it appeared metallic with no distinct markings or structural appendages. She did not see any windows nor did she hear any noise. She noted it was not like anything she had ever seen before, certainly not a helicopter or other form of flying craft she was used to seeing. She told me the light was all encompassing and seemed to penetrate every nook and cranny of her bedroom. Suddenly her explanation came to an abrupt halt. I waited for her to continue but at that moment she sat quietly and appeared to be staring into space. I turned to her and said, "Please continue Judy." She looked directly at me and told me she had nothing more to tell. That was the end of the episode. The next thing she recalled was waking up in the morning and feeling sick, almost like she had the flu. There were muscle aches and pains. Her skin was very dry and she felt slightly nauseated. In addition she was extremely thirsty. She got out of bed, went to the bathroom and peered into the mirror. She explained she thought she looked terrible, with bags under her eyes and looking as if she aged over night. She reached for a glass and filled it with water, put the glass to her lips and gulped the contents. She repeated this several times until her thirst was finally quenched. The more she stood there the worse she felt and decided at this point she would go back to bed. Sometime before she woke again, her friend had gotten up and left. She told me they had never talked with each other after the incident. She painfully got out of bed and decided to take a shower. As she applied the soap to her body she noticed there was a lump in her right arm. She had no recollection of anything like that ever being there before and was mystified. She reached over with her left hand and touched the object. She almost fell in the shower when she saw the object move.

About three years later she met her current husband. After almost seventeen years of marriage they never discussed this incident. She made it a point to tell me she had not discussed this with anyone. I was the first.

I inquired as how she heard about me. She explained that about three years ago she had a friend who asked if she wanted to accompany her to a lecture I was giving in the eastern United States. She thought it crazy but was intrigued by the subject. She listened intently to what I had to say but found no personal interest. She had obtained my address and telephone number at that time, kept it all those years and after much thought finally decided to call me.

By the time my initial examination was over I was very excited about her case. I asked her if the object caused her any pain. Her response was really not clear. She told me sometimes when it moved she could feeling what she called a "Creepy" or "Crawly" feeling under the skin and it bothered her very much. She also told me, it caused her psychological distress because she knew the object was there and because it moved when she touched it.

At that point I felt as she had met another one of the criteria for implant removal surgery. I asked her point blank, if she wanted it removed. She told me this was her wish, so I piped up and offered my services. What she told me next was also shocking and through me for a loop. She went on to explain she had already made arrangements with a surgeon in the San Fernando Valley to have the object removed. She continued by telling me the surgery date was coming up next week.

I knew at that point I had to do something fast if I was going to obtain any knowledge from this case at all. I asked her if she would mind if I was there when the surgery was performed. She told me she would be glad to have me there. I also offered to video the procedure and she voiced no objection to that also. Then I asked her the big one. "Do you suppose they would let me have the object after it was removed, so I might have the pathology done for them?" She told me she could only call her Dr. and ask about my requests. I thanked her, wished her luck and told her I would see her on the day of the surgery. She promised she would call me as soon as she spoke to her doctor.

That night I had a very restless night. Judy's case rolled over and over in my mind. It was a wonderful opportunity to retrieve more knowledge and I was afraid it was all going to slip away from me.

It was the very next day when I received a call from Judy. She told everything had been arranged with her surgeon and I could be there to film the procedure and also they would let me have the specimen. I was relieved and overjoyed. She gave me the date and time of the surgery. The procedure was going to be done in the Motion Picture Hospital, located in the San Fernando Valley. I had been there several times in the past. I called my office and had my secretary make notation of the time and date.

The days passed quickly. I arrived at the hospital early in order to meet Judy's surgeon and ask him some questions. I entered the hospital and made my way to the reception area. I was asked to wait in the waiting area until the Dr. came to get me. I carried my camera bag over my shoulder and settled into a comfortable stuffed chair. About ten minutes passed when I saw an older gentleman wearing a long white lab coat approaching me. He stopped at the reception desk and I overheard them mention my name. With that, I rose and walked over to greet him. "Dr. Soder, I'm Dr. Leir." We shook hands. I got right to the point and asked him if he had any x-rays of the object in Judy's arm. He told me he did not but if I insisted on having an x-ray taken, he would send her down to radiology and have one taken. I explained my thinking about these types of foreign bodies and he agreed to order the x-ray as soon as the patient arrived. He told me to have a seat and wait for the patient. This I gladly did without complaint.

I sat there nervously watching the clock. The patient was now five minutes late and it seemed to me more like an hour. As I thumbed through a magazine I kept glancing out of the corner of my eye to the individuals I saw coming down the hall. The minutes dragged by. The patient was now over a half an hour late. I got up and walked to the reception desk. The receptionist was very friendly and I engaged her in some light conversation. At one point I suggested she might try and call the patient to try and find out the reason she was late for her appointment. This very cooperative individual did just as I suggested. I could overhear the conversation and I surmised who ever it was on the other end of the line must have been telling her that Judy left some time ago. The receptionist confirmed what I had overheard.

I took up my look out point once again in the soft, comfortable chair I was in previously. I could not help but continue to glance at my watch. I was just about to question the receptionist again when I saw Judy hurrying down the hall. She rushed up to the reception desk and apologized over and over again for her tardiness. I arose from my chair and greeted her with a friendly greeting. I told her I had met her surgeon and as far as I knew everything was still a-okay. The receptionist asked us to both have a seat and informed us she would let the doctor know the patient was here. Only a few minutes went by when she came over to us and asked us to follow her. We proceeded to walk down a long hallway and followed her into a large typical examining room. I could not figure out whether this was the room where she was going to have her surgery or just be examined by the Dr. again. Judy and I chatted for a few moments, the door swung open and Dr. Soder entered the room. They exchanged greetings and she apologized for being late. He informed her I had requested an x-ray and explained he had made arrangement for her to go to radiology and have one taken. I asked him if I could accompany her and he told us there would be no problem. He gave us directions and together we walked through a number of intersecting hallways until we saw the sign, "Radiology". Judy approached the receptionist and filled out a short form. She was asked to take a seat and wait until her name was called. It took about twenty minutes until she was finally called. I wished her luck and picked a copy of Modern Romance magazine to look through. This was not my type of reading but was the only one available at the time. About ten more minutes went by and she was back. I asked her if they read the x-ray and she told me she didn't ask.   We arrived back at the original treatment room, went in and waited. Soon a nurse came in and informed us the Dr. would be there shortly. I looked at my watch and realized I had spent most of the day just waiting. I decided to keep this thought to myself. Suddenly the door flew open and the Dr. made is presence known. He told us he had talked with the radiologist and no foreign body was seen in the x-rays. hat was disappointing news to me but had I any inclining of what was about to happen next I would have probably turned a somersault.

The doctors beeper went off and he excused himself, leaving the room at a hurried pace. He was soon back and asked me to please step outside. I looked at Judy, turned and followed the surgeon into the hallway. He calmly told me he had just gotten some bad news from the administrative office. He explained to me he was told I could not film the surgery, and in addition I could not take the specimen to have it analyzed. I asked if I could at least be present during the procedure. He nodded his head and told me he was sure that would be all right.

I had no way of knowing, at that point that a surprising cascade of unseen events were about to unfold.

I followed the doctor back into the treatment room. Judy was still sitting on the table and a nurse was conversing with her. Dr. Soder pulled his hand out of his pocket, peered at is wristwatch and shook his head. He turned to Judy and said, "I am really sorry to have to tell you this, but I have to be in a meeting in one half hour. Being that is the case, I won't have time to do your procedure today." Judy's face turned bright red. She explained to him this was the only day she could have this surgery done because she was leaving in a few days on a flight to New York. The surgeon told her the best to time reschedule the procedure would be in a few weeks. He advised her to see the main receptionist to make another appointment.

I was probably as shocked as Judy was. I could see how disappointed she was and knew how much courage it must have taken to have her mind finally made up to have the surgery performed and then to have it canceled at the last minute. I turned to her and told her my feelings about the matter. Then it suddenly occurred to me there was an opportunity that had just presented itself. I asked her about having my surgical team do the procedure instead. She told me she was concerned because her insurance would only pay the bill if it was done in that facility. I assured her there was no charge ever made for any of the candidates in our research project. She looked at me with a surprised look and asked, "Do you mean to tell me you guys don't charge for anything? I reassured her there would be no charges for anything we do including all the lab analysis of the specimen following the surgery. She explained her tight time schedule and how she was committed to leave on a flight to New York on Friday. "Judy, if go back to my office and can arrange for all this to be done tomorrow, will you let us do it?" She looked at me with an engaging expression and calmly said, "Yes I will."

I called my secretary from my cell phone and told her to cancel most of my afternoon. I realized I would probably be on the telephone all the rest of the day.

This was a golden opportunity and I was bound and determined to make it work.

Just as I expected I spent most of the day talking on the phone. I not only had to arrange for the surgery itself but all the other peripheral elements that went along with it, including getting a professional videographer there to record the procedure.

Luck was holding true. By 5:00PM, I was making the last phone call. It was to Judy. I told her on the phone the surgery was all arranged and the procedure would be done at 10:00AM in the morning. I instructed her to bring all her medical records because the surgeon would need to review them prior to performing the procedure.

I had also arranged for someone to stop at the Motion Picture Hospital and pick up the x-rays. If indeed, there was no foreign body evident I would be violating one of my own established protocols. This was a risk I was going to have to take and felt it was justified.

It was now the following day, October 29, 2001. The surgery was scheduled for 10:00AM. I arrived at the surgeons office at 8:00AM to make sure all was in place and ready at the appointed hour. Because of time constraints involved in this case I was not able to use all the complex procedures that had been involved in the previous surgeries. There were no special invitations to witnesses, no catered lunches, no observation room monitors and no specialized equipment rented. There were just the basic essentials. We had our general surgeon, our specially trained operating room nurse, the basic equipment needed for the procedure and a professional camera man and his assistant to record the procedure. All personnel arrived without a hitch. Soon the patient was there and was introduced to Dr. Minor, the general surgeon we were using for this procedure. He examined the patient and reviewed her medical records. Since she had been previously scheduled for a surgery and because of this had all the required lab tests performed which turned to be all in the normal range. I reviewed her x-rays and also concluded there was no visible foreign body present.

The actual procedure itself was the least important aspect of this case. It was a relatively easy procedure with the exception of the fact the surgeon was required physically trap the object between two fingers in order to stop it from moving out of the way. One of the other most unusual gross findings was that the object itself did not seem to be attached to any of the surrounding tissues. It just popped into view, was clamped and removed. It appeared about the size of a pea and was a bright yellow in color. When inspected the object closely we noticed the outside coating was very smooth and noted the object was really composed of two halves connected on one side like a clam or bivalve. We could physically open up the object and pull the two halves apart. When this pressure was removed they closed again by themselves. On the upper edges we noticed a dark line, very uniform on the upper edge of each side. Exploration of the subcutaneous tissues did not give us a clue as to how this object was able to move about under the skin.

The patient seemed overjoyed the object had been removed. The following day she left on her appointed flight to New York without any physical or psychological problems. I have seen her several times following the procedure. She has a small scar in the area but no pain or other discomfort. I have asked her a number of times if she was interested in learning more about her abduction background with regressive hypnosis but she has not yet made up her mind. I also advised her that after we have collected some scientific data on the object we will give it to her and maybe it would help her to make a decision.

To date, we have not had the funds to do much analysis. A laboratory we had used in the past has looked at the object through the Atomic Force Microscope and Optical Microscope. The biologist at the laboratory stated she had never seen anything like this before. We also discovered that on one edge of the object were some small egg-like sacs, which were very similar to the sacs seen on the previous specimen. The previous sacs were filled with an unknown oil. We plan to continue an in depth investigation of this object and make the findings known at a later date.

With ten surgeries performed to date we have garnered a great deal of scientific information. Some of our questions have been answered but almost as soon as we understand one aspect, many more questions are raised. I have no personal doubt as to whether the human race is being tampered with by a non earthly civilization. It is happening as you are reading this material and is worldwide.

Appendix 1:

Biological Analysis Reports

In the following reports, the patients real names and the specific addresses and names of researchers and laboratories have been removed to protect anonymity. Persons interested in pursuing the details further may contact the author through the publisher. Research is on-going, and future reports may be available from other sources

HEALTH LINE CLINICAL LABORATORIES, INC   PAGE: 1

2249 N. Hollywood Way • Burbank, CA 91505 • Tel: (818) 954-0202 • 1-800-954-4588 • Fax: (818) 954-8895
Director and Pathologist: William W. Temple, M.D.
Laboratory Director: Gary L. Burkhartsmeier, HCLD

LABORATORY REPORT

	COLLECTED	RECEIVED	REPORTED
	02/17/2000	02/18/2000	03/01/2000

HLC-

CLIENT:
ROGER LEIR, M.D.
253 LOMBARD ST.
SUITE B
THOUSAND OAKS, CA 91360

HL00-01796

100625

PATIENT

AGE	SEX	PATIENT ID	01176407
DOB	M	ACCESSION	
PHYSICIAN			

Procedure	Outside of Reference Range	Within Range Result	Reference Range	Units

PATHOLOGY REPORT
  CLINICAL IMPRESSION / HX.
    NONE PROVIDED
  SPECIMEN / BIOPSY SITE
    SOFT TISSUE

ADDENDUM REPORT

GROSS DESCRIPTION:
  THE SPECIMEN CONSISTS OF TWO FRAGMENTS OF FATTY TISSUE
  MEASURING 0.6 CC AS AN AGGREGATE, TOTALLY EMBEDDED IN ONE
  CASSETTE.
MICROSCOPIC DESCRIPTION
  SECTIONS SHOW TWO PARTIALLY ROUNDED NODULES OF BENIGN
  FATTY TISSUE. BETWEEN THESE TWO NODULES IS AN AREA OF
  FIBROSIS. THIS AREA OF FIBROSIS CONTAINS SOME SMALL NERVE
  BUNDLES. THERE IS NO SIGNIFICANT INFLAMMATION AND NO
  GIANT CELLS ARE IDENTIFIED.
MICROSCOPIC DIAGNOSIS:
  BENIGN FATTY TISSUE WITH ADJACENT FIBROSIS, NO SIGNIFICANT
  INFLAMMATION (INCLUDING GIANT CELLS) IDENTIFIED

WILLIAM W. TEMPLE, M.D.
SIGNATURE ON FILE

FINAL   03/01/2000   01176407

Pathology Report Indicating
Nerve Tissue and Lack of Inflammation

INTERNATIONAL COLLEGE OF SURGEONS
United States Section

OVERNOR, INTERNATIONAL
OLLEGE OF SURGEONS

RNO A. ROSCHER, M.D.
C.A.P., F.A.S.C.P., F.I.C.S.
iplomal American Board of Pathology

LINICAL PROFESSOR OF PATHOLOGY
niversity of Southern California
os Angeles, California - U.S.A.

DIRECTOR OF PATHOLOGY & LABORATORY MEDICINE
Henry Mayo Newhall Memorial Hospital and
Granada Hills Community Hospital

10445 Balboa Blvd., Granada Hills, CA 91344
Phone (818) 831-6810 Fax (818) 360-8452

SURGICAL PATHOLOGY CONSULTATION

PATIENT:
TISSUE #:   S-1404-98
DATE RECEIVED: 8-25-98

SUMMARY CONCLUSION:

Specimen "A" and "B" represent soft tissue from the surgery performed.
Tissue removed is fibrocapsular tissue, fatty tissue, nerve trunk tissue
and interstitial fibrous connective tissue showing hemosiderin.

The absence of an overt inflammatory process and the absence of foreign-
body reaction is indicative that the structure removed from the hand is
of unknown nature at this time. The absence of a reactive inflammatory
process, acute, chronic and/or foreign-body, is indicative that the
structure must be rather inert not to elicit a foreign-body response.

Further determination of this structure is forthcoming through the
utilization of X-ray defraction pattern, atomic absorption spectro-
photometry, as well as possible electronmicroscopy. Immune marker
pathology on the tissue removed appears unlikely to yield any additional
findings.

AAR:jg
9-18-98

Pathologist
Arno A. Roscher, M.D.

(3)

FOUNDED IN GENEVA, SWITZERLAND, INCORPORATED IN WASHINGTON, DC ◆ A WORLD FEDERATION OF GENERAL SURGEONS AND SURGICAL SPECIALISTS, INC.

Pathology Report Indicating
No Inflammation

212 The Aliens and the Scalpel

Biopsy Report

REVISED REPORT

NAME: �_____   Age: 47   Sex: F
Roger Leir, DPM   95-MN-10884R   Recd: 8/22/95
Thousand Oaks, CA

SPECIMEN: BIOPSY, DORSUM OF LEFT HAND ADJACENT TO
                 FOREIGN BODY

GROSS: The specimen consists of two fragments of soft tissue ranging from 3 to
5 mm. The specimen is submitted in its entirety for microscopic examination.
WMG/pcs

MICROSCOPIC: Sections show minute portions of fibroadipose tissue. The stroma
focally exhibits macrophages with brownish granular pigment and mononuclear cells. No
malignancy is seen. Iron stain is positive. Melanin stain is negative. No acute or chronic
inflammation is present.

DIAGNOSIS: FIBROADIPOSE AND COLLAGENOUS TISSUE WITH FOCAL
                 RECENT AND OLD HEMORRHAGE. NO INFLAMMATION IS
                 PRESENT (DORSUM OF LEFT HAND).

REJ/pcs
File
8/25/95

Pathology Report Indicating
No Inflammatory Response to Foreign Body

Biopsy Report

NAME: ████████████
Roger Leir, DPM
Thousand Oaks, CA

Age: 47
95-MN-12444

Sex: M
Rec'd: 10-06-95

SPECIMEN: LESION, LEFT HAND

GROSS: The specimen consists of a 0.3 x 0.2 x 0.1 cm brown and tan shred of
tissue. The specimen is fully embedded.
REJ/eb

MICROSCOPIC: Sections show a strip of dense, eosinophilic fibrillary material
containing rare portions of superficial, degenerated epidermis and scattered, amber brown
pigment granules. No malignancy is identified. An iron stain confirms the presence of
hemosiderin.

DIAGNOSIS: LESION, LEFT HAND: PROTEINACEOUS COAGULUM
SUPERFICIAL DEGENERATED EPIDERMIS AND
HEMOSIDERIN.

GNP/eb
File
10/10/95

Pathology Report on Tissue Composing Membrane
Surrounding Metallic Object Removed from Hand

Biopsy Report

NAME: ██████████   Age: 52   Sex: F
Roger Leir, DPM   95-MN-12445   Rec'd: 10-06-95
Thousand Oaks, CA

SPECIMEN: LESION, FOOT

GROSS: The specimen consists of a 0.3 x 0.1 x 0.1 cm irregular piece of dull,
brown tissue along with a similar piece half that size. Both parts are submitted.
REJ/eb

MICROSCOPIC: Sections show a curved piece of proteinaceous, eosinophilic coagulum
admixed with keratinous material and coarse, amber brown granules. No malignancy is
identified. An iron stain confirms the presence of hemosiderin.

DIAGNOSIS: LESION, FOOT: KERATIN, PROTEINACEOUS COAGULUM
                  AND HEMOSIDERIN.

GNP/eb
File
10/10/95

Pathology Report Also Showing Composition of Membrane Srrounding Metallic Object Removed from Body

psy Report

NAME: ██████████   Age: 52   Sex: F
Dr. Roger K. Leir   95-MN-10911   Rec'd: 8-22-95
Thousand Oaks, CA

SPECIMEN: LESION, FOOT

GROSS: The specimen consists of eight tan irregular tan fragments measuring up
to 0.7 cm. The specimen is fully embedded.
REJ/e

MICROSCOPIC: Fragments of fibroconnective tissue and fat demonstrating peripheral
nerve and pressure receptors. The peripheral nerve segments show perineural fibrosis. There
are included fragments of hyperkeratotic stratum corneum. No foreign material is identified
by either plain or polarized light, except for a few small polarizing fragments with the
appearance of cotton fibers. No inflammation is present, and there are no atypical cell
changes.

DIAGNOSIS: 1)   PERIPHERAL NERVES WITH MILD PERINEURAL
                      FIBROSIS.
                2)   FAT, FIBROCONNECTIVE TISSUE, AND SKIN - NO
                      DIAGNOSTIC CHANGES (TISSUE FROM FOOT
                      ADJACENT TO FOREIGN BODY).

REJ/eb
File
MN
08/23/95

Pathology Report Indicating
Nerve Tissue in Surrounding Soft Tissue

Affidavit
Of
Custody of Foreign Object

Now comes **Dr. Roger K. Leir, DPM**, a person above the age of majority and a resident of and domiciled in the State of California and who does state, as follows:

1. That he is a medical doctor licensed in the State of California and at all times material was the physician to Timothy Lloyd Cullen and in particular was Mr. Cullen's physician on Saturday, February 5, 2000;

2. That his patient, Mr. Cullen, underwent a surgical procedure by a licensed general surgeon on Saturday, February 5, 2000 for the removal of an anomalous foreign object in Mr. Cullen's left forearm;

3. That the general surgeon did remove said anomalous object which was imaged by the C-Arm device as shown below:

4. That the general surgeon removed the object and placed the same in a plastic container along with small amounts of the patient's blood products and tissue and immediately thereafter handed the container to affiant;

5. That he has maintained custody, care and supervision of the container and its contents from that time forward and shall remain said custodian in the future;

Typical Affidavit Signed by Patient
Prior to Surgery

6. That the above facts are true and correct to the best of his knowledge information and belief.

_____

Dr. Roger K. Leir, DPM
Affiant

Sworn to and subscribed before me, Notary, on this 5th day of February 2000.

_____

Notary

Appendix 2:

Metallurgical Data

The University of Texas ★ San Antonio
Division of Earth and Physical Sciences

UTSA

September 14, 1998

6767 Forest Lawn Drive, Suite 100
Los Angeles, California 90068

Dear Mr.

On August 31, 1998, an unknown sample was given me for XRD analysis by you and Mr. Whitly Strieber. The sample was approximately 5-7 mm by 3-6 mm in size and somewhat rounded. We tried several runs on the XRD unit by setting the sample only on a glass slide. This yielded no major peaks, only background counts. It was then decided to crush the sample in a mortar and pestle. The sample turned out to be very hard, with only the surface coating being removed. This powder was ground as fine as possible and placed on a glass slide. Again, no major peaks were observed, only background counts. The sample was reoriented and run again, with one peak being observed at 2.454 Å (Sample rks100, see figure). Additional powder was added to the glass slide and the sample run a fifth time, but with no peaks being observed (Sample rks101). On September 1, 1998, I mixed the powder with 95% ethyl alcohol making a slurry on the glass slide and letting it dry. This dried slurry was then run and again no major peaks were observed, only background counts (Sample rks102, see figure). This same sample was run an additional two times. For each XRD run no major peaks were observed, only background counts (Samples rks 103 and 104, see figures). I then ran a single glass slide to compare the XRD traces (Sample rks 200, see figure). In all cases there is only background counts observed, except for Sample rks100. However, this peak could never be repeated in the additional runs.

It is my conclusion therefore, that the powdered material collected from the unknown sample is amorphous and therefore lacks any internal ordered arrangement of atoms or ions. The one x-ray peak located at 2.454 Å in Sample rks100 was not observed in subsequent XRD runs. I am not sure what to say about that, except that it may have been a piece of dust or some other foreign object on the slide during that one particular XRD run. Additionally, all the XRD traces look very similar to the one XRD trace for the glass slide. The Scintag XRD 2000 x-ray unit with the Peltier detector is a very sensitive system and would show most convincingly if an internal ordered structure existed for the unknown powder.

Best regards,

R. K. Smith, Ph.D.
Professor of Geology

6900 North Loop 1604 West ● San Antonio, Texas 78249-0663 ● (210) 458-4455 ● (210) 458-4469 fax

Metallurgy — Report Indicating Iron is Amorphous

Letter of Opinion (Samples T1,2 and T3)

The first theory on the origin of these samples was initiated due to the relatively high hardness value obtained for the iron core of sample T1,2. It is well known that very hard iron alloys can be found naturally in meteorite samples. In fact, several characteristics of the specimens are similar to certain meteorite-type materials. Meteorites can be a complex combination of many different elements (see for example, McSween, 1987). This is the case particularly for sample T3, which contains at the very least 11 elements: Na, Al, Si, P, Cl, Ca, Fe, Ni, Cu, Mo & Sn. Typical of iron and stony-iron meteorites is the classic "Widmanstatten structure", consisting of lamelae (plate or needle-shaped crystals) of kamacite (α-iron) and/or taenite (γ-iron), formed during the slow cooling of meteoroids [McSween, 1987; Budka et al., 1996]. Interspersed with the metal grains are other minerals rich in iron and/or nickel such as troilite, FeS, and schreibersite, $(Fe,Ni)_3P$. Based on my examination, the samples in question could possibly fit into this framework. Elemental analysis done by X-ray Energy Dispersive Spectroscopy (EDS) indicated iron and phosphorous as major constituents of the cladding material surrounding the iron core. The (EDS) patterns resemble those recently reported for iron dendrites found in pockets and veins of the Yanshuang H6 meteorite [Brooks, et. al., 1995]. In addition, I identified a calcium phosphate mineral as a possible phase within the cladding of both samples. Interestingly, chlorapatite, $Ca_3(PO_4)_3Cl$ is among the more common meteorite minerals [Wasson, 1974]. This would account for the presence of a substantial amount of calcium and smaller amount of chlorine detected. A problem with this theory, however, is that no nickel was detected in T1,2 and only a minute amount in T3. It has been stated that "most meteorites contain between 6 and 10 percent nickel" ... and "no iron meteorites contain less than five percent nickel" [McSween, 1987]. This may not be a problem after all, since the specimens could be just a small fragment of a larger meteorite body.

Brooks, C.R., N.E. Biery, L. Zhaohui, X.Xiande, and Z. Datong, "Surface Morphology of Iron Dendrites in the Yanzhuang H6 Meteorite", *Mat. Charact.* 35 p.165 (1995).

Budka, P.Z., J.R.M. Vierti, and S.V. Thamboo, "Meteorites and the Iron-Nickel Phase Diagram", *Adv. Mat. & Processes*, p.27 (July 1996).

Hench, L.L., "Bioceramics: from Concept to Clinic", *Amer. Ceram. Soc. Bull.* 72 [4] p. 93 (1987).

McSween, H.Y., Meteorites and their parent planets, Cambridge Univ. Press (1987).

Wasson, J.T., Meteorites, Classification and Properties, ed. P.J. Wyllie, Springer-Verlag, (1974).

Letter of Opinion from New Mexico Tech

National Institute for Discovery Science

4 June 96

Dr. Roger Leir
1155 E. Thousand Oaks Blvd.
Thousand Oaks, CA 91360

Dear Dr. Leir;

This letter is a necessary formality and a follow-up to the copy of the results we sent you regarding the testing of your material samples. As we made clear in our conversations, NIDS does not intend to release data until it meets scientifically acceptable standards. This letter provides our position about the current status of initial testing.

The samples were subjected to laser induced breakdown spectroscopy (LIBS) to determine the chemical composition of the exposed surface. To preserve the sample, no internal or destructive tests were done.

We feel that the test results speak for themselves. However, due to the preliminary nature of the testing, we anticipate further extensive testing and analysis. In view of this, at this point in time, it is premature to generate any public statements. We intend to proceed with a second more extensive round of testing at a second lab. With the completion of that testing a much clearer picture of the results will be available.

Sincerely,

M. W. (Pete) McDuff
Director of Operations
Aerial Phenomenology Division

1515 E. Tropicana Suite 400 • Los Vegas, NV 89119
Phone (702) 798-1700 • Fax (702) 798-1970 • EMail DiscSci@aol.com

Letter From N.I.D.S. Indicating Need for Further Testing

Let's 'talk' about the possibilities...
Sample # **RR3**, by the Nickel, Zinc and Silver ratios, may have extraterrestrial origins, but the Tungsten and Thallium ratios don't show any anomalies.
Sample # **007KT**, by the Nickel, Zinc, Ruthenium, Samarium, Europium and Tungsten ratios, may have extraterrestrial origins, but the Magnesium ratios (which have the largest signals) are consistent with earth origin.
Sample # **AL101** shows some anomalies, for example with Germanium and Tungsten, but others are inconclusive. I doubt that there is any extraterrestrial origin with this material.
Sample # **SM/DS** shows the earth origin ratios for Magnesium and Zinc. Within some small variation, the other elements which have multiple isotopes detected appear to be close to the earthly natural abundance ratios.

In Conclusion;
It is possible, but not conclusively proven, that both the **RR3** and **007KT** samples show some isotopic ratios consistent with an extraterrestrial origin. More test with a larger sample size would be required to know for sure. These samples were run without any idea of the chemical constitution of three of the samples. With the 'enclosed' data it would be possible to tailor subsequent tests to take advantage of this information.

Sincerely,

Russell VernonClark

Conclusion of Non Terrestrial Isotopes
by Dr. Russell VernonClark

Conclusions (Samples T1,2 and T3)

The samples referred to as T1,2 and T3 are not like any I have seen first-hand before. Nor are their analyses comparable to any analyses that I have previously conducted. To my knowledge, there are no such objects manufactured for any practical use. I conclude, therefore, that the specimens, in there present state, were formed via (a) natural process(es).

I found nothing particularly unusual about sample T1,2. The density fell somewhere between that of iron and that of a typical iron oxide or phosphide as expected. The needle shaped samples were magnetized along their long axis which is ordinarily the easy direction for magnetization. The one somewhat surprising characteristic was the high hardness of the iron core compared to other types of iron. The Vickers hardness value of 821 is one achieved only in high carbon tool steels, specifically formulated and heat-treated for machining applications.

Sample T3-A is a curious combination of at least 11 elements: Na, Al, Si, P, Cl, Ca, Fe, Ni, Cu, Mo & Sn.

Intermediary Non Conclusive Early Report

 **National Institute for Discovery Science**

July 25, 1996

Dr. Roger Leir
1155 East Thousand Oaks Blvd.
Thousand Oaks, CA 91360

Dear Dr. Leir:

As promised, enclosed is a copy of the results from New Mexico Tech for your review.

If you have any questions, please feel free to contact me.

Sincerely,

Robert T. Bigelow
President

RTB/db

enclosure

1515 E. Tropicana Suite 400 • Las Vegas, NV 89119
Phone (702) 798 1700 • Fax (702) 798 1970

Communication Letter From Robert Bigelow of N.I.D.S.

New Mexico Tech

July 19, 1996

Paul A. Fuierer
Materials Engineering Dept.
New Mexico Tech
Socorro, NM 87801

National Institute for Discovery Science, Inc.
1515 E. Tropicana Suite 400
Las Vegas, NV 89119

Dear Dr. Alexander,

Please find enclosed the final summary report as per the contract dated June 7 for analysis of samples T1,2 and T3. I hope it serves your purposes.

Paul A. Fuierer
Assistant Professor, Materials Engineering

Deapartment of Materials and Metallurgical Engineering • Socorro, New Mexico 87801 • (505) 835-5229 • FAX (505) 835-5626

New Mexico Tech is an Affirmative Action Equal Opportunity Institution

Letter to N.ID.S. from New Mexico Tech

Sample Description

Sample T1,2 contained two tiny rod or lamellar-shaped pieces, primarily gray-black in color with some brown-white deposits at several locations on the surface. Sample T1,2-A is approximately 4.4 mm long and 0.6 mm in diameter. Sample T1,2-B is approximately 5.75 mm long and 0.6 mm in diameter (See micrograph in Fig. 1). These two samples were observed to be rather strongly magnetized along their long axes.

Sample T3 also contained two small pieces. T3-A is long (~ 4.1 mm) and thin with an irregular geometry (see Fig. 2), while T3-B is essentially equiaxed with diameter of about 3 mm. T3-A has many interesting features visible under a 4X microscope. A yellow-white flake-like substance is attached to the surface. In the neck region of the sample there appears to be a high concentration of small, reflective aggregates with a copper-gold color. T3-B has several yellow-brown spots on the surface. T3-A was observed to be magnetized, while T3-B was not.

All samples were found to be non-conducting when the probes of a DMM were held to the surface.

Physical Properties

Density

Bulk densities of the samples were measured using an immersion technique (based on Archimedes' principle). By accurately measuring the sample mass, both dry and when submerged in a liquid of known density, one can calculate the bulk density of an unknown. In this case, toluene ($\rho = 0.862$ g/cm^3) was used rather than water to avoid any possible hydrolysis or oxidation reactions with the sample. A Sartorius precision balance was used for measurements to the nearest 0.00001 g. Mass and density values are tabulated below:

	T1,2-A	T1,2-B	T3-A	T3-B
m (g)	0.01070	0.01395	0.00657	0.00404
ρ (g/cm^3)	5.62	5.81	4.95	2.70

Despite the small size of the samples, repeatable values were obtained and are beleived to be accurate. The difference between T1,2-A and -B is probably within experimental error, and thus 5.7 g/cm^3 is taken as the bulk density of T1,2. The difference between these and T3-A is considered to be significant, suggesting some difference in material. Sample T3-B has a density roughly half that of the others.

Hardness

Two samples were chosen for hardness tests, T1,2-B and T3-B. About 1/3 of the length of T1,2-B was broken off and warm mounted in a slug for grinding and polishing utilizing standard metallographic techniques. The polished surface of the core material was highly reflecting and white-gray in color, clearly metallic in nature. While grinding through sample T3-B, a dull, black color is all that was observed, indicating the lack of a metallic core. This is in agreement with the very low density measured.

Complete Analytical Report from New Mexico Tech

Once the sample was polished to a very flat and smooth finish, a Vickers Hardness number was obtained from a Leco Tester using a diamond tip micro-indenter. Five indentations were made for each sample. The size of the resulting indentations were measured under a light microscope, and averaged. This average value, along with the known applied load were used to come up with the Vicker's Hardness number. The hardness values are tabulated below:

	Vickers	Knoop	Moh's	comparison
T1,2-B	821	821	7	SiO_2
T3-B	136	136	3	$CaCO_3$

Vickers corresponds to the Knoop hardness scale. A corresponding Moh's hardness (1-10 scale) is given for comparison. A huge difference in hardness is observed. T1,2-B is seen to be very hard, as Quartz or a very hard (carburized) tool steel. T3-B is seen to be relatively soft, as Calcite.

SEM and Chemical Analyses

Due to the small sample size, chemical analysis was limited to a qualitative analysis using X-ray Energy-Dispersive Spectroscopy (EDS)* as an auxiliary unit on a scanning electron microscope (SEM)**. The two samples T1,2-B and T3-A (shown in Figs. 1 & 2) were chosen for analysis. Since the samples were found to have an insulating outer shell, it was necessary to deposit a very thin layer of carbon (few angstroms thick) to avoid charging during imaging. Figure 3 gives the EDS analyses for various locations on sample T1,2-B. Major amounts of iron, phosphorous, and calcium, and minor amounts of chlorine were detected. The spectra shown were all obtained using a collection time of one minute. As there is virtually no difference in these spectra, it is concluded that the composition of the cladding material is uniform over the entire sample. Figure 1 (b) shows a higher mag shot of the cladding material near the central portion of the sample. The obvious cracking may be indicative of differential thermal expansion/contraction of cladding and core materials. A calcium dot map suggested an even distribution of calcium over the sampling area. A dot map taken from the protruding area on the lower left side of the sample also suggests no real preferential segregation of calcium (Figure 1(A)). Figure 1(C) shows some of the features of the surface in the divot area on the right side of the sample. This surface is a bit rougher and devoid of the clean craze-like cracks seen in Figure 1(B).

Both the microstructure and composition of sample T3-A varies tremendously across the sample. I identified primarily three different locations: the bulk region near the tip, the flaky deposit bottom right, and the neck region (Figure 2). The higher mag shot of the bulk tip region reveals a microstructure like that of sample T1,2-B; crazing-like cracks across a relatively smooth surface. The bulk tip region was found to be similar chemically as well, with major constituents Fe, Ca, and P, and minor amounts of Cl (Figure 4). However minor amounts of copper, and aluminum were also detected. The dark, bulk region near the center of the sample was found to be nearly identical.

* Tracor Northern
** Hitachi

As the difference in back-scattered intensity suggests, the "flaky" region has a very different composition and phase. It was found to contain a lesser amount of iron, with major quantities of silicon, phosphorous, molybdenum, chlorine, sodium, calcium and a trace of copper. The material may also contain a number of elements in between, since the peaks are broad and overlapping. Its microstructure seen in the higher mag shot is very interesting, the flake-like nature perhaps indicative of a layered silicate sheet structure.

The "neck" region appears to be highly metallic. EDS reveals a host of metals in addition to the major iron: copper, aluminum, tin, and nickel. The "balls" seen in the higher mag shot correspond to the gold-copper colored aggregates seen under the optical stereoscope at low mag. Individual EDS scans taken both directly on the "ball" and in the "rough" area at the center of the picture were essentially the same as Figure 4(A).

Phase Identification

X-ray Diffraction Experiments

Attempts at obtaining an x-ray diffraction (XRD) pattern from the samples using our Philips diffractometer were unsuccessful. Detection of any reflections at all from such small samples (without grinding to a powder) requires special instrumentation and conditions. Therefore, the samples were taken to an X-ray facility equiped with a state-of-the-art Siemens D-5000 diffractometer. The samples were mounted on "Zero-background" quartz slides, and scanned from 5 to 90° 2Θ at an extremely slow speed over a period of 10 hours using Cu Kα radiation. Both samples T1,2-A and -B were mounted side-by-side to maximize sample area. Sample T3-A was mounted and scanned alone. As seen from the print-out of the raw data in Figure 5, the two samples are not much different with respect to detected crystalline phases. Both T1,2 and T3 contain fairly well-defined peaks at about 21.2°, 23.6°, 28.1°, and 31.4° 2Θ. T1,2 however contains two additional peaks at about 32.2° and 53.0 ° which are significant. The broad hump at about 16° and the large rise in intensity at low angles indicates a significant quantity of amorphous phase. No reflections were detected above 60° 2Θ. Figures 6 and 7 show expanded views of the important range of angles with much of the background noise removed. The lattice spacing (d) is called out for each observed peak.

Search-match procedures were then conducted on these patterns to try and identify the specific *phases* present. A combination of the traditional hand search (Hanawalt Method) and automated search-match software (JADE 3.0) was used. The search was complicated by two factors: 1. the extremely low signal-to-noise ratio due to the small sample size, and
2. the presence of multiple phases in each sample
Despite these difficulties, a reasonable match was found for a mixture of three or four phases (see Appendix):

1. Anapaite, $Ca_2Fe(PO_4)_2 \cdot 4H_2O$
2. Goethite, $FeO(OH)$
3. Phosphorous oxide
4. γ-Iron phosphide, FeP_4

Iron phosphide may account for the two rather diffuse peaks observed in T1,2 but absent in T3.

Since the effective penetration depth of the x-rays is likely to be on the order of 25μm, most of the reflected signal is due to the cladding material rather than the core, which explains why there is no strong iron peak.

Metallography

In an attempt to learn more about the iron, or iron-alloy core of these samples, traditional metallography using an optical microscope was performed. The ground and polished cross-section of sample T1,2-B was etched using "Nital" (HNO_3 & methanol). The fact that nital etched the sample very quickly affirms the presence of an iron-rich alloy. Etching revealed a very fine (too fine to produce a good photograph) maze-like pattern of light and dark regions, reminiscent of a slowly-cooled eutectic composition. Although the microstructure did not reveal a "classic" Pearlite structure, the system is presumed to be iron-carbon, with the dark phase being perhaps cementite (Fe_3C) in a matrix of ferrite (α-Fe). A high percentage of finely dispersed carbon may account for the very high hardness (VH=821) as reported earlier. Ferrite is favored over austenite (γ-Fe) due to the fact that the sample core is apparently ferromagnetic.

Summary

Sample T1,2 can be described as needle or lamellar in shape, with a predominantly iron core and a non-conducting, dark gray-black coating. This coating or surface layer material has Fe, Ca, P, Cl and very possibly some lighter elements (ie. C, O) as its constituents. The phase analysis via x-ray diffraction was not absolutely conclusive due to the extremely small sample size, however the best fit to the obtained pattern suggests Anapaite, $Ca_2Fe(PO_4)_2.H_2O$, Goethite, $FeO(OH)$, iron phosphide, FeP_4, and phosphorus oxide, P_2O_3, as likely phases. The microstructure of the core (polished and etched) as observed under an optical microscope resembles an iron rich alloy with large amounts of carbon, probably in the form of iron carbide. The iron is likely to be α-Fe with a body-centered-cubic packing (bcc structure) since the samples are magnetized. The hardness of this core material is very high, in the neighborhood of high carbon tool steels.

Sample T3-A is a very complex mixture of materials. While the inner core is presumed to be similar to T1,2, the outer portion is comprised of a combination of many different elements and phases, depending upon the location. A majority of the cladding is the same as T1,2. However, a flake-like substance deposited on a portion of the sample is made up of Fe, Si, P, Mo, Na, and Ca. This may be some complex silicate mineral. The "neck" region of this sample may actually give a representation of the core metallic constituents: Fe, Cu, Ni, Al, & Sn. This alloy may have been oxidized for lack of protective phosphide coating. Sample T3-B was apparently a "chunk" of the amorphous/mineral cladding material with no metallic core, as evidenced by the very low density and lack of magnetization.

Returned Samples

Samples T1,2-A, and T3-A are returned in full to NIDS. Approximately 2/3 of sample T1,2-B is returned. None of T3-B is returned. These samples were ground and polished for hardness and microstructure analyses.

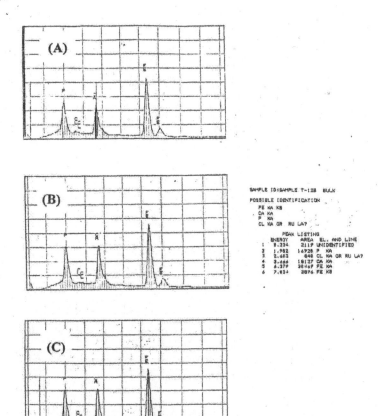

Fig. 3. EDS analyses of sample T1,2-B taken from locations labeled A, B, and C in Figure 1. Elemental composition is essentially the same over the surface of the sample.

EDS Analysis from New Mexico Tech

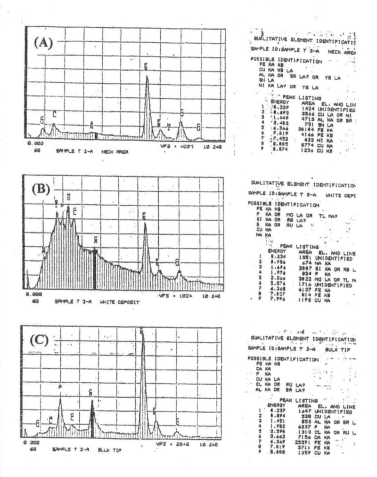

Fig. 4. EDS analyses of sample T3-A taken from locations labeled A, B, and C in Figure 2. The dark regions of the cladding are probably phosphides and/or phosphates, the flake-like deposit some complex mineral, and the neck region metallic or metal oxide.

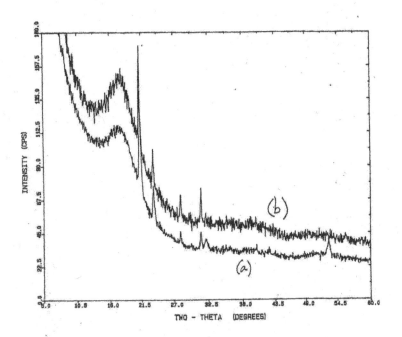

Fig. 5. X-ray diffraction (CuKα radiation) patterns obtained from (a) T1,2 and (b) T3-A. Both samples contain large amounts of amorphous phase, however some crystallinity is apparent. A majority of the signal is believed to come from the cladding material.

X-Ray Diffraction Analysis from New Mexico Tech

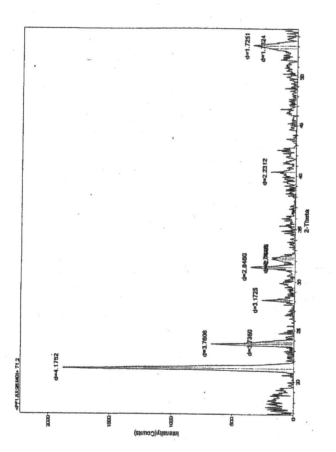

Fig. 6. XRD pattern for sample T1,2 with corresponding d-spacings given in Å.

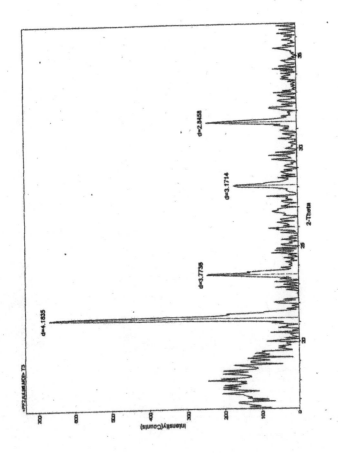

Fig. 7. XRD pattern for sample T3-A with corresponding d-spacings given in Å.

Appendix

Experimental XRD patterns
along with published patterns of possible cladding phases.

Experimental X-Ray Diffraction Patterns
of Outer Metallic Layers

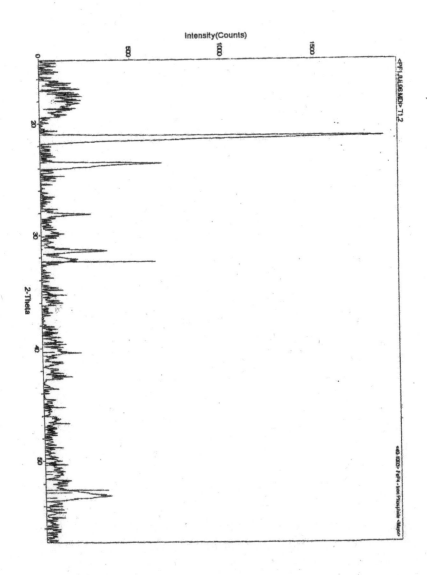

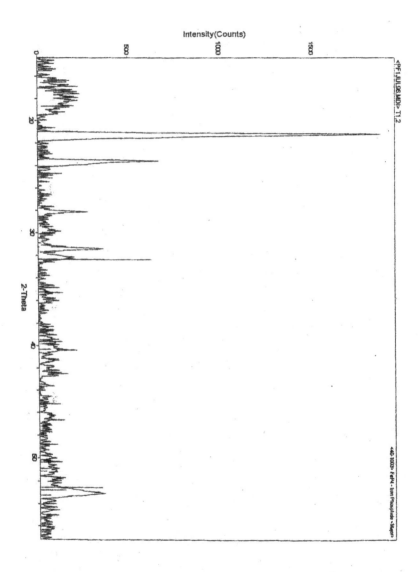

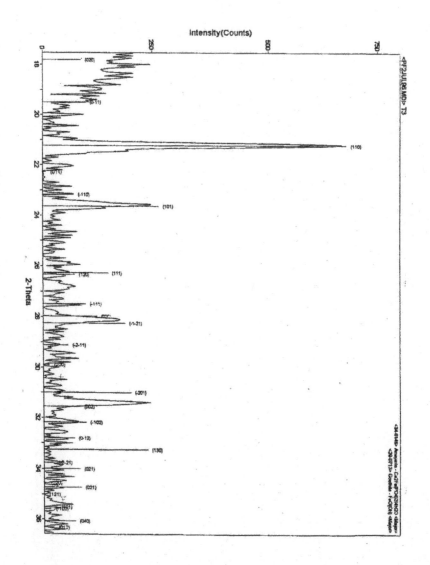

National Institute for Discovery Science

May 20, 1996

Roger Leir, D.P.M.
1155 East Thousand Oaks Boulevard
Thousand Oaks, California 91360

Dear Roger:

Enclosed, you will find the complete spectrographic analytical report.

In the future, we expect to receive information from other labs that is more thorough in the total menu, as we discussed over the phone, for things to be checked.

Yours truly,

Bob

ROBERT T. BIGELOW

RTB/db

Encl.

1515 E. Tropicana Suite 400 • Las Vegas, NV 89119
Phone (702) 798-1700 • Fax (702) 798-1970 • EMail DiscSci@aol.com

Letter from Robert Bigelow of N.I.D.S. Indicating Further Reports will be Forthcoming

MAY-15-1996 14:25   FROM CST 1 BLDG 41   TO   817624569404   P.01

UNCLASSIFIED fa X COVERSHEET

CHEMICAL SCIENCE & TECHNOLOGY DIVISION
GROUP CST-1, MS J565
LOS ALAMOS NATIONAL LABORATORY
LOS ALAMOS, NM 87545

TO: *Robert Bigelow*   (702) 456-9404
         NIDS   fax no.

FROM: **David Cremers**   (505) 667-1034 / 665-4180
                                          telephone

                                          (505) 665-6095
                                          fax no.

message:

*Report with spectra will be sent
via Express Mail.*

number of pages (including cover sheet): — 6 —

Cover Letter from Los Alamos National Labs

Identification of Elements in Samples t1, t2, t3, t4, and t6 Using Laser-Induced Breakdown Spectroscopy (LIBS)

Introduction

   Samples of unknown composition labeled tx were analyzed using laser-induced breakdown spectroscopy (LIBS) to determine the elemental composition. The samples were small rod-like materials 1-2 mm in diameter and less than 1 cm in length. Because of the small size of the samples and the non-uniform appearance of the sample surfaces when observed under a microscope, it was decided that LIBS was a suitable method to determine elemental composition because of its microsampling ability and relatively non-destructive analysis capabilities. Under microscopic examination some of the samples appeared to be metallic and all but one sample (t4) was observed to have areas of visually different appearance. These are labeled as the black, brown, white areas, etc. on the spectra recorded from these areas. Because of the microsampling capabilities of the LIBS analyzer, it was possible to interrogate these regions separately to obtain spectra corresponding to these distinct regions.

Analysis method

   LIBS is an elemental analysis technique in which powerful laser pulses are focused on the sample to generate a hot microplasma (10,000 K) [1]. Because the laser beam can be focused to a small area (0.2 mm diameter), the method has microsampling capabilities. The microplasma vaporizes a small amount of sample (<50 nanograms), and excites the resulting atoms to emit light. The light is collected, spectrally dispersed, and the resulting spectrum is recorded to determine the elemental composition. Because each element has a unique spectral signature, the elements can be identified by analysis of the spectrum. The intensity of the emission lines can be used to determine the concentrations of elements if the sample has uniform composition.

   A diagram of the experimental apparatus used for the analysis is shown in Fig. 1. The experimental conditions are listed in Table 1. Because of the small size of the samples, a specially constructed microscope-coupled LIBS analyzer was used to interrogate precisely selected locations on the sample surface. Videographic images of each sample were made for reference. Because of the visual non-uniform appearance of the samples, quantitative determination of the composition of the samples will be difficult. The samples were viewed through the microscope objective of the apparatus and the area selected for analysis was aligned in the microscope cross-hairs. The laser was fired to generate the microplasma and the light collected. The analysis was carried out for regions of each sample that appeared visually different from other surface areas.

   For these measurements, the spectral regions from 220-500, 560-590, and 740-770 nm were examined at moderate spectral resolution to record emission lines. This region contains the majority of analytically useful lines for element identification. The resulting spectra are appended to this report. The spectrum label indicates the file number, the sample number, and area of the sample interrogated by the microplasma. The spectra are also available on disk in ASCII format if requested.

1

Report from New Mexico Tech Identifying Elemental Composition of Unknown Sample

Data Analysis
    The spectra were analyzed and the major elemental emission lines were identified based on NIST (National Institute of Standards and Technology) wavelength tables. Elements were positively identified by monitoring several emission lines of each element to minimize the possibility of incorrect identification due to spectral interferences (overlapping lines). Some of the major lines identified on each spectrum are listed on the attached spectra but not all identified lines are listed because of space limitations. An element was detectable using LIBS if it was present at a concentration above the minimum detection level for the LIBS method. The LIBS method is generally suited to identify the major and minor elements in a sample. Typical detection limits for the elements identified in the tx samples range from 1-100 ppm(w/w).

Summary
    The elements identified in each of the samples are listed in Table 2 according to major and minor concentrations. The labels major and minor elements is only a relative term indicating the strength of emission lines from the designated elements. Because the sample appeared to be non-uniform, as noted above, a concentration analysis with LIBS is difficult because of its microsampling characteristics (i.e. it is difficult, if not impossible, to obtain a measurement representative of the average bulk sample composition). A review of the elements found indicates that:

(1) The spectra obtained appear moderately complex (density of emission lines) and are similar to spectra that charaterize soils, rocks, and some metal alloys. The spectra are more complex than those observed from most aluminum alloys.
(2) No unusual elements (i.e. those not normally found in common materials) or combination of elements were identified in the samples at major or minor concentrations. For example, refractory elements such as Mo and W were not observed in these samples from any of the areas sampled. Ti was observed, however, but again this is an element found in soils and minerals.
(3) The white regions of the samples have a visual appearance and a composition indicative of mineral formations containing of Ca and Al.
(4) Some lines in the spectra remain unidentified, but this is not unusual even for samples having a simple, known composition.

Therefore, the samples do not appear to have unexpected elemental composition. Additional tests, not performed by us may indicate some unusual properties. These tests could include x-ray crystallographic and metallographic analysis to elucidate the sample structure (grain boundary structure, unusual metal phases, preferential grain growth). The ability to perform some of these tests may be problematic due to the small sample size, however. Some tests will involve destruction of at least a part of the sample.

Reference:
1. D.A. Cremers and L.J. Radziemski, "Laser Plasmas for Chemical Analysis," in Laser Spectroscopy and Its Applications (Marcel Dekker, New York, 1986) edited by L.J. Radziemski, R.W. Solarz, and J.A. Paisner. Chapter 5.

2

Table 1. Experimental Conditions used to Analyze tx Samples

laser	Kigre, MK-367, 17 mJ/pulse 6 nsec pulsewidth, 1064 nm wavelength
Spectrograph	CHROMEX 500IS, 12000 I/mm grating, 50 micron slits
Detector	ORIEL InstaSpec V ICCD gating interval = 2-20 μsec after plasma formation
Data analysis software	ORIEL InstaSpec V

3

Table 2. Summary of Analysis Results

Sample	Area*	Major Elements	Minor Elements
t1	scaled**	Al, Ca, Fe	Ba, Cu, Mg, Mn, Na, Ni, Pb, Zn
	black	Ca, Cu, Fe	Al, Ba, Mn, Na, Ni
t2	black	Ca, Cu, Fe	Al, Ba, Mg, Mn, Na, Ni
	brown	Ca, Fe	Ba, Cu, Mg, Mn, Na, Ni, Si
t3	black	Ca, Cu, Fe	Ba, Mn, Na
	white	Al, Ca, Cu, Fe	Ba, Mg, Mn, Na, Si
	rust	Ca, Cu, Fe	Ba, Mn, Na
t4	black	Ca, Cu, Fe	Al, Ba, Mn, Na, Ni
t6	brown	Al, Ca, Cu, Tl	Mg, Na, Si, Zn
	white	Al, Ca, Cu	Fe, Mg, Mn, Na, Si, Zn
	beads on white	Ca, Cu, Fe	Al

* Under microscopic examination, some of the samples appeared visually to have areas of different color (e.g. black-colored, brown-colored, white-colored). These areas were analyzed separately. Different elemental compositions were found for the different areas. These are listed above.
** This area was of a larger diameter than the main rod. This area appeared glassy-like and scaled.

4

UFO Crash In Brazil:

A Genuine UFO Crash with Surviving ETs, by Dr. Roger K. Leir.

On a worldwide scale the country of Brazil is arguably the hottest UFO spot on the planet. News of their UFO sightings and related events seldom gets out to the rest of the world, but this story was too big to stop. Even the reputable *Wall Street Journal* reported it on July 12, 1996. After this, in America, the story disappeared.

In Varginha, Brazil, however, near the crash location, multiple witnesses were coming forward and creating a media frenzy. According to numerous eyewitnesses, an unidentified flying object did crash near Varginha on January 20, 1996 and at least two beings similar to those pictured on the front of this book were reported to have survived (one of them was injured).

Many of these eyewitnesses did not know each other, were credible people, and had no reason to lie – yet described these beings in exactly the same way. This was not a movie or a hoax. It was real.

Find out what happened and get this book! Join Dr. Roger Leir and follow in his footsteps as he takes you through the entire investigative journey. This is a truly bizarre, frighteningly real, yet extremely interesting series of events.

If you think UFOs are not real or that only crazy people believe in such things as aliens, think again. Consider the three girls who had the wits scared out of them by staring one of these creatures in the face, or medical staff that was forced to work on an injured being while the military stood guard, after virtually locking them into the operating room. Consider also the sudden, unexplained death of a healthy 23 year-old military officer who touched the creature without adequate protection or gloves. This could well be the most important UFO story to ever come out and is a must read for anyone interested in the subject.

ISBN 1-58509-105-7 · 152 pages
6 x 9 · trade paper · $14.95

Babylonian Influence on the Bible and Popular Beliefs: A Comparative Study of Genesis 1.2, by A. Smythe Palmer. ISBN 1-58509-000-X • 124 pages • 6 x 9 • trade paper • $12.95

Biography of Satan: Exposing the Origins of the Devil, by Kersey Graves. ISBN 1-885395-11-6 • 168 pages • 5 1/2 x 8 1/2 • trade paper • $13.95

The Malleus Maleficarum: The Notorious Handbook Once Used to Condemn and Punish "Witches", by Heinrich Kramer and James Sprenger. ISBN 1-58509-098-0 • 332 pages • 6 x 9 • trade paper • $25.95

Crux Ansata: An Indictment of the Roman Catholic Church, by H. G. Wells. ISBN 1-58509-210-X • 160 pages • 6 x 9 • trade paper • $14.95

Emanuel Swedenborg: The Spiritual Columbus, by U.S.E. (William Spear). ISBN 1-58509-096-4 • 208 pages • 6 x 9 • trade paper • $17.95

Dragons and Dragon Lore, by Ernest Ingersoll. ISBN 1-58509-021-2 • 228 pages • 6 x 9 • trade paper • illustrated • $17.95

The Vision of God, by Nicholas of Cusa. ISBN 1-58509-004-2 • 160 pages • 5 x 8 • trade paper • $13.95

The Historical Jesus and the Mythical Christ: Separating Fact From Fiction, by Gerald Massey. ISBN 1-58509-073-5 • 244 pages • 6 x 9 • trade paper • $18.95

Gog and Magog: The Giants in Guildhall; Their Real and Legendary History, with an Account of Other Giants at Home and Abroad, by F.W. Fairholt. ISBN 1-58509-084-0 • 172 pages • 6 x 9 • trade paper • $16.95

The Origin and Evolution of Religion, by Albert Churchward. ISBN 1-58509-078-6 • 504 pages • 6 x 9 • trade paper • $39.95

The Origin of Biblical Traditions, by Albert T. Clay. ISBN 1-58509-065-4 • 220 pages • 5 1/2 x 8 1/2 • trade paper • $17.95

Aryan Sun Myths, by Sarah Elizabeth Titcomb, Introduction by Charles Morris. ISBN 1-58509-069-7 • 192 pages • 6 x 9 • trade paper • $15.95

The Social Record of Christianity, by Joseph McCabe. Includes *The Lies and Fallacies of the Encyclopedia Britannica*, ISBN 1-58509-215-0 • 204 pages • 6 x 9 • trade paper • $17.95

The History of the Christian Religion and Church During the First Three Centuries, by Dr. Augustus Neander. ISBN 1-58509-077-8 • 112 pages • 6 x 9 • trade paper • $12.95

Ancient Symbol Worship: Influence of the Phallic Idea in the Religions of Antiquity, by Hodder M. Westropp and C. Staniland Wake. ISBN 1-58509-048-4 • 120 pages • 6 x 9 • trade paper • illustrated • $12.95

The Gnosis: Or Ancient Wisdom in the Christian Scriptures, by William Kingsland. ISBN 1-58509-047-6 • 232 pages • 6 x 9 • trade paper • $18.95

The Evolution of the Idea of God: An Inquiry into the Origin of Religions, by Grant Allen. ISBN 1-58509-074-3 • 160 pages • 6 x 9 • trade paper • $14.95

Sun Lore of All Ages: A Survey of Solar Mythology, Folklore, Customs, Worship, Festivals, and Superstition, by William Tyler Olcott. ISBN 1-58509-044-1 • 316 pages • 6 x 9 • trade paper • $24.95

Nature Worship: An Account of Phallic Faiths and Practices Ancient and Modern, by the Author of Phallicism with an Introduction by Tedd St. Rain. ISBN 1-58509-049-2 • 112 pages • 6 x 9 • trade paper • illustrated • $12.95

Life and Religion, by Max Muller. ISBN 1-885395-10-8 • 237 pages • 5 1/2 x 8 1/2 • trade paper • $14.95

Jesus: God, Man, or Myth? An Examination of the Evidence, by Herbert Cutner. ISBN 1-58509-072-7 • 304 pages • 6 x 9 • trade paper • $23.95

Pagan and Christian Creeds: Their Origin and Meaning, by Edward Carpenter. ISBN 1-58509-024-7 • 316 pages • 5 1/2 x 8 1/2 • trade paper • $24.95

The Christ Myth: A Study, by Elizabeth Evans. ISBN 1-58509-037-9 • 136 pages • 6 x 9 • trade paper • $13.95

Popery: Foe of the Church and the Republic, by Joseph F. Van Dyke. ISBN 1-58509-058-1 • 336 pages • 6 x 9 • trade paper • illustrated • $25.95

Career of Religious Ideas, by Hudson Tuttle. ISBN 1-58509-066-2 • 172 pages • 5 x 8 • trade paper • $15.95

Buddhist Suttas: Major Scriptural Writings from Early Buddhism, by T.W. Rhys Davids. ISBN 1-58509-079-4 • 376 pages • 6 x 9 • trade paper • $27.95

Early Buddhism, by T. W. Rhys Davids. Includes *Buddhist Ethics: The Way to Salvation?*, by Paul Tice. ISBN 1-58509-076-X • 112 pages • 6 x 9 • trade paper • $12.95

The Fountain-Head of Religion: A Comparative Study of the Principal Religions of the World and a Manifestation of their Common Origin from the Vedas, by Ganga Prasad. ISBN 1-58509-054-9 • 276 pages • 6 x 9 • trade paper • $22.95

India: What Can It Teach Us?, by Max Muller. ISBN 1-58509-064-6 • 284 pages • 5 1/2 x 8 1/2 • trade paper • $22.95

Matrix of Power: How the World has Been Controlled by Powerful People Without Your Knowledge, by Jordan Maxwell. ISBN 1-58509-120-0 • 104 pages • 6 x 9 • trade paper • $12.95

Cyberculture Counterconspiracy: A Steamshovel Web Reader, Volume One, edited by Kenn Thomas. ISBN 1-58509-125-1 • 180 pages • 6 x 9 • trade paper • illustrated • $16.95

Cyberculture Counterconspiracy: A Steamshovel Web Reader, Volume Two, edited by Kenn Thomas. ISBN 1-58509-126-X • 132 pages • 6 x 9 • trade paper • illustrated • $13.95

Oklahoma City Bombing: The Suppressed Truth, by Jon Rappoport. ISBN 1-885395-22-1 • 112 pages • 5 1/2 x 8 1/2 • trade paper • $12.95

The Protocols of the Learned Elders of Zion, by Victor Marsden. ISBN 1-58509-015-8 • 312 pages • 6 x 9 • trade paper • $24.95

Secret Societies and Subversive Movements, by Nesta H. Webster. ISBN 1-58509-092-1 • 432 pages • 6 x 9 • trade paper • $29.95

The Secret Doctrine of the Rosicrucians, by Magus Incognito. ISBN 1-58509-091-3 • 256 pages • 6 x 9 • trade paper • $20.95

The Origin and Evolution of Freemasonry: Connected with the Origin and Evolution of the Human Race, by Albert Churchward. ISBN 1-58509-029-8 • 240 pages • 6 x 9 • trade paper • $18.95

The Lost Key: An Explanation and Application of Masonic Symbols, by Prentiss Tucker. ISBN 1-58509-050-6 • 192 pages • 6 x 9 • trade paper • illustrated • $15.95

The Character, Claims, and Practical Workings of Freemasonry, by Rev. C.G. Finney. ISBN 1-58509-094-8 • 288 pages • 6 x 9 • trade paper • $22.95

The Secret World Government or "The Hidden Hand": The Unrevealed in History, by Maj.-Gen. Count Cherep-Spiridovich. ISBN 1-58509-093-X • 270 pages • 6 x 9 • trade paper • $21.95

The Magus, Book One: A Complete System of Occult Philosophy, by Francis Barrett. ISBN 1-58509-031-X • 200 pages • 6 x 9 • trade paper • illustrated • $16.95

The Magus, Book Two: A Complete System of Occult Philosophy, by Francis Barrett. ISBN 1-58509-032-8 • 220 pages • 6 x 9 • trade paper • illustrated • $17.95

The Magus, Book One and Two: A Complete System of Occult Philosophy, by Francis Barrett. ISBN 1-58509-033-6 • 420 pages • 6 x 9 • trade paper • illustrated • $34.90

The Key of Solomon The King, by S. Liddell MacGregor Mathers. ISBN 1-58509-022-0 • 152 pages • 6 x 9 • trade paper • illustrated • $12.95

Magic and Mystery in Tibet, by Alexandra David-Neel. ISBN 1-58509-097-2 • 352 pages • 6 x 9 • trade paper • $26.95

The Comte de St. Germain, by I. Cooper Oakley. ISBN 1-58509-068-9 • 280 pages • 6 x 9 • trade paper • illustrated • $22.95

Alchemy Rediscovered and Restored, by A. Cockren. ISBN 1-58509-028-X • 156 pages • 5 1/2 x 8 1/2 • trade paper • $13.95

The 6th and 7th Books of Moses, with an Introduction by Paul Tice. ISBN 1-58509-045-X • 188 pages • 6 x 9 • trade paper • illustrated • $16.95

Printed in November 2024
by Rotomail Italia S.p.A., Vignate (MI) - Italy